# Learning from Robben Island

T0307879

# Learning from Robben Island

## THE PRISON WRITINGS OF
# Govan Mbeki

In association with the
UWC Historical & Cultural Centre Project
(UWC Mayibuye History Series No.1)

JAMES CURREY: London
OHIO UNIVERSITY PRESS: Athens, Ohio
DAVID PHILIP: Cape Town

First published 1991 in southern Africa by David Philip Publishers (Pty)
Ltd, 208 Werdmuller Centre, Claremont 7700, South Africa

Published 1991 in the United Kingdom by James Currey Ltd,
54b Thornhill Square, Islington, London N1 1BE

Published 1991 in the United States of America by Ohio University Press,
Scott Quadrangle, Athens, Ohio 45701

The University of the Western Cape is setting up an Historical and Cultural
Centre, which will include a museum on the apartheid era, and an archive
of the South African liberation struggle. The UWC Mayibuye History Series
is a part of this project.

ISBN 0-86486-166-4 (David Philip)
ISBN 0-85266-366-0 (James Currey)
ISBN 0-8214-1007-5 (Ohio University Press, pb)
ISBN 0-8214-1006-7 (Ohio University Press, cased)

Printed by Clyson Printers (Pty) Ltd, 11th Avenue, Maitland, Cape Town

British Library Cataloguing in Publication Data:

Mbeki, Govan
   Learning from Robben Island : the prison writings of Govan Mbeki.
   1. South Africa. Political movements
   I. Title
   322.4092
   ISBN 0-85266-366-0

Library of Congress Cataloging in Publication no.: 91 – 3198

# Contents

# Acknowledgements

A number of people have contributed to the publication of these essays. Priscilla Jana played an important role. Without the willing assistance of Ilona Tip, Lesley Hudson and Colleen Taylor, who typed the essays from handwritten manuscripts, they would not have seen the light of day. Tembisa Xundu and Bongani Buta assisted greatly in reading and correcting the first typed copies. My thanks go to Harry Gwala for his foreword, to Linda Zama, and to Thole Majodina and his staff for the assistance and cooperation they gave.

# Foreword
*by Harry Gwala*

The essays by Comrade Govan Mbeki come at the most appropriate time, when serious doubts are being cast on the labour theory. Events in Eastern Europe are being used as ammunition by enemies of Socialism.

When comrades were incarcerated on Robben Island a crying need was felt for a theory that would correctly interpret the world. Such a theory was the labour theory as propounded by Marx and Engels and developed by Lenin. To organise this theory for our comrades required material, which we lacked; consequently we had to rely on memory. Comrade Govan's memory was aided by the fact that he was doing his Honours in economics.

These essays, as already explained, were a collective effort intended for discussion. They helped lay a foundation for our young comrades who needed to be armed with a correct theory. This was particularly so in an environment where bourgeois ideas reign supreme and are taken as the law of God. When Comrade Govan deals with capitalist development in South Africa he reveals that so-called *laissez-faire* or what is generally known as free enterprise is after all not free, that it only reached its height when the bourgeoisie themselves captured state power both in Europe and the United States. In South Africa it was only when the National Party captured state power on behalf of the Afrikaner bourgeoisie and farmers that Afrikaner capital started making heavy inroads into the world of big capital.

For this to happen the National Party government embarked on the most oppressive racist laws South Africa had ever seen. The first was the Suppression of Communism Act. This was followed by the Bantu Authorities Act, which created reservoirs of cheap labour for the young Afrikaner border industries. Comrade Govan examines the so-called homelands, which in fact are certain forms of colonies for Afrikaner capital and shows why it is imperative that our people in these ghettoes must be organised. It is only through organisation and hard work that the liberation of our people can be realised. But for that liberation to be realised the masses must be armed with a correct theory. Without so saying, the essays convey that message to our people.

Today the great debate revolves round the content of liberation. The ruling class is at pains to show that freedom and prosperity lies in free enterprise and deregulation. In other words, in *laissez-faire*. But they have not explained to us why in over 300 years of free enterprise in this country the rich have become fewer but richer and why the vast majority of the people have remained poorer. The people are convinced that monopoly industries, which have now become a state within a state, must be taken over by a people's state in order to generate wealth for society as a whole. If these essays convey this to our people they will have contributed a great deal in our struggle for liberation.

# Introduction
*by Colin Bundy*

## Govan Mbeki: intellectual activist

The dining-room table in Govan's parents' home was beautifully carpentered: fully extended, with all its leaves in, it could seat sixteen. Even in its more compact form for everyday use, the table would have been surrounded by a good number of chairs. Govan was the youngest of eight children: he had three half-sisters by his father's first marriage, while his own mother bore three daughters and two sons. He was born on 8 July 1910, in Mpukane, a straggling village in Nqamakwe district in that portion of the southern Transkei known as Fingoland. His parents named him Govan Archibald Mvunyelwa ('he for whom people sing') Mbeki.

The furniture – like the handsome stone-built house which it occupied – was probably built by students from Blythswood mission school in nearby Nqamakwe, the seat of the magistracy. Pigs and poultry were in pens around the house; at a little distance was his father's farmland, about sixteen morgen, held under Glen Grey title and all fenced. Govan's father, Fkelewu Mbeki, owned a quantity of livestock: cattle, horses, sheep and goats. Before East London and Umtata were linked by rail, Fkelewu Mbeki had run a wagon transport service between Kingwilliamstown and the Transkei. He had also earned a modest salary from the government of the Cape Colony when he served as a headman.

Furniture, home, farm and livelihood: in every respect, Govan was born into a typically 'progressive' or modernising peasant family characteristic of the region at the turn of the century. Like most other members of this modest elite, his parents were Christians. His mother was the daughter of a Methodist evangelist; Govan is not sure when his father was converted, 'but the missionaries evidently had great influence on him'.[1] Govan himself was named after one of the most famous missionary educators of the Eastern Cape, William Govan, a Presbyterian minister and principal of Lovedale College from its inception in 1841 until 1870. (An indication of William Govan's standing amongst African Christians in the Eastern Cape and Transkei is that Govan – named 35 years after the Scot had died – had among his acquaintances two others similarly baptised.)

Fkelewu was a devout Methodist, a teetotaller who would say grace even before drinking a glass of water. Did anything of the family ambience rub off on Govan, who left the church when still a student? Certainly, those who worked with him politically between the 1940s and early 1960s speak about his self-discipline, his dedication to the task in hand, and a certain austerity in his life-style. A further defining characteristic of the stratum into which he was born was the premium placed upon education. Govan's own family exemplified this. Most of his sisters became teachers; his brother also trained initially as a teacher before becoming a demonstrator at the Tsolo school of agriculture.

Govan himself was not only encouraged in his schooling, but also excelled in it, rapidly ascending the rungs of the best education available to a bright young Transkeian of his generation. He began at the local Methodist primary school, a church hall given over on weekdays to this use. In a single large room, six classes were conducted simultaneously: the Sub A pupils chanting out their alphabet while older children scratched their sums on slates – and looking back, Govan wonders with amusement how he learned anything. He also remembers how he enjoyed school and 'never played truant'. In his teens, he left Nqamakwe for boarding school at Healdtown, near Fort Beaufort, a leading Methodist institution. At Healdtown he was introduced to Latin – which he loved, later studying it for two years at university – and also studied history, physical science, biology, and English.

From Healdtown, Govan was awarded a *Bunga* (United Transkeian Territories General Council) scholarship to Fort Hare,[2] where he first completed his Senior Certificate and then enrolled as an undergraduate. He was at Fort Hare from 1932 to 1937 – and these years constituted a formative period of his life, intellectually and politically. (His student life was not all politics. Govan was an accomplished footballer and an enthusiastic ball-room dancer. Years later, held in solitary confinement in Port Elizabeth's North End prison, Govan exercised and amused himself by twirling through the remembered steps on the impromptu dance-floor of his tiny cell.)

There had been glimpses of organised politics before 1933 – Govan remembers attending an ANC meeting in the Transkei when he was in his teens, held by an African minister. He also acted at some point in the late 1920s as an interpreter for a cousin, Robert Mbeki, who was a member of the ICU (Industrial and Commercial Workers' Union). The ICU, which grew mightily in rural areas between 1926 and 1928 to become the first mass organisation of black South Africans, was briefly active in the southern Transkei. (Thomas Mbeki, a prominent Transvaal ICU leader, was not related to Govan's family.) But Fort Hare, when he arrived, was not yet the political hothouse that it became in the 1940s: he cannot recall 'any real political work' there in 1932.

In the winter of 1933 there took place an encounter which was a decisive political turning-point in his life. Eddie Roux, a member of the Communist Party of South Africa, and his bride Win embarked on 'a sort of busman's honeymoon'. They had recently begun producing a monthly magazine, Indlela Yenkululeko – The Road to Freedom – which they sent to various educational centres 'and especially to students at Fort Hare'. Now, with camping gear and a donkey, they tramped through the Ciskei. When they reached Alice they camped by the Tyhume River – and from this base they went to hold outdoor meetings at Fort Hare. The students (recounted the Rouxs) 'told us of their life in college and of how they were disciplined and treated as schoolboys. We told them of the movement and of Indlela Yenkululeko.'³ Among those students was a rapt Govan Mbeki, immediately attracted by the clarity and radicalism of what he heard. He was most impressed by Roux, and began an association that was to last until the 1950s, long after the older man had broken with Marxism and the Party.

There were other influences, too, at Fort Hare that shaped Govan's politics. He majored in political science and psychology; and his political science lecturer invited Max Yergan to lecture on fascism and communism. Yergan was a black American who served as a representative of the American Young Men's Christian Association between 1921 and 1936. Politically, he moved from evangelicism to left-wing activism and then (during the Cold War) to a right-wing anti-communism. In 1934, after an absence during which he had visited the USSR, Yergan returned to Fort Hare. He drew on this experience to preach a riveting sermon (after which he was debarred from the pulpit at Fort Hare!) on the text 'I have come that ye may have life, and have it more abundantly' (John 10: 10). Govan became 'very close' to him, visited his home, and was introduced by Yergan to Marxist literature in the shape of the Little Lenin Library.

In 1935 and 1936, student politics at Fort Hare was galvanised by the fascist invasion of Ethiopia, by the Hertzog Bills and the 1936 Native Land and Trust Act, and by the calling of the All-African Convention in December 1935. Govan spent each holiday during these years in Johannesburg, where he lodged with one of his half-sisters. There he was drawn further into political discussions and reading, and encountered for the first time the realities of poverty and police repression in a black township. In 1935 he joined the ANC. He was also influenced by socialist ideas, and became personally close to Edwin Mofutsanyana, a leading African member of the CPSA. (Thabo, Govan's oldest son, was named after Mofutsanyana.) Govan did not, however, join the Party: in fact, he did not become a member until much later, when the banned CPSA regrouped underground in 1953 as the SACP. Govan explains that, while sympathetic to the aims of the Party and friendly with individual members, he differed with them as to where the primary focus of their organisational efforts should be:

My view was, look, if we want to make an impact on the government let us organise around labour. And we cannot organise on the mines. We must go and organise in the rural areas. . . . That was my approach. Let's go and organise in the Transkei, let's go and organise in Zululand so that when they come to Jo'burg they are already reached – we are able to guide them to take certain actions.

During his vacations in the Fort Hare years, Govan Mbeki worked in a branch of the Central News Agency, in Johannesburg. He set about trying to organise his co-workers there into a trade union – and was promptly fired by the Irish manager of the branch. This was his first dismissal on political grounds. A series of such sackings, mainly from teaching posts, peppered his employment history.

He graduated from Fort Hare in 1937. Almost immediately the three main strands from which his working life was woven became visible. These were teaching, journalism, and political organisation. The first teaching appointment was at Taylor Street Secondary School in Durban, and from there Govan moved to teach at Adams College, near Amanzimtoti, under Edgar Brookes. While at Adams, in 1938, he received a telegram from Clarkebury Institution – a teachers' training college in the Transkei – and he jumped at the chance to live and work there. In addition to teaching educational psychology and economics at Clarkebury, Govan also became increasingly politically active – especially in meetings of the Transkeian African Voters' Association. Towards the end of 1939, he was dismissed from Clarkebury.

By then, he had just published *Transkei in the Making*, a book he had drafted as a series of articles in 1937. Dedicated 'To the youth of my race', it was written partly as a rebuttal of a 1933 booklet, *Transkei Enquiry*, written by the Quaker and liberal, Howard Pim. Mbeki criticised the form of local government – indirect rule – operating in the Transkei, and examined economic conditions in the reserve. Introducing themes which his later writings would revisit and amplify, he identified the ways in which migrant labour and peasant farming on tiny plots generated rural poverty so that the majority of the territory's population were 'wallowing in a permanent slough of debt'. Although the argument is couched for the most part in measured tones, there is a decidedly radical edge to a passage warning against cattle culling imposed from above:

It should really be an unfortunate state of affairs if the rigours and vices of a capitalist society will be deliberately imported into the African territories – any attempt to destroy the people's cattle is no less than a declaration of that most iniquitous system which enables a chosen few to be possessors of all the means of production in the Transkei to the entire exclusion of the masses. . . .[4]

He was now approached by the African printers of *Transkei in the Making*, who invited him to edit a newspaper that they were launching in the Transkei, the *Territorial Magazine*. While he was still editor, the publication was renamed *Inkundla ya Bantu*, a more overtly political newspaper. In 1943 or 1944, *Inkundla* fell into financial difficulties, and a new board decided that Govan's opinions were too radical, and replaced him as editor. Another important journalistic connection was his appointment in 1940 as one of the directors of the *Guardian*, a left-wing weekly close to the Communist Party.

Another major event in Govan's life during these years was his marriage. He first met Epainette Moerane in Durban when they both taught at the Taylor Street School. She came from an essentially similar background to his own. Her parents, Sotho-speakers, lived in Mount Fletcher district near the border between Lesotho and the Transkei. Her father was a lay preacher and a prosperous peasant farmer. Her parents saw to it that Epainette and her six siblings received the best available education. All three of her brothers were university graduates; she had obtained the Cape Senior Certificate. She remembers Govan as an unostentatious, rather lonely young man: 'particular about how he dresses, particular about how he speaks'.[5]

When they spoke together, it was frequently about politics. Together, they moved in circles close to the Communist Party in Durban: Epainette had been impressed initially by Betty du Toit, an Afrikaner woman and Party member, who came to Natal to organise workers in the sugar industry. She became a member of the Party in the late 1930s − and must have been one of only a handful of African women in its entire membership. When Govan departed Natal for Clarkebury, she spent a year in the Orange Free State, and the pair saw each other during school holidays. They married in January 1940 − and had four children (Linda, Thabo, Moeletsi and Jama) between 1941 and 1948.

They lived in Idutywa district, a few kilometres south of the town of the same name. Govan's journalism did not bring much money into the home, and they supplemented this income in various ways: they ran some livestock; Epainette baked scones and cakes for a coffee shop; and, especially after Govan left *Inkundla*, they relied upon the small shop run from their home. This venture sprang initially from a political enthusiasm of Govan's: an interest in cooperatives. He had read about them while studying privately for his B.Comm., and also read Father Bernard Huss's pamphlets urging cooperative self-help. In 1946 Govan published a booklet, *Let's Do It Together*, in a series edited by Eddie Roux. He identified existing collective practices amongst African peasants, in ploughing land or building huts, and argued that greater cooperation could lessen dependence on white traders for credit. The cooperative aspect of the store dwindled as the other partners fell away, and it became a Mbeki family concern.

The 1940s have won considerable scholarly attention for their watershed quality in the history of organised black resistance in South Africa: Tom Lodge, in particular, has chronicled the reorganisation of the ANC under Dr Xuma and the radicalising influence of the Youth League; the growth of war-time trade unionism amongst black workers; the volcanic underclass pressures exerted by township residents and squatters; the exemplary effect of campaigns against the pass laws and against the Pegging Act; the emergence of new left-wing political groupings like the Non-European Unity Movement − and so on. In all these elements, this phenomenon is almost entirely an urban one. There is another, parallel history that has not yet been adequately researched or written: an account of how politics in rural areas – the reserves in particular – was also radicalised.

The process was patchy and uneven. Peasant politics, in South Africa as elsewhere, tends to be parochial, atomised and defensive: rural producers are conscious of their weakness relative to other classes and to the state. But during the 1940s, in a number of areas, the scale and intensity of rural resistance broadened significantly. The Transkei was one such area; and Govan Mbeki was not only caught up in the process, but also helped shape it.

He became increasingly active in Transkeian politics, on a number of fronts. He was elected secretary of the Transkeian African Voters' Association in 1941; served for a session in the *Bunga* as councillor for Idutywa; and in 1943 was a founder member of the Transkeian Organised Bodies. The TOB linked a number of disparate organisations: Vigilance Associations, the Chiefs' and People's Association, welfare societies, women's groupings, and so on. It also exemplified the changing tone and content of politics in the Transkei. It shifted from an emphasis upon specific reforms in favour of educated Transkeians to distinctly tougher and more radical public utterances. At its 1946 conference, the TOB called for 'full citizenship rights for all the people'; supported a cash collection for victims of the miners' strike on the Witwatersrand; and pledged its support for a boycott of the Natives Representative Council.

Govan corresponded with the ANC head office in Johannesburg a number of times during this decade: requesting Xuma's help in launching Congress in the Transkei; suggesting that the ANC take over *Inkundla* as an official publication; urging that the national movement should provide a clear lead to its potential followers in the reserves. In 1941 he described the Transkei as 'to be frank, politically in midnight slumber'; but due in no small measure to his own efforts, an awakening of sorts occurred. A letter from Mbeki to Xuma in September 1946 is vibrant with optimism. He described fund-raising efforts for the Anti-Pass Campaign and added, 'what a joy it is to be alive in these days when history is being made all around us.' A few months later he wrote again, enquiring what plans were being developed by the ANC 'to clamp down on Advisory Boards, Councils, and individual chiefs?' His concern went beyond the details:

Writing a letter like this I feel I must be frank. Our fears here are that we may work up the people only to find that the rest of the country does not attach much significance to its resolutions. Country people have a way of being honest. We have already lost face in the Anti-Pass Campaign which was just dropped when we were working up the people, and that was immediately seized on by the gradualists as one of these 'paper fires' which do not last . . . .[6]

It must have been a source of frustration that, for all his clear-headed urgings, there was negligible response on the part of the urban leadership of the ANC.

In 1953, Govan took up another teaching post – in Ladysmith, Natal. Once again, he was dismissed for political activities, including his opposition to the Bantu Education Act and his efforts at organisation amongst local coal-miners. While he was still in Ladysmith, he was approached by Fred Carneson and Ivan Schermbrucker in 1954 with the suggestion that he move to Port Elizabeth as local editor and office manager of the newspaper New Age.[7] He did so – and thus commenced a decade of intensive, unremitting political activism.

Time and again, when interviewing Govan Mbeki about his years in Port Elizabeth, one is struck by how hard he drove himself. In the first place he was a full-time journalist, running the New Age office, attending meetings and fund-raising events and then filing news stories through to the head office in Cape Town. He also wrote more analytical and theoretical pieces for the left-wing periodicals Liberation and Fighting Talk. In particular, he wrote a major series on the Transkei (which was subsequently incorporated into his best-known book, The Peasants' Revolt) for Liberation, then edited by Michael Harmel. As these articles had not been commissioned, Govan worked on them in what spare time he had: 'On Sundays I would come and write what I could – in the afternoon. Sunday after Sunday. Sunday after Sunday.'

Secondly, he was deeply involved in organisational politics in Port Elizabeth. The M-Plan, proposed by Nelson Mandela in response to the state's crackdown after the 1952 Defiance Campaign, sought to equip the ANC to run at least some of its activities beyond surveillance, to establish certain underground structures and practices. The only urban area in which real progress was made towards underground politics before the ANC was banned was Port Elizabeth. From 1953 to 1956, meetings of more than ten Africans were banned in New Brighton (the municipal 'location') – and so the ANC held its meetings in Korsten and elsewhere. But in 1956, the ban was extended to the entire magisterial district of Port Elizabeth: 'Now it was during this time, 1956 to 1960,' recalls Govan, 'that we perfected methods of working underground.' Almost all organisation work was done at night. A task dear to Govan's own heart was political education: with ANC membership in Port Elizabeth growing rapidly, he set up scores and scores of study groups. He also wrote, cyclostyled and distributed a booklet of about fifty pages, in Xhosa, outlining the aims and policies of the movement.

Thirdly, his urban base did not deflect Govan from his long-standing involvement in rural politics. The Port Elizabeth ANC established links with smaller branches in Ciskei villages like Peddie and Middledrift, particularly through organising in migrant hostels. Govan also maintained an active interest in the Transkei, hammering away in *New Age* against the Bantu Authorities system – precursor to bantustan 'independence'. In 1960 (after he had been detained during the State of Emergency) Govan received an invitation to visit Pondoland. A militant popular protest movement had developed there against chiefs who supported the Bantu Authorities, and the young ANC activist Anderson Ganyile now sought Govan's assistance. To reach Bizana meant slipping through a heavy police presence in Pondoland; and Govan achieved this disguised as a chauffeur, driving the car of a white Communist Party member from Uitenhage. Contact between the ANC and the Mpondo resisters was maintained through subsequent meetings in Durban.

Fourthly, the organisational abilities and intellectual energies displayed by Mbeki during this period won recognition, and he became increasingly involved in ANC and Communist Party leadership at national level. Much of this had to be behind the scenes, as his movements were restricted by banning orders. By the time of Sharpeville, the banning of the ANC and the State of Emergency, the balance of his activities had already swung from journalism towards organisation. From April 1960 to June 1963, this pattern of political activism in the face of state harassment intensified. He was detained for five months during the Emergency; arrested in 1961 on charges of furthering the aims of a banned organisation; arrested again in 1962 under the Explosives Act; and served on his acquittal with an order of house arrest.

During this same period he was on the National Executive Committee of the ANC (before the banning) and on the National

Action Committee (its underground leadership structure after the banning); he was directly involved in the decision to turn to armed struggle and a founder member of High Command of Umkhonto we Sizwe. He recruited and ran a sabotage group in Port Elizabeth, travelled to Durban for meetings with the Mpondo rebels, and – after being served with a house arrest order – he went fully underground. Underground, but still working prodigiously. He prepared scripts, with Ruth First, for broadcasting on Radio Freedom; worked on the manuscript of *The Peasants' Revolt*; served as treasurer and secretary for the underground organs; maintained contact with MK units inside and outside the Transvaal; and attended meeting after meeting. Talking about these months, Govan chuckled and said emphatically, 'I was *very* fully occupied.' Underground, active – and living on the farm Lilliesleaf, in Rivonia.

Govan spent some months on the farm, before moving early in July 1963 with the rest of the political leadership to another property that had been acquired. A meeting was called, and it was decided 'alright, let this be the very, very last meeting that takes place at Rivonia'. So, on Thursday, 11 July 1963, Govan and the others had actually returned to Lilliesleaf only shortly before a dry-cleaner's van entered the driveway. It was full of armed Special Branch policemen. Govan, followed by Sisulu and Kathrada, jumped out of a back window but had not moved far when the command rang out: 'Stop – or we shoot.' Govan was in the clothes he had used while living on the farm: old overalls and a woollen balaclava, so as to resemble a labourer. A photograph of him with the balaclava rolled up as a cap – reproduced many times since then – was taken by the police.

The arrest at gunpoint brought an abrupt end to one phase of a remarkable political career. As a Fort Hare student, he had become a member of the ANC and a student of Marxism. Thirty years later, he was one of the most influential leaders of the underground structures of the ANC and the Communist Party. Throughout that period, Govan Mbeki's political theory and practice were inseparably fused. The dedicated organiser and activist was also a versatile intellectual – commentator, analyst, reporter and historian. More, perhaps, than any other African politician of his generation he experienced and reflected the tensions and complexities of both rural and urban life. He worked in Johannesburg, Durban and Port Elizabeth but also devoted enormous energies to the Transkei and rural Eastern Cape. As a theorist, he occupied a distinctive place on the South African left for his insistence on the potential importance of rural mobilisation and struggle. As a practising politician, he contributed mightily to the urban organisation that made Port Elizabeth a rock-solid centre of ANC support.

Hilda Bernstein provides this pen portrait of Govan during the Rivonia trial:

Govan Mbeki admits to being a member of the National High Command of Umkhonto; to membership of the African National Congress and the Communist Party. Perhaps 'admits' is not the word; rather he declares proudly that he has played a substantial role in these organisations.

'As you have answered in the affirmative to questions or actions concerning all four counts against you, why did you not plead guilty to the four counts?'

'First, I felt I should come and explain under oath some of the reasons that led me to join these organisations. There was a sense of moral duty attached to it. Secondly, for the simple reason that to plead guilty would to my mind indicate a sense of moral guilt. I do not accept there is moral guilt attached to my actions.'

. . . Something in Govan's quiet and courteous way of speaking arouses in Yutar [the state prosecutor] a greater antagonism than he has yet displayed to the accused . . . He returns again and again to questions of identities, places, names, which Govan refuses to answer.

Although Govan's admissions make it unnecessary for Yutar to press his cross-examination of Govan – there is no question of the verdict in his case – he continues to question him for three more days, interspersing questions about documents with the questions that seek information. He is like an angry fly hitting himself again and again against a pane of glass; because the glass is transparent he believes he only has to hit hard enough and he will reach the other side. Govan steadfastly refuses to answer any question which might implicate anyone else.[8]

Life sentences for eight of the nine accused were handed down in the Pretoria Supreme Court on 12 June 1964. As a huge crowd filled Church Square with the strains of 'Nkosi Sikelele', the police van left the court behind its convoy of cars and motorcycles. That night, apart from Denis Goldberg (held in the whites-only Pretoria Central Prison), the men of Rivonia were flown to Cape Town. The next morning the Dakota aeroplane crossed the wintry waters of Table Bay to the flat, windswept island that was to house them for so many years. It was also to become their 'university', the site of an extraordinary programme of political education. It is a portion of that programme which makes up the body of this book.

## Political education on the Island

Michael Dingake (an ANC operative jailed from 1966 to 1981) published an account in 1987 of his years on the Island. The prison was – he suggested – 'a laboratory of a major political experiment': here, 'the political fibre of the oppressed' was to be tested. And, despite the controls available to the experimenters (over diet, mail, study rights, and punishment) the attempts to destroy that fibre failed.[9] Instead, the ANC re-established itself as a political organisation with identifiable leadership, underground structures, ingenious communication channels, and committees with a wide range of responsibilities. Committee structures existed for day-to-day administration amongst the political prisoners on the Island, for organisational discipline, for developing a programme of study, for devising leisure activities – and more. The full story of how this 'complete underground organisational machinery' (as Mbeki refers to it) was set up on Robben Island awaits its own history.

Two educational initiatives were mounted on the Island: academic education and political education. Govan Mbeki speaks proudly of the attention given to academic study on the Island:

We took people from the lowest level, who came to the Island illiterate, and they had to be taught. I remember one group I had – I started with them when they were illiterate – started them up. And by the time they left Robben Island they were able to write letters home – they didn't require anybody to write letters for them, and to address their envelopes. And they spoke English. And, so we did that. Most people when they came to Robben Island were at about the JC [Standard 8] level, and by the time they left they were doing degrees and things like that. Take one case, you had a special case like Eddie Daniels. Now Eddie Daniels when he came to Robben Island was starved of education. But when he left Robben Island he had a B.A. and a B.Comm.

On another occasion he spoke again about the academic educational programme.

We encouraged people to study. It is good for them. It is good for our discipline too. It is good for them to improve their qualifications. It is also good for their parents. Like before I was released, there was a young chap from UWC [the University of the Western Cape], Leonard. We asked for a report from the section: 'Who are studying of the new chaps? Who are studying and what are they doing?' So we are given the report and it shows that Leonard is not studying. So we make an enquiry why is Leonard not studying. Leonard replies, saying, 'Look, here's Comrade Mteto in this section' (it was section B), 'here's Comrade Mteto, he has no degree and yet he is up and up in his politics and he has given us guidance here. Why should I bother? I want to concentrate on political studies.' So we replied, 'Leonard, when your parents took

you to the UWC they expected you to come out of there with a degree for your good
and for their own good, and their satisfaction as parents – and now that you are here,
the organisation stands in loco parentis! You've got to study![10]

But as well as encouraging educational activities from literacy
skills to post-graduate degrees, the ANC leadership on the Island
also devised a programme of political education. A good deal of
less formalised political education took place in earlier years, but
it was mainly after 1979 and especially in the early 1980s that a
full-blown course of studies was devised, material prepared and
circulated, and study groups set up. The project was both more
necessary and more feasible at this time.

The necessity arose from the influx of political prisoners in the
late 1970s and early 1980s. By the beginning of the eighties,
explains Mbeki,

a new crop of very young comrades started streaming into the Island. Most of them
were MK cadres, but also among them were BCM [Black Consciousness Movement]
members whose leadership stated that they had no time 'for the dusty manuscripts of
Marx and Engels' . . .
It did not take long to establish the fact that as enthusiastic as the young ANC
cadres were about the national democratic revolution, they were not well informed
about the history of ANC, nor were they clear about its policies and how they
differed from those of the Communist Party.[11]

These circumstances had two implications for the senior ANC
prisoners. First, they wanted to equip their own members with an
adequate knowledge of their own history and struggle; secondly,
in doing so they would also be able to counter the claims of rival
groups on the Island, particularly the Pan-Africanist Congress.

Several factors made it possible to implement political education on the desired scale by the end of the seventies. A major
barrier to a successful programme was the difficulty of developing
communication channels between the various sections. (When the
Rivonia trialists arrived on Robben Island in 1964, they were
housed in an antique building originally used as a prison by the
Cape colonial government, and segregated from other political
prisoners in the 'zinc tronk' – a cluster of buildings constructed of
wood and corrugated iron. Prisoners worked on the Island to
quarry the stone which went into the construction of the new
maximum security wings, divided into seven sections, named 'A'
to 'G'. High walls were erected between the sections, so that
inmates of one could not even see those of another.) Gradually, the

prisoners devised ways of breaching their isolation and making effective contact between the sections.

One man is credited, in particular, with defeating the system of isolation between the sections. 'The transfer of the late Joe Gqabi from the main section to the B section where the Rivonia group was isolated' (Govan Mbeki narrates) 'was one of those inadvertent mistakes the jail authorities committed.'[12] Gqabi belonged to the first group of Umkhonto we Sizwe cadres sent out of the country for training as military commanders, and his instruction had included covert communication methods. 'He was *absolutely* good, very good, at it!' recalls Mbeki. Joe Gqabi immediately set about devising all sorts of communication channels – and with this breakthrough, it became possible to prepare material and to smuggle it from one section to another.

Moreover, if we laid our hands on any book, however thick, it was copied out and distributed to our membership throughout the various sections. On occasion, newspapers and even small portable transistor radios fell into our hands, and the information derived therefrom was immediately written out and despatched to all the sections. Sometimes during searches that took us by surprise, 'banks' of the material were confiscated from the prisoners, and sometimes the authorities acting on information dug it up from the yard. But whatever losses we incurred in one section were made up for by the materials that were kept in 'banks' in other sections.[13]

The political prisoners fought year after year to improve conditions on the Island; and as the years passed these struggles helped to win small privileges. An important policy change that directly benefited the political education programme took place in 1980, when access to newspapers became regular (although they were still often subject to censorship and arrived mutilated by the warders' scissors). The study programme through the University of South Africa also provided both content and cover for political education. Govan Mbeki drew directly for several of the essays in this book upon material gathered towards his courses in business economics, economics Honours and a Masters degree in economics. The UNISA assignment pads also housed those portions of the political education programme that Govan brought with him when he left the Island in 1987.

The perceived need for an enhanced programme of political education thus intersected with factors making it possible. Govan and others set about drawing up a two-part syllabus. The first part, called Syllabus A, was a history of the ANC. It was far from perfunctory. It commenced in the mid-nineteenth century, with the Wars of Dispossession, and provided an analysis of the social context from which the educated proto-nationalists emerged, who in 1912 were to become the founders of the organisation. It dealt with the subsequent history of the ANC, decade by decade, with particular attention devoted to a study of the Freedom Charter. It also examined closely the 'reasons which decided the organisation to embark on the armed struggle' and 'showed the relationship between the ANC and the SACP, devoting considerable attention to the distinction between the two organisations – the character of the alliance between the two'.[14] Mbeki estimates that it took about three years of study to work thoroughly through Syllabus A.

Syllabus B was essentially a materialist history of the development of human society. It outlined the writings of Marx and Engels, especially with reference to the rise of capitalism, and introduced concepts of class struggle and socialism. In addition to these two syllabuses, other documents were also prepared for the political education programme: essays were commissioned from individuals or groups of prisoners on specific topics and topical issues.

Political education material was circulated and discussed in two main ways: through the clandestine structures that had been set up in all the sections, and during work in the quarries and elsewhere. Small groups of three to five people conducted classes: 'As the prisoners would say, they had a greater number of eyes and ears than the jail authorities.'[15] In producing the material, it was essential that it could be hidden, copied, and passed on. (In one of the essays Govan notes the need to keep it 'within a tolerable length and transportable proportions'!) The essays were written on the thinnest paper that could be found, in the smallest possible script. Govan's eyesight did not permit him to compress his own handwriting, so many of his essays were dictated to 'scribes'. Terror Lekota, he recalls approvingly, 'could write so small the chaps would want magnifying glasses!' As material circulated from one section to another, it would be copied and stored.

The writings in this book are only a sampling of the material written by ANC historians and theorists. They are not even a complete collection of Govan's own contributions, but are the ones he was able to preserve. They are discussed briefly in the final section of this Introduction.

**The Robben Island writings**

South Africa has jailed so many gifted men and women that there already exists a sizeable body of prison writing. Bosman's sardonic *Cold Stone Jug* begins the genre – and alongside it one might shelve Breytenbach's *True Confessions of an Albino Terrorist*. Ruth First's *117 Days* and Albie Sachs's *Jail Diary* both describe detention without trial – and they are also linked by the terrible bombings which took life and limb from these opponents of injustice. Prison memories by Idris Naidoo, Moses Dlamini and Michael Dingake recreated the cell blocks and rock quarries of Robben Island. Hugh Lewin and Tim Jenkins took readers into (and in the latter case out of!) Pretoria Central. So did the taut verse of Jeremy Cronin's *Inside*. Helen Joseph (treason trial and house arrest) and Frances Baard (prison and banishment) described their lives in other parts of the apartheid gulag. *Drum* magazine's photo-essay on life in the Johannesburg Fort and the *Rand Daily Mail*'s publication of Harold Strachan's revelations (for which he was promptly re-imprisoned) are journalistic classics.

The essays by Govan Mbeki which comprise this book add to this distinguished list. Yet they differ in important respects from all the others: they were written, circulated and preserved in prison. They were never intended for publication but to be read by other prisoners; their aim is not to share an experience but to educate politically. They are remarkable documents. The circumstances of their production and nature of their initial audience are intriguing enough; but their content and scope mean that they possess far more than mere curiosity value. Ranging over history, politics and economics they draw upon their author's learning and his life as an activist.

Govan Mbeki agreed that these documents should be reprinted as they stand, and not reworked with hindsight and at leisure. He points out that they will contain gaps and silences. The essays represent only a small portion of the total material produced. Some of the essays were not based on research; in other cases, sources could not be identified lest they fell into the hands of the authorities. Over the years, the Robben Islanders had built up a collection of Marxist texts – and the authors of the political education material were unwilling to draw attention to these.

A couple of the shorter pieces ('A Note on the Comment on the Paper on Apartheid' and 'The ANC and Student Organisation') are written in the first person, responses by Mbeki to written communications from other inmates. Many of the others appear at first glance completely impersonal. Yet even in these, there are constant glimpses of Govan, echoes of his experience. There is the highly educated man: quoting Wordsworth, Kipling, Mqhayi, Cicero and Vegetius (although in this last instance, half a century after his Latin courses, Govan ascribes 'Let him who desires peace, prepare for war' to Caesar). There is the teacher: present in almost every essay, in the deft use of the Socratic question and in the measured emphases 'we stress the following significant points' ('The Rise of Afrikaner Capitalism', III). At one point Govan suggests that political leaders need 'the patience of a conscientious class teacher', and in the same document he reflects, with characteristically gentle humour, upon his schoolmasterly approach:

You complain that my Note was full of 'provocative assertions, hints and undeveloped points' which have set your mind a thinking. Blame my training as a teacher, which was entrenched in my mind by having to teach others to be teachers. One of the most important lessons in Psychology of Education and in School Method was the injunction to draw the answers from the pupils. They should work out answers from hints thrown out. When I write I so often forget that my position is no longer that of a teacher. ('A Note on the Comment')

First cousin to the teacher, there is the scholar. This is most evident, perhaps, in those essays dealing with formal economic issues ('Notes on the Business Cycle, Unemployment, Inflation and Gold', 'Movements in African Real Wages' and, the longest essay in the book, 'Monopoly Capitalism in South Africa'). Govan completed an Honours degree in economics on Robben Island, took other courses in business economics, and planned to embark (in his seventies) on a Masters degree. He effectively recycles data and arguments from his UNISA coursework in these essays. Even where he is dealing with a topical issue – explains Govan in 'The Rise of Afrikaner Capital, III' – he is not reporting as a newspaper does: he is 'on the contrary, seeking to get to the bottom of the underlying forces and factors that have been building up over a period of time'.

Not writing a newspaper – but present too is the journalist. A moving 'In memoriam' to Ruth First contains a valuable assessment of the historical contribution to the liberation movement of the *Guardian* and its successors, with 'the story behind the story' of major exposés, and an acute comment on the importance of photographs. It is a journalist's eye that remembers and describes a picture thus: 'the then Minister of Justice towering above a group of giggling Nationalist parliamentarians as he fondled a cat-o'-nine-tails'. And it is a most effective pen that produces passages like this:

'Operation Apartheid!' thus went out the order. Apartheid, Apartheid, was the war, cry. Hardboiled officials steeped in racist ideology leapt to work with crowbars and bulldozers, while close behind them were menacing Saracens, police armed with submachine guns, police holding in leash fierce Alsatian dogs no less bloodthirsty than their masters. . . . . ('Rise of Afrikaner Capital' II)

In these writings, as in Mbeki's life, there are also the unmistakable tones and temperament of a political tactician.

Go to the masses of the oppressed and exploited peoples of our land. Work among them; work with them to prepare the way for a take-over of power. Expressed briefly this is to say: Go – organise.

From this point of departure, the two-part essay on 'Good Organisation: The Key to Success' proceeds in the accents of the Port Elizabeth veteran. It is worth looking more closely at how the argument develops. Mbeki begins by posing the problem in the most general terms. If oppression and exploitation are man-made by minority interests, what must the majority do to turn things in their favour? The collective organisation of a beehive or ants' nest is driven by instinct, but in human society consciousness can be sharpened and harnessed by a political movement. The process focussing political consciousness involves 'two closely related pillars', building an organisational machinery and rallying mass support.

From these general precepts, the essay shifts to concrete, practical illustrations. In South African conditions, operating underground, 'it is a hard and exacting exercise' to recruit a strong, closely knit membership into an organisational machinery. Mbeki spells out the value of working to a schedule, meeting tasks and targets. He stipulates different approaches to various sectors – labour, educational institutions, sports organisations, professional bodies, and churches.

The second half of 'Good Organisation: The Key to Success' shifts the focus from urban to rural areas, and concentrates on the challenge of creating an organisational machinery in the bantustans. Suggestions are made about organising in migrant workers' hostels and about establishing a presence in rural areas (both to create supportive structures and to recruit and train military cadres). The essay concludes with detailed practical advice.

Cadres must produce a news sheet in the vernacular; compile a mailing list by obtaining names and addresses from migrant workers; and despatch small parcels of the publication wrapped in 'as many calendars, catalogues, sales promotion bills as they can lay their hands on'. The essay closes with these words: 'Difficult? Yes. But if the job has to be done, it must be done.'

Another striking essay is the three-part study on 'The Rise and Growth of Afrikaner Capital'. Part I is a tour de force: an historical analysis of 'the process of capital accumulation by the Afrikaner operating consciously as a group within the overall framework of the development of capitalism in this country'. Summarised thus, it will remind many readers of one of the most influential 'revisionist' monographs by a Marxist scholar — Dan O'Meara's *Volkskapitalisme*. This book was published in 1983; but Mbeki produced his study, on Robben Island, in October–November 1981.

He begins by identifying the proletarianisation of significant numbers of Afrikaners in the early years of this century, and links to this the role played within Afrikaner nationalism by an emergent intelligentsia. Then, in a passage which adumbrates O'Meara, Mbeki traces the emergence of 'business enterprises which were to be the main pillars around which in the future large concentrations of Afrikaner capital were to take shape'. He details the particular benefits extended by Hertzog to unskilled Afrikaner workers, to manufacturing enterprise, and to farmers. This provided a launch-pad from which, after 1940, 'the phenomenal growth of Afrikaner capital and its widely spreading tentacles' took place.

Part II deals with the 'socio-political-economic effects' of the rise of Afrikaner capitalism, and specifically with the responses by the oppressed peoples. Mbeki looks sternly at 'petit bourgeois misconceptions': the attempts by an emergent black middle class to cushion themselves against the blows of apartheid. Their basic error is to assume that they can replicate the success story of the Afrikaner petite bourgeoisie and clamber up the ladder of capitalist success. They fail to recognise that the objective conditions favouring the growth of Afrikaner capitalism are absent for the black middle class. The alternative response advocated is to mobilise 'all available forces to engage actively in a struggle to rid the country of the cancer of apartheid'. The paper concludes with a survey of the various forces that might be knitted together in a broad front.

Part III (written in February or March 1982) is in effect an analysis of the Botha administration's reformist initiatives and its attempted co-option of black middle class groupings via the new constitution. ('A new dispensation! Power-sharing! Words. Words.') He concludes that the new constitutional proposals are 'like a diseased foetus' that must be rejected. What did this mean in practical terms? Mbeki distinguishes between short-term and longer-term aims. In the short term, if tricameral elections were to take place, 'the task of the progressive forces' would be to mount a mass boycott so as to render hollow any claims to representivity by those elected. Long-term objectives are summed up in the slogans, 'Overthrow the fascist dictatorship. Set up a democratic people's republic.' In a telling sentence, the essential dynamics of the mid-1980s are identified – in advance. 'Inevitably, the new phase of the birth of the UDF will fuse with the on-going politico-military struggle conducted under the ANC–SACP alliance.'

Finally, there are the writings concerned with theoretical issues and generated by theoretical disputes. In various places, there recurs an explication of the relationship between the ANC – usually referred to as Inqindi ('the fist') – and the Communist Party. In 'Economic History: South Africa' Mbeki is mediating between positions taken in two other documents circulating on the Island. He argues that while the basic contradiction in capitalist societies is that between opposing classes, the imperialist epoch introduced a 'complementary contradiction', that of national oppression. The immediate project of the liberation movement led by the ANC, he argues, is to concentrate upon the complementary contradiction.

'A Discussion Document' and its companion, '3/B: A Supplement', were also written in response to formulations by others. At the heart of the exchange was the issue of what kind of society would be ushered in by an implementation of the Freedom Charter. Govan's adjudication works at several levels. It identifies practical political problems raised by a theoretical clash: he urged that the existence of conflicting views must not allow them to become rallying points for factionalism, and stressed the need to follow agreed procedures. He then sets out the two positions – which he summarises as envisaging 'Bourgeois Democracy' or 'People's Democracy', and then comes down firmly in support of the latter. He marshals a number of arguments against the proposi-

tion that the Freedom Charter would permit a flowering of
African capitalists. 'Can anyone realistically expect', he asks at
one point, 'the bourgeoisie to man the scaffold to hang themselves
by nationalising banks, monopoly industries and finance houses?'
And he spells out a vision of People's Democracy as a 'national
democratic republic', and a transitional phase towards a socialist
society.

Many, today, might disagree with Govan's radicalism. He
would respond, one suspects, much as he did on Robben Island.
Here are my positions, and here are my arguments in support of
them. You may not accept them; there may be differences of view,
but let them be discussed. 'If anything, there should emerge at the
end a clearer understanding. . . . In that way the discussion will
have borne fruit.' ('Discussion Document') What is certain is that
the issues under debate, and their outcome, are not less important
today than when the exchanges took place on Robben Island.

Govan Mbeki's prison writings – the lessons from Robben
Island gathered in this publication – offer to historians and political scientists valuable raw material for any study of the ideas and
ideology of the ANC–SACP alliance. They provide activists with
a distillation of practical lessons about political organisation,
learned in the most testing conditions. They include extended
historical, political and economic analyses that must be read
alongside Mbeki's other writings in any assessment of the intellectual history of the South African left. And they are pages in a truly
international literature – a record throughout the ages of the
creativity and indomitability of people imprisoned for their
beliefs. These prison essays mark a victory in the continuing
contest between the pen and the sword.

1. Govan Mbeki, interviewed by Colin Bundy, in Port Elizabeth, 1988. Unless
otherwise indicated, all quotations by Govan Mbeki in this Introduction are taken
from a series of interviews conducted in 1988 and 1989.
2. Fort Hare, founded in 1916 as the South African Native College, and until the
1960s the only university expressly intended for Africans. Up to 1938, Fort Hare
admitted students who were completing high school in addition to those registered
for undergraduate studies.
3. E. and W. Roux, *Rebel Pity: The Life of Eddie Roux* (London, 1970), 147, 150.
4. G. Mbeki, *Transkei in the Making* (Verulam, 1939), 13, 23.
5. Mrs Epainette Mbeki, interviewed by Colin Bundy, in Idutywa, December
1988.

6. Xuma Papers (microfilm, University of Cape Town library): G. Mbeki to Dr A. Xuma, 7 May 1941; Mbeki to Xuma, 11 September 1946; Mbeki to Xuma, 27 June 1947.

7. Carneson and Schermbrucker were members of the SACP. *New Age* was a weekly newspaper printed in Cape Town. After the *Guardian* was banned in 1952, it was followed by the *Clarion*, the *People's World, Advance, New Age* and *Spark* – each publication eventually banned. (See 'In Memoriam: Ruth First', infra.)

8. H. Bernstein, *The World That Was Ours* (London, 1989, originally 1967), 218-220.

9. M. Dingake, *My Fight Against Apartheid* (London, 1987), 203.

10. Names have been altered in this quotation.

11. From 'How They Came To Be', typescript by G. Mbeki. (This was written in 1990 to give brief details about the origins and context of the prison writings: the typescript has been a major source for this section of the Introduction).

12. Ibid.

13. Ibid.

14. Ibid.

15. Ibid.

# PART ONE

# Ruth First: In Memoriam

*'We must be free or die'*

The above words appear in a different and narrower context in a sonnet by William Wordsworth. We dig them out of that obscurity not to give them a new connotation but to apply them to a wider, nay, international setting in which the life of Comrade Ruth – now no more – may be seen. In the course of the last forty years her life has been bound up with the struggles of the oppressed and exploited peoples of this country. Freedom does not come without a struggle. And because she struggled to be free she paid the highest price which those who hold back the masses of the people here at home and the world over exact from those who strive to restore man's heritage, his birthright: freedom. Bearing in mind the South African situation, Comrade Ruth over the years consistently acted from a deep conviction of the ultimate ascendancy of the interests of the many who create wealth over those of the few who filch it. Now for a few snapshots of her in action in her crowded lifetime.

## The journalist and writer

*Her work milieu*

Comrade Ruth spent all her years as a journalist with the newspapers that were published by The Guardian Newspapers, which was succeeded by Real Printing & Publishing Co. (Pty) Ltd, both of them registered as private companies. Under their wing were published the *Guardian* (banned 1952), the *Clarion* and the *People's World* (both of which were banned in quick succession after operating for a couple of months), *Advance* (banned in 1953), and *New Age* (banned at end of 1962). *Spark*, the last of this famous line, operated for a few months and folded in March 1963. It closed after all the editorial staff in the four offices – Cape Town,

Durban, Jo'burg and Port Elizabeth – were served with banning orders that stipulated they were not to write for any newspapers or enter any premises where a newspaper was printed or published. Some of the editorial staff were served with house arrest orders.

Comrade Ruth served as the Jo'burg editor of all six of the Guardian line of newspapers (GLONS), which were in the forefront of the struggle to expose the fascist character of the National Party government. Each in its time – week after week – brought before the public of this country, and public opinion the world over, the sufferings of the oppressed and exploited peoples of this country and the masses of legislation and decrees (proclamations) churned out by the National Party government aimed at crushing all opposition among the oppressed. The GLONS went further and rallied the people to fight back.

We may pause at this moment to point out that while the National Party government – under the pretext of ridding the country of 'foreign Communist ideologies' – was attacking freedom of speech and assembly as well as the freedom of the press, the bourgeois press and politicians looked on without raising a finger. The Guardian line of newspapers warned the white opposition parties and their press that true to the Nazi tactics of taking out opponents one at a time, the Nationalist government's vicious attack on the Communist Party (CP), the Congresses, progressive trade unionists, and the GLONS would, in due course of time, be unleashed against all opponents of its policies.

After banning the CP, the government turned its guns relentlessly not only on the GLONS but on the personnel. Comrade Ruth's name, like those of many others, was placed on the roll of listed Communists. When the government made a midnight swoop in 1956 on 156 political activists who were charged with treason, Comrade Ruth was one of them. The proprietor of Pioneer Printing Press which printed *New Age* was also charged with treason as was the manager of Real Printing & Publishing Co. In this way, the paper was itself charged with committing treasonable acts.

In addition to the battles in which the GLONS was locked with the government, there was always the problem of financing the papers. From month to month and year to year there always loomed the problem of meeting the expense bill. As would be expected, the GLONS did not get any advertisements. They survived on donations from those who were in sympathy with the cause for which these papers stood or from those who supported them directly. The editorial staff had to take off time from ferreting for news or from their desks to raise donations. But the main attack came from the government – sometimes harassment in the offices by the Special Branch who confiscated material including books of accounts, sometimes interference with the sellers. For twelve years (1951–63) the GLONS fought gallantly in the front line against the rise of fascism in this country. And Comrade Ruth was always in the thick of it.

*Some highlights*

And now for a glimpse of some of the great stories covered by this line of newspapers – stories of conditions which affected millions of people so adversely and vitally as a result of laws aimed at entrenching white supremacy or, put differently, the supremacy of the interests of the whites. During the 1946 African mine-workers' strike it was the *Guardian* which went beyond the skimpy reports of the bourgeois press to show the brutality of the police in suppressing the strike: the shooting and killing of defenceless miners, the indiscriminate police attacks on miners in their compounds, flushing them out at the point of the bayonet and marching them to the shaft-head to disappear into the bowels of the gold-bearing earth. Gold – that scarce metal around which the currencies and economies of the capitalist world have revolved. The price which thousands of workers have paid to prop up capitalism and its vast machinery of exploitation is incalculable. Thousands have died a quick death from rock falls, thousands a slow painful death resulting from inhaling fine stone dust, hundreds of thousands have died miles and miles from the point of gold production where families of contract labour live in dire poverty. The mine wage structure is based on the notion that the determination of the wage should not take into account the miner's dependants because they live on subsistence farming, and that in any case a high wage would be a disincentive as mine workers would take a long time in the reserves before offering themselves for labour on the mines again. In other words, a high wage would affect the supply of mine labour unfavourably.

The shootings in Jo'burg in 1950 received full coverage in the *Guardian*. By 1952 when the Defiance Campaign got under way, press photography had already established its role. Photographs of group after group of volunteers were a tremendous visual aid that made even illiterate people buy the paper because they could read the message of the struggle from the grim faces of the volunteers and what was then the Congress salute.

In the campaign to publicise the Congress of the People, the GLONS was alone in the field explaining tirelessly what the people should do to express their views and what a future South Africa should look like. In a way it was a referendum, the result of which is the Freedom Charter.

Then came the period of the great exposures which infuriated the government. Here was a photograph of Charles R. Swart (Mnyamana), the then Minister of Justice, towering above a group of giggling Nationalist parliamentarians as he fondled a cat-o'-nine-tails after he had piloted through parliament a Bill which prescribed flogging for offences associated with those living in conditions of poverty – in other words, the oppressed.

Under Hendrik Verwoerd, then Minister of Native Affairs, the implementation of pass laws was intensified. A special police section – the Ghost Squad – was set up. Its function was to keep a tight check on passes and to arrest pass law offenders. Almost from nowhere the Ghost Squad sprang on Africans on busy streets, at odd places and times. Droves of African males were caught in this dragnet. The Native Commissioner's Courts, especially in Jo'burg, could not cope with the flood of arrests. One of the concomitant results of this drive was that a large number of such pass offenders were pressed into labour on the farms without going through the legal court procedures – such as these are. The GLONS hunted for the Ghost Squad, as they in turn, unaware they were being tracked down, hunted for and swiftly bundled their victims into closed vans. In the meanwhile people on the crowded pavements went about their business without so much as throwing a second glance at an African man who was stopped and led to the edge of the pavement, ostensibly by friends. To white South Africans all seemed normal.

The GLONS caught the Ghost Squad in action and splashed their photographs. Thus exposed, the Ghost Squad was stripped of its ghost mask. From week to week the story, accompanied by photographs, told of the disappearance without trace of men who had left the township in the morning to go to work. The people were awakened to the brutal reality of the new type of pass: the

*Dom Pass*. To check the *Dom Pass*, police had to thumb through its many pages and one was lucky not to be caught out in one or other of the various sections.

Quietly the editorial staff of GLONS was trying to solve the mysterious disappearance of law-abiding men who failed to return home after work. A number were traced to the potato farms of the eastern Transvaal in the Bethal area. Photographs of some of the lost men dressed in grain sacks were splashed. One story told of how the men were whisked away, how they lived on the potato farms, how those who died at the hands of the foremen were buried in furrows and covered under the soil as the tractor ploughed through into the furrow where the corpse lay. The unfolding of the ghastly truth was so shocking that the government did not make any attempt to deny it. Instead they explained it away by saying: those are Jewish-owned farms.

The anger of the people found immediate expression in the as yet most successful nationwide economic boycott: the potato boycott.

During periods when there was considerable unemployment in the townships, the government employed convict labour especially on the railways (at the loco). It also hired out convict labour at a fee which was far less than the average wage of unskilled labour – itself far below subsistence level. When the GLONS reported on this practice, cabinet ministers dismissed it as Communist propaganda. The GLONS took photographs of convict labour working at premises of private concerns, such as wool-packing houses. Challenged by captions such as 'The Camera Does Not Tell Lies', the government fell back on its last line of defence. It passed legislation making it a criminal offence to take and publish photos of prisoners or prisons without the permission of the minister.

In covering the march of 20 000 women to the Union Buildings to protest against the extension of pass laws to women, the GLONS captured this historic event by filming it so that it could be shown on the screen.

It is to be hoped that at some time the role that the GLONS played in advancing the cause of the struggle for liberation in this country will be shown more fully, and that a collection of some of Comrade Ruth's main articles will be compiled.

*Editor of* Fighting Talk

As editor of *Fighting Talk*, Comrade Ruth's ability as an organiser blossomed. In addition to the exacting work in GLONS, she called on her inner springs of energy to marshal a wide range of writers for the monthly *Fighting Talk*. It required one with the push she had to have ensured the regular publication of the high standard of *F. T.* She drew contributors from both within the Movement and from outside its ranks. One would have imagined that her fork already carried more hay than it could. No! In addition to finding diverse contributors who required some prodding to observe the deadlines and the general editing work involved, she had to keep an eye on the financial side and distribution of the magazine.

**A political activist**

The role which Comrade Ruth played in building and guiding the CP, especially after it was forced to operate illegally, can only be mentioned in passing here. She had one of the sharpest brains and played a vital role in solving some of the most knotty problems. At the highest decision-making levels she participated in shaping policies that will vitally influence the future course of events in this country. The CP does not operate in a vacuum. It works amongst the masses of the oppressed and exploited, and to that end she applied herself as devotedly in advancing the cause of national liberation as in advancing that of the working class. As the expression goes, *yimazi ephala neenkabi* (a mare that holds her own in the race with steeds).

Always nurturing, she worked hard to set up an illegal printing press for the Movement, and when an illegal radio was commissioned, she played an important part in the preparation of the script for broadcast. She lined up material for an illegal publication which was intended for translation into the main African languages: *Why You Should Be a Communist*. Under trying conditions she kept a steady nerve. When the post-Rivonia 'Mfecane/ Difaqane' gathered momentum and she had herself spent about four months in detention, she left the country to continue the struggle from outside the borders. This gave her an opportunity to develop yet another dimension in her varied contribution to the struggle. She engaged in research work, on the basis of which she wrote books on problems affecting the African continent.

**At home**

Those who knew her as the tough politician she was or as the journalist who used her pen so effectively to destroy the myth of the race superiority of the whites, might have found it difficult to think of her as a woman who had a home to run and a mother who had children to rear. She invited friends to her home and as a host she was always warm. Her idea of what a new South Africa should look like was reflected in the relaxed atmosphere one experienced in her home.

## Weep no more

Comrade Ruth is no more, but to those who would shed tears we say: Weep no more. She lived a full and fruitful life. Her life holds lessons for us, the living: to hold back nothing of ourselves to ensure ultimate victory for the cause of the struggle against fascism. Comrade Ruth dedicated her life to this noble cause, and in thinking of her, let our resolve to bring about the liberation of the masses of the oppressed and exploited peoples of this land - whatever the price – be strengthened. She has shown us: 'We must be free or die.'

Forward to Freedom.

*Amandla! Matla!*

[Ruth First died on 17 August 1982]

# Reply to P.W. Botha's Offer to Release on Condition We Renounce Violence

All of us endorse fully the reply made by Nelson Mandela [February 1985] to your offer of a conditional release. In doing so we would like to emphasise that our organisation, the African National Congress, was founded on the policy of non-violence in its search for freedom for the oppressed people of South Africa. This policy of non-violence was borne out by almost fifty years' record of peaceful struggle.

With the coming into power of the National Party in 1948, the ANC was subjected to all forms of harassment by the police. It was the NP government that set up, for the first time in South Africa, a special branch of the police, similar to the secret police of Nazi Germany and Fascist Italy. Our leaders were subjected to police harassment and many of them were banned, house-arrested or banished to remote areas of the country.

The reign of the National Party saw the worst forms of racism in the country. The blood-baths of Sharpeville and Langa stands as a ghastly record of NP rule by the gun. When the ANC decided to protest against the blood-letting on 28 March 1960 by destroying the pass – that badge of bondage – the NP government replied by banning our Organisation. The peaceful protest of the people against the declaration of a Republic, without a mandate from the people of South Africa, in May 1961, was visited with police mass raids and the mobilisation of the army.

All this showed clearly that the NP government did not countenance any opposition by the oppressed to its apartheid regime. When it should have heeded the just and democratic demands of the people, the NP government went ahead with the implementation of the bantustans and Urban Bantu Councils, which were established on the same model as the ghetto Jewish authorities under Nazi Germany.

Even the longest road has a turning. The oppressed had to decide whether they were to live and perish on their knees or stand up and fight rather than surrender.

You, Mr President, are now saying we must desert our people and all that we have lived for; we must desert what our people are struggling for at this very moment. You say we must undertake not to be arrested again. Who of the oppressed black people and democratic white people can escape the wide dragnet of the draconian apartheid laws?

Only those who have sold their souls can imagine they are safe; only the puppets can imagine they are safe. The vast minefield of apartheid laws makes your offer a mockery. It is patently clear that you do not intend your offer to be accepted by an organisation as principled as the ANC is. Your offer is intended to provide your imperialist friends with a pretext to continue to support the National Party regime.

Our people are today dying daily of police bullets in the townships. School children are undergoing the rigours of indefinite detentions. All this takes place despite the fact that we are arrested and kept away for more than twenty years. It is clear therefore that it is apartheid that is the cause of all this violence in our country. It is apartheid that must be renounced and dismantled if there is to be peace in this country.

[September 1985]

# Comrade Moses Mabida: In Memoriam

**Comrade Moses Mabida: his origins**

In paying our last respects in memoriam to Comrade Moses, it is well to remember that it is not the amount of words we say here that will measure the depth of our feelings at the loss to the liberation struggle of the peoples of our land. His life and struggles are an open book for all to read and evaluate.

Often we walk along the pavement, stop at a display window and admire a beautifully tailored woollen suit – a finished product. It never occurs to us at that moment that the finished product is made from the wool shorn from a sheep, leaving it exposed to all the weather changes.

Comrade Moses was born and brought up in his early years in a small peri-urban location which, for all practical purposes, borders on peasant areas outside Maritzburg. Look at the lifeless, uninspiring conditions in which the children born and bred there live. Look at the drab surroundings into which the children of our oppressed peoples are born and reared: the slum conditions of our ugly townships in the urban areas. But the weight of such squalor and oppression has not overwhelmed them. They have risen to stake their rightful claim to their birthright: *Inkululeko, Tokololo, Vryheid,* Freedom.

And Comrade Moses emerged from their ranks and they elevated him to the highest positions to lead them.

Comrade Moses – the secretary of the working class party, the CP. Comrade Moses – a member of the National Executive of the ANC – the spearhead of the struggle for national liberation.

**Comrade Moses: the man**

Comrade Moses Mbeki Mabida will long be remembered by those who knew him personally. He was modest and unassuming in his daily relations with those who came his way. I don't know how much his teacher at school – Comrade Harry Gwala – contributed towards this quality which endeared Comrade Moses to all who met him. At almost all the Organisation's meetings Comrade Moses was a delight to listen to when interpreting from English to Zulu. Invariably he improved on the English version.

## Comrade Moses: in action

His public life started at an early age when he was still a student. He joined the CP and the ANC. After leaving school he became an organiser of the Transport Workers' Union in Maritzburg. During the early 1950s he moved to Durban where he became the secretary of the Railway Workers' Union until he left the country in 1960. In Durban he rose to the provincial executive of the ANC where he worked very closely with Chief A.J. Luthuli, then President-General.

By the end of the 1950s the ANC had mounted, through its anti-government campaigns, such tremendous pressures that the National Party government blundered into a declaration of a state of emergency. A strange and happy coincidence took place. On the day the police swooped on the leading members, Comrade Moses had gone to Maritzburg and managed to escape arrest. Up north, as Comrade Wilton Mkwayi left the Treason Trial court, he saw police standing at the door of their transport. He asked: 'What's going on here?' A policeman threatened to arrest him for 'obstruction'. He apologised and the policeman ordered him to go away, and so he escaped detention under the Emergency. The government has lived to rue the day these two trade unionists were not drawn into the police dragnet. SACTU [the South African Congress of Trade Unions] lost no time in sending them overseas to establish a mission at the headquarters of the World Federation of Trade Unions.

During the years that Comrade Moses headed this mission abroad, it carried out a campaign to draw the attention of the world's organised working class to the plight of the black working class in South Africa. Comrade Moses soon gained the respect and confidence of those with whom he came into contact. At international conferences the delegates from Africa always elected him to be the spokesman for Africa. The combined campaigns on various international fronts by the ANC, SACTU and the CP have ripened into today's massive international pressures to destroy apartheid.

**Comrade Moses: the lasting lesson he taught us**
The problems created by legalised racism, the institutionalised separateness between blacks and whites in South Africa, are not often well appreciated. The fact that over the years each of the four main racial groups has built up its own organisation purporting to advance its own interests has kept apart groups that should have been bound together to fight the common enemy. This problem has spilled over even into the CP, which has been non-racial throughout the years. Some of its members are white and enjoy all the privileges of whites while the black members suffer all the hardships of oppression and special exploitation.

It has been the task of the members of the CP, especially the black members, to lay bare the tricks of the oppressors and themselves be a living example of how a member of the CP can work in the national liberation organisation in a manner that inspires confidence and trust. It was on this absolute trust between the ANC and the CP that these two organisations have built the alliance that has shaken the very foundations of apartheid, and the National Party government is today fighting for its very survival.

To his very last breath Comrade Moses has been foremost in bringing about the successes we see today.

Let us take up the lesson and accomplish what he has taught us.
Our condolences go to his family.

[Moses Mabida died on 8 March 1986]

# PART TWO

# The Rise and Growth of Afrikaner Capital
## I

### AN OUTLINE OF THE PROBLEM

In this paper we seek to initiate, hopefully, an in-depth study on the rise and growth of Afrikaner capital. On reading the title the reader may, as a first reaction, be taken aback and might understandably ask the question: Why that of the Afrikaner, and not of any other white ethnic group? Or alternatively, why not deal with the rise and growth of capitalism in South Africa? But why that of the Afrikaner?

In the course of this study we hope to be able to uncover some unique aspects in the process of capital accumulation by the Afrikaner operating consciously as a group within the overall framework of the development of capitalism in this country. The fact that the Afrikaner constitutes about 60 per cent of the homogeneous capital-accumulating group should be expected to have far-reaching implications for socio-politico-economic relations within the body politic.

The problem we are setting out to study is wide and complex. Failure to grasp its essentials can and does lead to a great deal of confusion among the populace. And without a clear understanding of the complex nature of the problems that bedevil not only the political but also the socio-economic relations among the peoples of our country, it would be difficult to reach decisions about what to do and how to bring about a basic change in the status quo if we are to survive.

To keep the paper within a tolerable length and transportable proportions we have decided to divide it into two parts. In Part I, we shall concentrate on dissecting and laying bare the whole process of capital accumulation by the Afrikaner bourgeoisie. In Part II we propose to deal with the aspects suggested by the subtitle: the socio-politico-economic effects arising out of the creation of exclusive group capitalist structures in order to achieve ends that place a small Afrikaner bourgeoisie, acting in the name of the Afrikaner as a 'nation', in a domineering position over all the peoples of South Africa.

## THE MOBILISATION OF THE AFRIKANER

Up to the discovery of diamonds (*circa* 1870) in Kimberley and gold (1886) along the Witwatersrand, Afrikaners concentrated mainly on subsistence farming. They produced largely to satisfy the immediate requirements of the family. For almost two decades thereafter there was no great influx of Afrikaners into the towns that were springing up around the mining activities in Kimberley and Johannesburg. The English-speaking people, consisting largely of immigrants from Britain, formed the main white population group in the towns and cities that developed. It was largely as a result of the increasing destitution of the Afrikaner on the land that a significant drift to the towns took place, especially after 1910. Right up to the end of the First World War there was hardly any Afrikaner bourgeoisie worth talking about. In the 1920s when the poor white problem, which in reality was essentially a problem of poor Afrikaners, had assumed alarming proportions, the Dutch Reformed Church (DRC) mounted the campaign 'Back to the Land'. The DRC said the answer to the breakdown of Afrikaner 'traditional moral standards' in the urban areas was a return to the isolation and stagnation of the impoverished *platteland*. The tragedy today for all the people of this country is that the DRC, which still exercises tremendous influence on the Afrikaner in-group, has hardly advanced sufficiently to face the socio-economic problems associated with an industrialised environment, other than the stereotyped thinking that was designed to serve the moral and religious requirements of the *plaasboer* more than half a century ago.

While the Afrikaner bourgeoisie had scarcely emerged in the 1920s the exclusively Afrikaner universities existing then — Stellenbosch and Grey University College (OFS) — were turning out intellectuals in increasing numbers. In addition, a stream of Afrikaner students at the post-graduate level were studying at universities in the Netherlands and to a lesser extent in Germany. On their return, the role played by those intellectuals largely shaped, if not determined, the political course which made South Africa what it is today.

In the period following the Boer War, the rallying call to the

Afrikaner was to repair the damage which British imperialism and the cruel years in the concentration camps had done to the dignity of the Afrikaner. But by the 1920s and especially after the National Party take-over as the government, with the support of the Labour Party, in 1924, the National Party had to find a new rallying point which would not alienate the English-speaking whites. It now called upon the Afrikaners to stand together to fight against *die swartgevaar* [the black peril]. Thus a common fear and common hatred were generated against a common enemy – the African. It is this fear and hatred of a common enemy that the Afrikaner intellectuals so skilfully exploited to mobilise the Afrikaners as a homogeneous group to seek their salvation in their ethnic homogeneity. They shifted the emphasis of their attack against British imperialism and projected an image of the Afrikaner striving to preserve 'white civilisation', when in reality to them 'white' was synonymous with the Afrikaner, and 'white civilisation' with Afrikaner hegemony. The non-Afrikaner whites fell for it. Politically they became indifferent, concentrated on business and thus gave the Nationalist Afrikaner a free hand to carry on with his allotted mission to put *die kaffer in sy plek*.

With fanatical devotion the Afrikaner intellectuals set about mobilising the Afrikaner through a number of societies or associations which sought to mould Afrikaners, in every walk of life, into an undifferentiated mass. The following are the main, exclusively Afrikaner societies or associations through which all Afrikaners were finally herded into the Afrikaner laager:

1. The Dutch Reformed Church (DRC)
2. The Broederbond
3. Die Suid-Afrikaanse Buro vir Rasse-Aangeleenthede (SABRA)
4. Die Federasie van Afrikaanse Kultuurvereniginge (FAK)
5. Die Afrikaanse Handelsinstituut (AHI)
6. Die Afrikaanse Studentebond (ASB)
7. Die Reddingsdaadbond
8. Die Instituut vir Christelike Nasionale Onderwys
9. Die Onderwysers Unie
10. Die Federasie van Vakbonde.

Let us deal briefly with a few of these associations with exclusively Afrikaner membership to show how the strategy of Afrikaner intellectuals to mobilise the Afrikaners unfolded in the period between the two World Wars.

From a study of the above-mentioned list of associations some of the most glaring examples of race or ethnic exclusivism stand out. Even in those cases where there were already existing associations – as far as whites were concerned – the Afrikaners broke away to form exclusively Afrikaner ones. The Federated Chambers of Industry (FCI) and the Association of Chambers of Commerce (ASSOCOM) were to serve the interests of industry and commerce, but the Afrikaners formed the Afrikaanse Handelsinstituut (AHI) and the Sakekamer. Instead of the South African Institute of Race Relations they set up SABRA. The Afrikaner students broke away from NUSAS to form the ASB. The SA Federation of Trade Unions was formed to cater for the exclusive interests of Afrikaner workers like the Mine Workers' Union organized by Dr Albert Hertzog so as to keep them out of the South African Trades and Labour Council. The reason behind the formation of these exclusive Afrikaner associations was to organise the Afrikaners in order to assert themselves as a group instead of establishing their position on individual merit within the capitalist system. What justification is there today for these exclusive Afrikaner associations?

**The Dutch Reformed Church**
The DRC is based on the teachings of Calvin, whose central theme is the doctrine of predestination. This teaches that man's life on earth is charted by God from birth to the grave. From this the Afrikaner religious leaders have evolved the idea that they are God's chosen race and have been endowed with a special destiny to rule over groups in South Africa. By far the greatest majority of Afrikaners are members of the DRC, which is committed to race domination. For a long time, the DRC played a dominant role in determining and guiding the policy of the National Party. Even in this day it continues to exercise a significant influence on the Nationalist government in implementing the apartheid policy in all spheres of life in the country.

**The Broederbond**
This was formed in 1919. According to a statement issued by the Broederbond in 1934 its primary aim was 'Whether Afrikanerdom will reach its ultimate destiny of domination in South Africa.' In charting the course of the Broederbond the statement was precise in defining what it aimed to achieve: 'Our solution of South

Africa's ailments is . . . that the Afrikaner Broederbond shall govern South Africa.'

Towards the end of World War Two, the Broederbond had come under attack by General J.C. Smuts as a 'political fascist organisation'. In defence, the secretary I.M. Lombard replied in a manner whose meaning was to be appreciated in less than five years when the NP won the 1948 elections. He stated: 'The Afrikaner Broederbond is born out of a deep conviction that the Afrikaner nation was put in this land by God and is destined to continue in existence as a nation with its own nature and calling.'

Of the seven ideals which the Broeders are called upon to strive for, we single out two, because they spell out without mincing words what a National Party government dominated by members of the Broederbond must aim to achieve as a matter of principle and top priority. The Broeders must strive to achieve:

(a) 'Separation of all non-white races in South Africa, leaving them free to independent development under the guardianship of the whites.'

(b) 'The Afrikanerisation of our public life and our teaching and education in a Christian National spirit while leaving free the internal development of all sections of the nation in so far as it is not dangerous to the State.'

In itself the Broederbond is a small compact organisation consisting of highly disciplined and utterly committed members drawn largely from a cross-section of the Afrikaner population. But its influence permeates surreptitiously the whole being of Afrikanerdom. In other words, its invisible hand guides the policies and actions of all exclusively Afrikaner organisations from the government down to a *jukskei* club. The Afrikaner must dominate in accordance with God's will. This lesson is tirelessly and relentlessly driven into the mind of the Afrikaner from the cradle to the grave.

## Die Federasie van Afrikaanse Kultuurvereniginge (FAK)

This was set up in 1929 to coordinate and direct a wide range of Afrikaner associations, e.g. women's and youth organisations, especially on the farms and in the churches. It also sponsored the formation of Afrikaans dramatic societies, scientific study circles, and welfare organisations. It held conferences from time to time to discuss matters relating to the advancement of the Afrikaner cause, e.g. fostering the use of Afrikaans, Afrikaner literature, etc.

## Die Reddingsdaadbond (RDB)

The RDB is another of the major Afrikaner organisations set up, like the FAK, at the instance of the Broederbond. Its primary task was to break down the Afrikaner farm mentality, to launch him into the urban, industrialised life, to orientate him towards capitalism, to establish his own industries, to launch commercial enterprises, and in the workplace 'to keep the Afrikaner worker away from foreign elements, i.e. to keep him in his church, language and own environment'. In other words, even in the work situation the Afrikaner workers were urged to club together, insulate themselves from influences that encourage the solidarity of the working class and therefore seek to bring them close to and to cooperate with non-Afrikaner workers on a class basis. Rather, the watchword for them was to belong to the Afrikaner group and to strive to advance Afrikaner group interests. About two years before the end of the Second World War, one Fritz Steyn bemoaned the fact that 'The Afrikaner Nation is the poorest element in the white population of our country, and is even poorer than the Indian.'

He estimated that not more than 5 per cent of the total capital in industry was controlled by Afrikaners and pointed out that Indians possessed 5 000 more general dealers' licences than the Afrikaners, in spite of the fact that comparatively speaking the Indian population was smaller than that of the Afrikaner group. Is it any wonder that after the war the National Party mounted a campaign to boycott Indian and Jewish shops on the *platteland*? Thus the Afrikaners were strongly reminded that their salvation as a nation lay in greater cooperation among themselves as a group. They were exhorted to spend their earnings in Afrikaner enterprises. Some of the most outstanding activities of the RDB were to grant loans to young Afrikaners who took up commercial and technical training; counsel Afrikaners in the running of business; and finance some Afrikaner businesses from its own capital resources.

As a result of these activities, small business enterprises which had been in the hands of the English-speakers and the Jews on the eve of World War Two in the small country towns had, by 1950, almost entirely passed into the hands of the Afrikaner.

## Die Suid-Afrikaanse Buro vir Rasse-Aangeleenthede

SABRA came into being in the late 1940s and was formed by a group of intellectuals at Stellenbosch. Its first conference took place in 1950. It was set up with the special purpose to bring together Afrikaner intellectuals to develop a theoretical framework for the apartheid policies as accepted and practised by the National Party government and the overwhelming section of the Afrikaner community.

SABRA issued every month a scholarly journal on racial affairs and masses of other propaganda material to justify apartheid. Some of the best Afrikaner brains from the Afrikaans-speaking universities and others outside such universities used SABRA as a gathering place from which to hatch out the most repugnant theories on race superiority. The SABRA intellectuals spun a notion based on statistics concocted out of the blue that the 'native reserves' were capable of supporting an African population far in excess of 10 million. It was here that this Afrikaner 'brains trust' showed its intellectual dishonesty as it stooped to provide justification for the genocidal measures of the Nationalist government in forcing Africans into a mass death trap – the bantustans. Towards what end were the Afrikaner intellectuals in conjunction with the National Party mobilising the Afrikaners?

## AFRIKANER ENTRY INTO BUSINESS

From the time that the National Party assumed power it has been difficult to draw a clear line between National Party policy and the activities of the Afrikaner intellectuals in pursuing measures that aimed at advancing goals exclusively for the benefit of the Afrikaners. To attain those goals it did not matter what the cost was to anyone else outside the Afrikaner ethnic group. The foremost task which both the Afrikaner intellectuals and the National Party government set themselves to tackle in the 1920s was to lay down clear guidelines for the elimination of the poor white problem. Over the years the Afrikaner population on the farms had increased considerably. Farms were subdivided as each of the farmer's sons came of age. The process was carried on to such an extent that even when conditions for commercial farming came with the increasing urbanisation around the mining areas and the seaports, the agricultural units were too small to ensure a regular income to live on. Poverty among the Afrikaners had become so widespread that the Nationalist government appointed the Carnegie Commission on the Poor White Problem (thus named because it was financed by a grant from the Carnegie Trust of the USA). It was estimated that 50 per cent or more of the Afrikaners on the farms were destitute.

The two decades between the two World Wars saw the unfolding of a two-pronged plan. On the one hand, the intellectuals set up business enterprises which were to be the main pillars around which in the future large concentrations of Afrikaner enterprises were to take shape. On the other hand, the Nationalist government led by General Hertzog lost no time in creating a legal framework in which the plans of the Afrikaner intellectuals could be given free play. Let us examine in broad outline the role each played in this period and how the two roles complemented each other.

## The role of the intellectuals

The first big Afrikaner business enterprise, although it had a small beginning, was Sanlam, which was established in 1918. For its premium income from insurance policies it relied on the support of Afrikaners. Although its premiums were higher than those of the then English insurance companies (whether South African or foreign-based), it appealed to Afrikaner sentiment to make such sacrifices in order to ensure the survival of Afrikaner business enterprises. The campaign claimed that only Afrikaner businesses could guarantee employment to Afrikaners then, as well as in the future. Establishing an insurance company which, it was calculated by its founders, would depend on the incomes of Afrikaners for its business was regarded as an act of faith by those whose business decisions were influenced by no other consideration than well-conducted market surveys. In those days the Afrikaners were by and large destitute and those on the farms barely literate. But Afrikaner intellectuals would take no excuse if it obstructed the prosecution of their grand plan. In the course of the years, Sanlam has grown by leaps and bounds into the giant which, according to a recent report, was able to increase its assets in a matter of twelve months by R500 million from R2 500 million to R3 000 million.

The second pillar which these intellectuals, working through the Federasie van Afrikaanse Kultuurvereniginge (FAK), set up was Volkskas (1934). Another act of faith. The country had scarcely come out of the 1929–33 economic depression; the Afrikaner had not then made a mark in the main sectors of the economy (mining, manufacturing and commerce) and agriculture was in a chaotic state. In short, the Afrikaner bourgeoisie had not then emerged.

A sceptic might well have doubted the viability of Volkskas – a commercial bank established to serve exclusively Afrikaner banking interests – and reserved judgement. But Volkskas today is one of the five commercial banks in the country and heads a big conglomerate, i.e. a large group of unrelated business concerns. In addition, it provides some sophisticated services in the banking field, e.g. merchant banks and others.

In the uncertain international climate of 1939 the Afrikaner intellectuals launched the Ekonomiese Volkskongres. It was at that conference that the late Professor Schumann, head of the Faculty of Commerce at the University of Stellenbosch, set the tone by stating the problem the Afrikaner intellectual had to seek to understand and to find a solution. At that conference he said: 'It cannot be sufficiently strongly emphasised that our position in the first place depends on ourselves – on our physical, spiritual and moral strength. It is in the final analysis the deciding factor.' The role of the intellectuals was, he continued, 'To examine soberly and honestly the factual position; we must try to find out whether that position is the result of inherent characteristics, or weaknesses from unavoidable historical happenings or of the peculiar capitalist system as it has developed in our country.'

Around this third main pillar a wide range of Afrikaner business enterprises mushroomed – mining, manufacturing, commerce services, finance banking – all carrying the stamp of an Afrikaner-dom thrust along the capitalist road.

**The role of the government**

The coming into power of the National Party in 1924 placed it in an excellent position to carry out a legislative programme which coincidentally and, perhaps, by design dovetailed with the plans of the intellectuals, namely to develop the Afrikaner in all fields of economic activity, in order to prepare for the day when he would have the monopoly of political power firmly in his hands. After all, the National Party government and the Afrikaner intellectuals have worked towards the same goal even though they may appear to be operating at different levels. Professor Schumann was for many years adviser to the Hertzog government, as Dr Riekert was after 1948 and until recently adviser to the Nationalist government, and presently Dr S. S. Brand.

The following are some of the measures the Hertzog government, with the support of the Labour Party, took to improve the position of the Afrikaner:

(i) It pressed for the recognition of Afrikaans as an official language. Once this was attained it was a short step before separate Afrikaans-medium schools sprang up. In turn this stepped up the enrolment of Afrikaner pupils as well as teachers and those qualifying sufficiently to enter the civil service. The increasing numbers of Afrikaners entering the higher-income sectors of the economy provided a rich field for Sanlam agents to hunt. Principals of schools, police station commanders and others in strategic positions on the railways, became recruiting agents for Sanlam.

(ii) The adoption of the 'civilised labour policy' placed the unskilled Afrikaner — and most of the Afrikaner workers then were unskilled — at an income level that was arbitrarily fixed to be in keeping with the 'civilised standards of a white man' rather than with his productivity.

(iii) In 1925 the government passed protective tariff legislation to encourage the establishment of a manufacturing industry. Such protection was not without strings. Manufacturing enterprises were called upon to give priority of employment to whites and this virtually meant Afrikaners, who were fleeing in droves from the poverty of the *platteland*. To impress the government and the white consumers, some employers, especially those manufacturing tinned foods like jam, used wrappers marked in big black letters against a white background: 'Manufactured by white labour'. The government employed hundreds of thousands of unskilled Afrikaners in the public sector, e.g. on the railways, roads, and in the post office.

The adoption of the manufacturing policy with the strings attached to it was so effective that by the outbreak of World War Two the poor white problem was virtually wiped out.

(iv) In 1926 the government passed the Wage Act, in terms of which a Wage Board was set up to determine the wages of unskilled white workers. This ensured that employers were forced to pay unskilled Afrikaner workers not only a living wage but a wage that would enable them to maintain a standard expected of a white man.

(v) The government also turned its attention to the hopeless position of the farmers. Farming was bedevilled by chaotic conditions and large-scale impoverishment. To stem this, the government stepped in to regulate production, marketing and pricing of agricultural products. It passed the Marketing Act (1937), in terms of which the Maize Control Board and other control boards in respect of a wide range of products determined price levels that would ensure the farmer a sufficiently high income compatible with a decent standard of living.

These sweeping measures by the Nationalist government to pull the Afrikaner out of dire poverty cleared the decks for the launching of Afrikanerdom on its economic trajectory.

## THE BUILD-UP OF AFRIKANER CAPITAL: 1940–80

It should assist our study to preface the examination of the build-up of Afrikaner capital with a brief comparative comment on the early development of capitalism in a few leading capitalist countries. Hopefully this approach should throw into clear perspective the peculiar aspect of an exclusive capitalist structure taking place within a developing capitalist framework.

In Britain the early stages of capitalist development were based on individual efforts by the merchant class, who subordinated the domestic handicraftsmen to capitalism on the 'putting-out system'. In the course of time this development resulted in the crystallization of classes depending on the position in which they came to stand in relation to the means of production.

In America much of the capitalist development in the early stages was given impetus by massive investment from Britain in such basic projects as the railways.

At the beginning of the nineteenth century the German economy was mostly agricultural, and the country was divided into many principalities, each of which levied taxes (tariffs) on products crossing the border from other German provinces. On the other hand, goods from Britain with its comparatively highly developed capitalist economy entered Germany free of duties. In the words of Germany's foremost nationalist protectionist, Friedrich List: 'While other nations cultivated the finance and the arts whereby commerce and industry are extended, German merchants and manufacturers must devote a great part of their time to tariffs and taxes.'

After the unification of Germany the urge to place Germany on a footing to compete with more developed capitalist countries, especially Britain, became overriding. Rather than looking to individual capitalists, the banks entered commerce and industry to build the economy. All the three capitalist countries in whose image capitalism has developed world-wide share this feature in common: that capitalism is developed on a national basis. The national bourgeoisie strive to advance their interests on the one hand, while on the other, the working class create structures to defend their interests as a class on a national level, e.g. trade unions.

Where and how does the departure from the trodden path occur in the development of capitalism in South Africa?

## The multi-sector thrust of Afrikaner capital

In the period from 1940 to 1980 the number of Afrikaner-owned and -controlled companies listed on the Johannesburg Stock Exchange (JSE) has increased to about forty. But that figure in itself tells only a very small part of the phenomenal growth of Afrikaner capital and its widely spread, grabbing tentacles. This part of the story – generally unknown to the public – is only told by a study of the subsidiary companies falling under the main companies like Federale Volksbeleggings, Volkskas, Sanlam, etc. Then, in turn, some of these subsidiaries strike out on their own and acquire their own subsidiaries, which are not all listed on the JSE. The result is that hundreds and, it may even be, thousands are owned or controlled by Afrikaner capital. Add to these numerous thrusts which Afrikaner capital makes through investments in non-Afrikaner-controlled companies, and then the projects undertaken in association with other non-Afrikaner-controlled national and international enterprises. Another important feature is that the business name in which a company is registered and licensed does not necessarily give an indication of the financial group interests behind it. For instance, a number of businesses bearing English names are in fact controlled by Afrikaner capital. And where Afrikaner capital operates in areas like Botswana, the businesses carry Tswana business names. Obviously this practice is a hedge against boycotts. Another important feature is that intellectuals still play a major role on the directorate of the main groups, and also serve on the directorates of a number of subsidiaries controlled by Afrikaner capital. This suggests that the bourgeoisie are still thinly spread. Below we make a closer study of a few selected companies or groups.

*Federale Volksbeleggings (as at 31/3/79)*

The parent of this is the Sanlam group and associated companies.

Subsidiaries and associated companies number 314, while it has investments in 14 listed companies and 55 unlisted companies. The group has substantial shares in Federale Kunsmis, Irvin and Johnson, Durban Cement, Veka, Siemens (South Africa), and Sentrale Chemiese Beleggings. By spreading its investments in many non-Afrikaner-controlled companies, it is able to get valuable information on their operations. Among its subsidiaries we mention a few: Grahamstown Potteries, SA Television Manufacturing, Botswana Bonemeal Factory, Bechuanaland Malt and Milling Company, Selebi-Phikwe Wholesale, Sefalana SA Botswana Ltd.

## Volkskas Group (as at 31/3/79)

This group has two subsidiaries and has spread its operations to merchant banking, industrial banking and insurance broking. Volkskas group has also given rise to Volkskas Property Trust Management Ltd.

## Federale Mynbou (as at 31/3/79)

Its major parents are the Sanlam and Volkskas groups.

The subsidiaries of the group include General Mining, which in turn has interest in 40 listed subsidiaries. The Federale Mynbou group has effective control of 61 companies. In addition this group has interests in the following: 14 subsidiaries in Namibia; 17 in Luxembourg; 258 in Zimbabwe; 10 in the UK; 1 in Brazil; and 1 in Swaziland.

The group has investments in 100 other companies and has substantial investments in certain gold, coal, and platinum mines.

## South African Druggists (as at 31/3/79)

The parent of this group is the Federale Chemiese Beleggings, itself a subsidiary of Federale Volksbeleggings. This group has 97 subsidiaries and has investments in 34 other companies. This places this group in a commanding position in the manufacture and marketing of medicines in the country.

We have given brief notes on only four of the main groups spawned by Afrikaner capital. Among some of the biggest groups are:

1. Bank Holding Corporation of SA: parent, Sanlam.
2. Assura: parents Federale Volksbeleggings and Sentrust, the latter spawned by Federale Mynbou and Sanlam.

3. Bonuskor: parent, Volkskas group.
4. Federale Voedsels (Fedfoods): parent, Federale Volks-beleggings (FVB).
5. General Mining: parent, Federale Mynbou. Of interest is that Harry Oppenheimer is one of the directors of General Mining.
6. Rembrandt Group: parent, Rembrandt Controlling Investment. Of interest is that Prof R.E. van der Ross, Rector of UWC, is one of the directors.
7. Sentrachem: parent, Federale Chemiese Beleggings.
8. Veka: parent, FVB.
9. Impala Platinum Holdings: parent, FVB.
10. Trust Bank: parent, Bank Holding Corporation.

## Factors favouring the growth of Afrikaner capital

To what does this phenomenal growth and spread of Afrikaner capital owe its success? We single out five factors – and there are others – which favoured such growth. We may very briefly deal with them in turn:

### Protective tariffs

Before and after 1925 when legislation to foster the development of the manufacturing industry was passed, custom and excise duties had been levied, and they were one of the sources of revenue for the state. The purpose of protective tariffs, however, is not to raise revenue but to protect selected industries (infant industries) against competition from abroad. While the legislation was not intended to protect exclusively Afrikaner manufacturing concerns, such as sprang up benefited considerably from the raising of protective tariff walls. In addition, the growth of the manufacturing industry opened opportunities of employment for a large number of impoverished Afrikaners whose incomes were shepherded into Afrikaner business concerns.

### World War Two

The war conditions created a favourable climate for the growth of Afrikaner capital. The shortage of shipping forced the pace of industrialisation to supply not only the civilian demand for manufactured products but also the Allied armed forces operating in Africa. A number of business concerns sprang up during the war years. In the years following the war, the government still gave the newly established industries a protective umbrella to encourage them to manufacture goods to replace imported goods (substitution industry). The release after the war of the pent-up demand (i.e. funds which could not be spent during the war years owing to unavailability of supplies) kept business lively for the new industries as the government regulated the flow of imports of goods through import control regulations.

The shortage of white labour during the war years caused a phenomenal increase in their income. As they could not spend much of this owing to lack of supplies, the Afrikaner financial institutions siphoned it off for investment in commerce, industry, property and services under Afrikaner business control.

## Decentralisation

Primarily the purpose of embarking on decentralisation was to carry out part of the Nationalist government's master plan: to implement the apartheid policy. By forcing industry to establish in the border areas, the Nationalist government hoped to reduce the flow of African labour to the main established industrial concentrations in the country. The incentives the government offered were an attractive bait for small labour-intensive industries. Here are a few of the main incentives:

(a) The government would provide the infrastructure in the border area, i.e. roads, railway facilities, water, electricity.

(b) The wages of African labour in these areas would not be subject to determination by the Wage Board and Industrial Council agreement. Thus African labour in these areas depended on the mercies of the employers, who in practice saw to it that their wages were kept at barely a subsistence level. Add to this the fact that the trade unions were frowned upon by the police until only about three years ago when the Wiehahn Commission report was adopted. Only in a few border areas close to a metropolitan centre was there any trade union activity, e.g. Hammarsdale. To show to what extent African labour in the border industry areas was being exploited, the ratio of salaries and wages to net output was only 38,5 per cent compared with 49,5 per cent in the main industrial areas. The table below further illustrates the discrepancy in the wage scales between the border areas and the metropolitan centres.

# Average earnings of production workers in manufacturing

|  | Year | Males | Females |
|---|---|---|---|
| East London | '56/7 | R312.00 (1 666.60) | R132.40 (694.40) |
| Cape Border Areas | '56 | R206.40 (1 453.20) | R94.00 (713.80) |
| Durban–Pinetown | '56 | R319.60 (1 401.40) | R238.40 (922.80) |
| Natal Border Areas | '56 | R238.80 (1 942.40) | R134.60 (858.20) |

In fact the government pledged itself to maintain lower wages in border areas, i.e. for African labour. The figure in brackets in the table represents the average earnings of white workers in the respective areas shown in the table.

This disproportionately big gap between African and white workers represents the extra surplus value raked off by the employers, from which white wages were subsidised. The effect is that in South Africa white workers have, in practice, some common interest with the capitalist and thus defend apartheid structures.

(c) *Easy loans.* The Industrial Development Corporation (IDC) was always ready to provide long-term loans at low interest rates. And in addition the IDC was prepared to buy shares in border industries which it readily sold back as soon as there were buyers or the firm was in a position to stand on its own. What new manufacturing concern would not jump at such heaven-sent opportunities and other attractive incentives to establish itself? Afrikaner capital rode on the wave that was to carry it to a bourgeois earthly paradise. Witness its presence in Newcastle, Tukela Basin, Rosslyn, Brits, etc.

(d) *Regimentation of African labour.* The determination of the wage level of Africans, as they were drawn into the manufacturing industry, was largely influenced by the level of wages on the gold mines. Both the government and the Chamber of Mines were strongly opposed to the creation of competition for African labour on a wage basis. Two related considerations were decisive. Firstly the price of gold was fixed by international agreement at $35 per fine ounce and it was sold to central banks only until 1971–72.

Secondly, gold sales were the main source of foreign exchange to pay for machinery required for the manufacturing industry as well as for imported consumer commodities demanded by whites long accustomed to a life of unearned ease and comfort.

The Wage Board, as we saw above, was initially set up to ensure the wages of poor whites were in keeping with the maintenance of a standard of living expected of the white man. But by the end of the war the Wage Board was no longer required for this purpose, and white workers had largely been drawn into trade unions for whose members they negotiated wage agreements under the Industrial Conciliation machinery. The Wage Board, however, still continued to carry out its function to determine wages for unorganised labour. But the big difference was that after the war the unorganised labour was black, not white, and in addition Afrikaner capital was finding its feet in a capitalist environment in which the English and the Jews had already had a head start. Under some legalistic pretences the Wage Act was now used to block any upward movement in African wages.

Salaries and wages constitute the main element in a firm's costs of operations. Keep this element on the lowest level and even a firm with poor management may make the grade. As soon as price control was lifted after the war, prices immediately rose on a wide front. This in turn gave a spur to the establishment of new manufacturing enterprises under protective cover to rush for profit harvest, much like the rush of people to scoop from shoals of sardines as they swim close to the shore. As the prices continued to rise, building up to an inflationary trend to this day, the wages of white workers were adjusted to keep pace. But the real wages of African workers did not only stagnate during the decade of 1946–56 but between 1953 and 1957 there was even a negative increase of -1,5 per cent. Writing in 1962 even the chairman of the Wage Board was forced to admit grudgingly that: 'In secondary industry and metropolitan commerce the real income of Bantu employees showed a tendency to stagnate in the post-war period.'

To make matters worse, when the Nationalist government took over in 1948 it embarked on a determined programme to regiment African labour by tightening pass laws through the establishment of labour bureaux. By a combination of measures to block an upward movement in real wages and apportioning labour through the labour bureaux, accompanied by brutal police steps to break up strikes, the Nationalist government delivered the African workers bound hand and foot to employers who grabbed the opportunity to accumulate capital in the shortest possible time. It was during this decade – the dirtiest in South Africa's economic history – that Afrikaner capital spread to all the sectors of the economy.

During the latter half of the 1950s SACTU mounted an intensive campaign for a national minimum wage of a pound a day. But this and the debate for or against it, as well as government reaction, fall outside the scope of our inquiry.

(e) *Afrikanerdom's firm hold on political power*. The coming into power of the National Party in 1948 created the situation for which the Afrikaner nationalist intellectual in the DRC, in academic institutions and within the machinery of the National Party itself, had been planning. The NP had firm control of the reins of political power without having to accommodate, in carrying out their mission of Afrikaner domination, the view of outsiders. General Hertzog had had to join hands with the Labour Party (1924–29) and with the SA Party under Smuts in 1933 to form the United Party from which he was ousted by Smuts in 1939, then he was rejected by the *ware* Nationalists and driven into the political wilderness where he died a lonely death. After 1948 the Nationalist government intervened in the running of the capitalist economy in such a way that Afrikaner capital was given an opportunity to expand and consolidate. Job reservation and confining African and, to a lesser extent, coloured and Indian unskilled labour categories suited Afrikaner capital in the early stages in so far as manufacturing industry was forced to be labour-intensive for a long time, while Afrikaner financial institutions were building up financial muscle to enable them to finance Afrikaner enterprises and let them compete with the non-Afrikaner capitalist in a capital-intensive industry.

Afrikaner capital today has joined the mainstream of capitalism but in spite of that it still maintains the exclusively Afrikaner AHI and the Sakekamer. Why? Today it is not uncommon for Afrikaner capital to pair up in big business with the erstwhile 'enemy of Afrikanerdom', whom they once caricatured in their press as 'Hoggenheimer'. Thus today the Afrikaner ethnic group is not the undifferentiated mass the early Afrikaner intellectuals sought to portray it as. They have used it as a battering ram to crash through the barriers to economic and political power. Today there are Afrikaner bourgeoisie, upper middle class, top professionals, white- and blue-collar workers, big-time farmers. Yet exclusively Afrikaner associations are still going strong. To what purpose?

While the Nationalist government applied brakes to slow down the rate of development in the private sector, it set up state enterprises on a scale which the protagonists of 'free private enterprise' see as an encroachment on private enterprise. By taking this step, the Nationalist government built up vast public sector machinery which presently employs almost 40 per cent of economically active whites. And that in practical terms means mostly Afrikaners. The public sector does not only ensure the National Party a loyal bloc vote in a strategic position for election purposes but it is a training ground at public expense for personnel that continually drifts to Afrikaner enterprises in the private sector.

[October–November 1981]

# The Rise and Growth of Afrikaner Capital
## II

# The Resultant Socio-Politico-Economic Effects

*OPERATION APARTHEID*

In Part II of this paper we propose to deal with the socio-politico-economic effects resulting from the fact that Afrikanerdom has attained the twin objectives of political domination and economic power. But to stop at that would render the whole effort a fruitless academic exercise. If this study is to be meaningful at all, we must also examine how the oppressed people set about to marshal counter-measures to ensure their survival in the face of the apartheid onslaught.

When the National Party came to power they set about with unsurpassed thoroughness to build barriers between the people of this country. The purpose was that all potential opponents should be broken into so many racial or ethnic groups, that no one by itself could mount effective resistance to apartheid measures. On the other hand, the Nationalist government sought to weld the Afrikaners into one solid bloc which would draw to itself, on its own terms, the other non-Afrikaner whites. The first step towards this end was partly to illegalise non-racial political organisations, as in the case of the Communist Party which it banned in 1950 under the Suppression of Communism Act, and partly to make it illegal for blacks (Africans, coloureds and Indians) and whites to be members of one organisation. Under the revised Industrial Conciliation Act (1956), mixed trade unions were illegalised and could only function as separate white and coloured – Indian unions or separate branches with a white executive committee. This requirement had to be fulfilled irrespective of what the ratio is of whites to coloureds and Indians in the trade union concerned. The following table illustrates as of 1973:

## Mixed membership unions

| No. of unions | Membership | | Total |
|:---:|:---:|:---:|:---:|
| | Whites | Coloureds & Indians | |
| 41 | 45 188 | 130 355 | 175 543 |

Of the total membership of the mixed unions, the white membership constituted roughly a third, yet in terms of the law executive power had to be in the hands of the minority simply because they were white.

On the basis of the report of the Industrial Legislation Commission, set up when the National Party came to power, the Industrial Conciliation Act was revised to regulate the relations within the recognised and therefore registered trade unions in accordance with the apartheid scheme of things. But as far as Africans were concerned, the Nationalist government was not prepared to accept even a recommendation that would have left the government in effective control of such trade unions. The commission recommended: 'It would be in the general interest of South Africa as a whole to grant Native trade unions recognition under separate legislation, to subject them to a measure of reasonable control, and to give them sympathetic guidance.'

Even 'sympathetic guidance' such as one would have expected from a government of a Hans Strijdom, a Hendrik Verwoerd, a Balthasar Johannes Vorster, the Nationalist government would have none of it. Instead it passed the Native Labour (Settlement of Disputes) Act, in terms of which it resorted to naked brute force to suppress any industrial action by African labour.

Also the National Party government would not countenance political parties with a racially mixed membership. Thus under the Improper Interference Act of the sixties, both the Liberal Party and the Progressive Party had to jettison their black membership. On the question of relations in any sphere between black and white racial groups, the National Party government adopted in a literal sense Kipling's polarisation:

East is East
And West is West
And ne'er the twain shall meet.

'Operation Apartheid!' thus went out the order. Apartheid,

Apartheid, was the war cry. Hard-boiled officials steeped in racist ideology leapt to work with crowbars and bulldozers while close behind them were menacing Saracens, police armed with sub-machine guns, police holding in leash fierce Alsatian dogs no less bloodthirsty than their masters and handlers.

White-collar workers – the civil servants – sat at their desks wielding pens and rubber stamps to sign and affix the stamp of authority to forms that bore the final judgement which con-demned hundreds of thousands, if not millions, of people. The winnowing winds of apartheid were blowing, uprooting people from homes and areas they had lived in for generation upon generation. They were turning millions into human chaff. Dejected, many a family went to make representations to stay the order to remove. Invariably the answer from the pen-wielding gentlemen sipping coffee in their offices was 'It is the Law'. What inhuman excesses have been committed in the sacred name of apartheid laws. Millions of Jews and others in Eastern Europe disappeared in the name of the racist laws. In South Africa millions of black people are subjected to untold hardships, indignities and downright humiliation in the name of racist laws.

'Apartheid!' rang out the war cry. In Johannesburg Africans were flung out of Sophiatown, Newclare, etc. to Meadowlands; coloureds from Doornfontein to Coronationville; Indians from Newlands, Pageview and Sophiatown to Lenasia. In Port Elizabeth Africans were thrown out of Korsten to site-and-service lease land where the only structures were rows of bucket latrines and the order was 'Zakhele' [Build for yourself]; the coloureds out of South End and North End to Gelvandale and Bethelsdorp; the Indians out of the centre of the city to Malabar. In Durban Africans were flushed out of Cato Manor to KwaMashu in the bantustans; Indians from Clairwood, Cato Manor, Mayville and various other parts in the centre of the city to Chatsworth and Phoenix. In Cape Town, Africans were thrown out of Kensington and Retreat to Nyanga East; coloureds were uprooted from District Six, Mowbray, Claremont and other southern suburbs to outlying areas such as Bonteheuwel, Mitchells Plain, Manenberg.

Before the apartheid storm was unleashed from the Afrikaner Mount Olympus, the people lived happily and peacefully side by side as a cross-section of what the South African population really is. Now the various race groups have been sorted out to live each by itself. Points of contact have been reduced to the barest minimum so that a member of one group feels a stranger in another group's area. But the worst, the ultimate in techniques of dividing the potential 'enemies of Afrikanerdom' was to break up the Africans into a number of ethnic groups – ten of them. Can the National Party government make an about-turn, move away from apartheid, repair the damage they have done to South Africa's social fabric? Can they?

Judged by the increasing number of NP members of parliament elected since 1948, apartheid policies have been receiving increasing support not only from Afrikaners but also from non-Afrikaner white voters.

## PETIT BOURGEOIS MISCONCEPTIONS

After years during which the policy of white race superiority (*baasskap*) has been trumpeted in and out of season, it is not surprising that certain sections of the oppressed people, especially the emergent middle class, have begun looking for ways of cushioning themselves against the harsh blows that apartheid was raining on all the oppressed people without exception. Frequently the business circles of all three black racial groups express the hope that the answer to the discrimination suffered under apartheid policies lies in building their economic strength in much the same way that the Afrikaners have done. Behind this argument lies the belief – nay, the misconception – that if the black business community builds economic strength it would be in a position to provide employment to large numbers of its people.

Sensing the aspirations of the emergent middle class, especially the business section, the Nationalist government established Development Corporations for each of the black race groups and, in the case of the Africans, for each of the main ethnic groups. Until the Carlton Conference of November 1979, the Development Corporations for the various ethnic groups were prepared to grant loans only to people operating small one-man businesses in the bantustans. Even though a decision was taken at the Carlton Conference to establish a Small Business Development Corporation, it is only beginning to take shape by way of financing backyard artisans in Soweto.

What is of foremost importance with regard to the emergent middle class is to show them that their efforts to establish themselves in business do not contribute to the struggle to defeat apartheid. If anything, the argument they advance is misleading.

The financial assistance which the National Party government is to commit jointly, with the leaders of monopoly capital, to the emergent middle class, acts as a brake to slow down the momentum of the revolutionary ferment amongst the oppressed people of this country.

It must be clear that we are not, in the least, suggesting that those in business should not be there. But for them to advocate that they should take a leaf from the way the Afrikaners built their economic strength is in the first place a misconception, since the conditions that favoured the growth of Afrikaner capital are just not there for the oppressed people, as we pointed out in Part I. Secondly, the methods which the Afrikaners used are undesirable since they built on arousing ethnic and/or race sentiments. In addition, the economic conditions in the country are such that the market is dominated by a few giants who have spread their tentacles to cover 'virtually every aspect of business that affects consumers'.

## FACTORS IN ORGANISATIONAL STRATEGY
The National Party has all along been aware of the fact that the oppressed people of this country would not be paralysed at the sight of the massive build-up of an awesome coercive machinery. There is hardly any imaginable loophole left in their legislative network to enforce apartheid and to impose Afrikaner political domination on the peoples of this country. But opposition over the years built up until a stage was reached when Inqindi (ANC) had explored all channels for non-violent forms of struggle. Like an animal at bay, it had to engage in a survival struggle and call upon all who valued freedom to support it. The formation of MK [Umkhonto we Sizwe] in alliance with the Communist Party to repel the violence which the National Party government has mounted against four-fifths of the population was timely and just.

Thus there has emerged a clearly defined polarisation. On the one hand, the National Party government committed to white supremacy is seeking to line up forces to ensure continued Afrikaner political domination. Internationally, except for inaudible noises that the Nationalist government has only to make a statement of intent to move towards a modification in the application of apartheid, the Nationalist government with its racist policies has the support of the imperialist countries under the leadership of the Reagan–Thatcher administrations. On the domestic scene,

both the government and the non-Afrikaner national bourgeoisie
have succeeded in cutting the white working class adrift from the
mainstream of the working class. Thus in this polarised situation,
the white working class has linked its fortunes with white supremacy and capital. The government is part of the American-led
global anti-communist crusade, which is also supported by the
non-Afrikaner national bourgeoisie. Although there may be differences with the Nationalist government in the manner in which
the protagonists of 'free private enterprise' would like to see the
capitalist game played, they are not deep-rooted. In the final
analysis they will stand by the National Party government against
the forces of freedom whom they characterise as communist.

The government is not underestimating the potential strength
of the forces of freedom under the leadership of the Inqindi. In its
desperation it is now seeking to create special machinery to
accommodate coloureds and Indians in the apartheid structures,
albeit in a subservient position to white supremacy. The price the
coloureds and Indians will be expected to pay will be to stand
together with the white supremacists in defence of apartheid.

As regards the Africans: in much the same way that migrant
contract labour is recruited to go and work for a wage in the
'white cities and farms', they are being offered a wage to fight in
defence of apartheid. How functionally do they differ from
mercenaries?

This is the line-up which the National Party government is
working feverishly to establish. And what is the answer?

**Total mobilisation**

Inqindi, in alliance with the Communist Party, has emerged as
the main opposition to the country's fascist regime. This fact is
conceded by friend and foe alike. The acceptance of this fact
places a tremendous responsibility on Inqindi and its membership.
It must mobilise all available forces to engage actively in a
struggle to rid the country of the cancer of apartheid, which in
essence is based on racism. In the two papers, 'Good Organisation:
Key to Success', in which we dealt with the mechanics of organising in the urban and rural (bantustan) areas respectively, we
emphasised the vital need for Inqindi to rally mass support. In this
paper we are concerned chiefly with identifying the forces that
Inqindi must line up against those which the National Party
government is seeking to muster.

We must now examine and evaluate the forces on which Inqindi can count. Firstly, what prospects are there that the Nationalist government will succeed to rally the coloureds and the Indians around the apartheid colours? It seems inconceivable that these two black groups will succumb to the blandishments of the racist regime. The National Party government, for all its big talk about reforms, stands firmly for 'white self-determination'. This means that it is not contemplating any move away from the existing position in which political power is exclusively in white hands. Any arrangement short of including coloureds and Indians in a common voters' roll (with the right to elect representatives or to be elected as representatives on a non-racial basis to a single parliament) is not the genuine article. It will only be another version of the representative council system which the people have already rejected. If it is only a question of tinkering here and there with the superstructure of the council system without changing the substance of discrimination on racial grounds, it is difficult to see the coloureds and Indians lining up with the racist regime to the extent of making the supreme sacrifice to defend something in which they have no stake. This is, however, not to say there will not be individuals and even political groupings which will attempt – as best as they know how – to win the masses of the oppressed over to the acceptance of the fraud, thus selling the people's birthright for the proverbial mess of pottage.

In the discussions that took place in 1977 in which the National Party was seeking to trim its sails to meet the increasing pressures for change by the oppressed peoples in the country, John Vorster – then Premier – assured the National Party government that as far as Africans were concerned, *'Ons het klaar gepraat'* – i.e. everything that had to be said about them had been said. In other words there was to be no change in the bantustan policy. The political aspirations of all Africans could only find expression in the bantustans. His successor, P.W. Botha, has not shifted one step from this position. All the political parties, including the PFP, have accepted the fact that the Africans must satisfy their political aspirations in the tribal structures that the government has established in those areas. The Progressive Federal Party is making a case for finding a political formula only for the Africans in the urban areas. Yet in spite of it all, Magnus Malan – the Defence Minister and mastermind behind the scheme for the realignment of forces under the banner of apartheid – counts on the Africans, too, to lay down their lives in defence of Afrikaner political domination.

Within the ranks of the oppressed people there are still those who think and strain every nerve to convince those around them that there is still room for negotiation between themselves and the Nationalist government. The leading protagonist of this line is Chief Gatsha Buthelezi, the leader of Inkatha – a tribal politico-cultural organisation – and of the South African Black Alliance, consisting of Inkatha, the Labour Party and the Reform Party. Gatsha is working within the framework of the apartheid policies. Gatsha is in a dilemma. He would like to cut an image as a courageous opponent of apartheid, but at the same time he is directing the machinery of apartheid as the Chief Minister of the bantustan in his area. He agreed to implement the apartheid policy through the bantustan, and did that because the National Party government was in no mood to negotiate with him or anyone else on the application of its policy. Now that he has been harnessed to pull the bantustan chariot, he pleads for negotiations with those he allowed to harness him. And their answer is: 'for you *ons het klaar gepraat*'.

Nothing to negotiate. And Badenhorst, a National Party member of parliament who has not been schooled in the velvet art of diplomacy, said in a recent debate in parliament in which reference was made to the Buthelezi Commission Report, that Buthelezi as Chief Minister of KwaZulu knows that he is a citizen of KwaZulu and not of the Republic of South Africa. It takes more than one to negotiate. The government has made its position crystal clear. The most it will do is to upgrade the Urban Community Councils and link them up with the various bantustans, which will in turn be ultimately admitted to a confederation, over which a National Party government will preside.

'Peaceful negotiations!' Gatsha keeps on mumbling. In the meanwhile the National Party government recruits young men from his bantustans to fight MK and he is helpless to do anything about it. In the war situation the Organisation must bypass Gatsha to get to the people he is misleading. It must convince them that as Caesar experienced more than two thousand years ago:

> 'Let him who desires peace
> Prepare for war'.

# Forces to mobilise

The situation is serious and calls for utmost vigilance and preparedness on the part of Inqindi and the Communist Party. It calls for selfless exertion on the part of its cadres and the rank-and-file membership to ensure that the Organisation musters mass support in the struggle to defeat apartheid. It is of vital importance that the Organisation must be able to identify the forces who in one way or other must be roped in. Below we single out these forces. It must be noted that our categorisation refers to all the oppressed peoples of this land.

## The masses

The message of freedom must be carried to the masses. They must be shown and convinced that nothing short of the application of the Freedom Charter offers any solution of the country's complex problems. But resourcefulness to carry Inqindi to the masses is necessary. We are faced with a situation which is not of our making. The residential areas of the three main black groups are apart, as are also the white areas. In the vast African townships it is illegal for persons belonging to other groups to enter without a permit. Even in those townships that do not have such barriers, regular comings and goings or organising teams belonging to another race group will soon attract the attention of *impimpi* [informers]. And we do not mean anything that will attract the police. The situation seems to suggest that the Organisation must first build a nucleus of cadres who live in the area. Then the main burden of organising the area must rest on the shoulders of such cadres.

For the mechanics of organising in these townships the cadres will find it useful to study 'Good Organisation: Key to Success' as well as any other relevant material. A co-ordinating regional machinery on which each of the main townships in the area has a representative, will ensure uniformity of application of policy as well as discuss and resolve problems both of a particular and general nature.

## The working class

The role which the working class can play in the organisation cannot be measured in terms of their numbers only. But a politically conscious working class which, in addition, is conscious of its class position in the society, will lend a special quality to the

Organisation. It is of vital importance for the Organisation to rope in the workers in large numbers. It is not enough to recruit them into the Organisation in the course of the routine recruiting campaigns in the townships. An important auxiliary step should be to reach out to them at the work place through the Organisation's factory committees suggested in the paper 'Good Organisation: Key to Success'.

Yet another problem facing the Organisation is that a large number of workers in factories that are dominated by TUCSA [the Trade Union Council of South Africa] affiliates are discouraged, in terms of policies pursued by TUCSA, from taking part in politics. What is worse is that now that African workers are free to organise themselves into trade unions that may be recognised under the country's industrial relations legislation, TUCSA has insisted on the Wiehahn Commission's making a recommendation to provide for a closed shop. In this way African workers who had been unorganised before in TUCSA-dominated industries are forced willy-nilly to become members of TUCSA-affiliated unions, whose leaders like Arthur Grobbelaar, Lucy Mvubelo *et al.* play ball with the National Party government. In pursuance of its strategic objectives, it seems the Organisation should work towards rescuing black workers presently in trade unions affiliated to TUCSA.

## The professional people

An increasing number of men and women drawn from the ranks of the oppressed people are in the professions, including doctors, lawyers, teachers, nurses and others who are being drawn into industry in the lower and middle-management positions. Each of these groupings occupies a key position and exercises some significant influence over fairly large sections of the population. But in approaching them we have to take into account not only the fact that the Organisation is operating under illegal conditions but also the vulnerable position of the professionals vis-à-vis government pressures. For instance, under the influx control laws African doctors and lawyers are only allowed to practise in an urban area if, in the eyes of officials, they are not affected by the Inqindi or Communist virus. Otherwise they are classed as 'undesirable Natives or Bantu' and endorsed out. Similarly, teachers are so readily dismissed from their jobs that even without participating in any political activities they are not secure in their jobs. How much worse is their position if they should be suspected of engaging in Inqindi activities?

It does not assist the Organisation in its tremendous task to muster support against an enemy that has already drawn up battle lines to dismiss these sections of the oppressed people as 'reactionaries' and thus 'give a dog a bad name and hang him'.

That is so easy to do, but such a sweeping characterisation of sections of the oppressed people in key positions, such as the teachers, does not assist the Organisation in its task. Special hand-picked contacts to work among these sections will reassure them. And in a variety of useful ways they will play a significant role under the leadership of Inqindi.

## Students

In mobilising the forces under the leadership of Inqindi, the students must receive serious attention. Properly guided and armed with a sound theoretical grounding, the students can be a tremendous source of inspiration, through all the ranks of the forces lined up against those of the fascist regime. At the lower primary school and secondary school levels a committed body of teachers can play a vital role – all on the quiet – in infusing a fighting spirit among the pupils under the leadership of Inqindi. The teachers' role would supplement the work done by the Organisation's cadres. At the tertiary level of education all efforts must be made to win the students to support Inqindi policy as set out in the Freedom Charter, as well as recruit among the youths for MK.

Another important task for the students is to forge links with white students at white universities and their main student organisation, NUSAS. There are increasing numbers among white students who are coming out strongly against taking up arms for the defence of apartheid. They require encouragement, and this can be most effectively done by the students from the ranks of the oppressed people, who would put across clearly the policy of Inqindi as embodied in the Freedom Charter as an alternative to the apartheid policies.

## Other forces

To keep this paper within reasonable limits we must now mention other potential forces in the ranks of the oppressed that should be drawn into the ranks that oppose apartheid. To defeat apartheid, the Organisation must win this political battle to rally all the oppressed under the banner of Inqindi. The National Party has nothing to offer the oppressed, but support for the Freedom Charter and the acceptance of the leadership of Inqindi comes of hard work by the Organisation and its entire membership. Some of the forces that require attention are: (i) women's organisations; (ii) youth organisations; (iii) sports unions; (iv) professional associations like teachers' and nurses' associations; (v) religious organisations.

A considerable amount of work remains to be done in the rural areas, i.e. the bantustans and farm labour.

### Among the whites

Inqindi is not engaged in a race war of black versus white. Inqindi is determined to build a South Africa in which all its peoples will live in freedom. In the words of the Freedom Charter, which deserve to be written in bright shining letters across the length and breadth of this country for everybody to ponder seriously, 'South Africa belongs to all who live in it'.

Armed with the Freedom Charter the Inqindi cadres should sally forth, and marshal support for the principles embodied in the Freedom Charter. Already progress in this direction is being registered among some sections of the white population. The Organisation should redouble its efforts to popularise the Freedom Charter and to enlist commitment to its principles. The immediate targets are the students, the Black Sash, and intellectuals (both English- and Afrikaans-speaking). Those who are not prepared to accept the leadership of Inqindi, should rather adopt a neutral stance than line up with the apartheid forces which the National Party government is presently mobilising.

## CONCLUSION

In Part I we attempted to show how Afrikaner nationalism sought to express itself in the course of the last 60 years – from 1920 to 1980. Our limiting ourselves to this period does not mean that before 1920 Afrikaner nationalism had not then emerged. In the pre-1920 period the economy was largely based on primary production – farming and mining, and although the scope for trekking away from problems had already become very limited by the end of the Boer War (1899–1902), yet the farms could still be subdivided and sons were able to subsist.

From the 1920s the industrialisation process was under way. Large numbers of unskilled Afrikaners were drifting away from the land to the industrial centres to take up employment under foreigners, and to work side by side with foreign elements and black workers. Afrikaner leaders feared that the result of such mingling would have deleterious effects on the Afrikaner traditions of exclusivity.

To effect this, Afrikaner intellectuals in all walks of life, working hand in hand with the National Party, created all sorts of associations to cater for the exclusive needs of the Afrikaner. In the course of this period under review, Afrikaners were bombarded from the pulpits and all available platforms with hatred of anything and everybody outside the Afrikaner fold – the *laager*. Africans were singled out especially as a danger to Afrikanerdom. Behind the barrage of race hatred, the Afrikaners attained their twin objectives, viz economic strength and political domination.

It could not be expected that those who are at the receiving end of the apartheid whiplash, would not seek ways and means of bringing to an end the era of white terror. Part II of this paper examines the ways of doing so. Under the leadership of Inqindi, MK in alliance with the Communist Party was formed to give effect to the people's wishes to rid this country and its peoples of the scourge of apartheid.

The National Party government is determined to maintain its position of Afrikaner political domination, and towards that end it is seeking to forge an alliance to gang up against the *'swartgevaar'* – the Africans. Inqindi, on the other hand, offers the people of this country permanent peace and freedom as embodied in the principles set out in the Freedom Charter. But the first step towards that end is that all the freedom-loving peoples of this country should stand together to fight and defeat apartheid. The situation is serious.

*Amandla! Ngawethu! Matla ke a rona!*

[May 1982]

# The Rise and Growth of Afrikaner Capital
## III
# The Birth of a Fascist Dictatorship

### ESTABLISHING THE LINK

The reader might have found it annoying that there has been a wide gap in time in releasing the three parts of this paper. Part I became available in October–November 1981. It was not until May 1982 that Part II was released. And now, almost a year thereafter, Part III is released. We owe the reader an apology for the inconvenience caused by such long breaks between the appearance of these, which are linked to one another to form a definite unity. But in the circumstances it had to be because while we are dealing with a topical problem we are not seeking in this paper to fulfil the function of a newspaper. We are, on the contrary, seeking to get to the bottom of the underlying forces and factors that have been building up over a period of time, but are now erupting like a volcano in a manner that is bound to affect profoundly the lives of the people of our land.

In Part I we saw how the National Party from its inception set itself the two objectives of building economic power and taking over political power exclusively for the Afrikaner. To attain these ends, it used any means at its disposal – fair and foul – and more often than not foul.

In Part II we outlined how the liberation struggle, led by the ANC, was marshalling all freedom-loving people into a force to defeat the apartheid regime and seize power to establish a 'democratic people's republic' around the goals set out in the Freedom Charter.

In Part III we propose to examine the prospects in the event of the NP government succeeding, however partially, to get some political groupings amongst the ranks of their target groups – coloureds and Indians – to agree to join the apartheid camp as the Labour Party has already done.

## A BRIEF HISTORICAL BACKGROUND

To be able to appreciate the rationale of the various tactics employed in the last 35 years by political organisations within the three black oppressed national groups, it is necessary to unravel the tangled skein of sustained government attacks on the rights of the people. The technique of deprivation has followed a similar pattern but the act of deprivation itself has been applied separately to the three groups – Africans, coloureds and Indians.

### Africans

The notorious Hertzog legislation of 1936 fixed the group areas of Africans as those known today as bantustans, and as municipal locations in the urban areas; it removed African voters in the Cape from the common voters' roll and placed them on a separate roll. In terms of special legislation, the Representation of Natives Act, provision was made firstly for indirect representation in parliament, and secondly for the establishment of the Natives Representative Council (NRC) to advise the Minister of the Department of Native Affairs on matters relating only to Africans.

To meet the situation two views emerged. One supported a boycott of the parliamentary and provincial elections as well as the NRC on the basis that these were dummy institutions. The other view was that the people should go into these institutions to make representations to the government. The case for participation was built on a guideline suggested by Dr Kwegyir Aggrey: 'Use what you have to get what you want.' Yet another version in support of participation was to break the dummy institutions from inside. Although this debate started among the registered voters it soon became a burning issue throughout the country and among all the oppressed groups as the government in turn created separate representation machinery for each of the oppressed groups.

By the early 1950s the ANC had made its position clear. It was to engage in extra-parliamentary struggle. The realities of the South African political situation under a National Party government had taken such a turn as to make it unrealistic to rely on the use of parliament to redress the grievances of the Africans, to say nothing of dummy institutions such as the NRC. As from the time the National Party assumed power in 1948, parliament devoted so much time to churning out legislation to regulate the lives of the Africans that, in despair, Margaret Ballinger proclaimed: 'All South African politics is native affairs.' The Nationalist government dissolved the NRC and abolished representation of Africans in parliament. Instead it passed the Bantu Authorities Act which set the stage for the establishment of tribal territorial authorities. This machinery destroyed the case of those who argued for participation in government-created institutions in order to improve the lot of the oppressed. They went into the machinery on Nationalist government terms, to wit what is happening in the bantustans.

## The coloureds

No sooner did the government start implementing the legislation that dealt with Africans as a separate group than it turned its attention to the coloureds. As from the early 1940s it set up the Coloured Affairs Department (CAD) to carry out among the coloureds what NAD did among the Africans.

The new organisation that sprang up to oppose the CAD was the anti-CAD. Its membership was by and large drawn from the ranks of teachers. Their tactics took on mainly the form of boycott. But as in the case of Africans there were those who felt that they would serve the cause of the coloureds better by working in such institutions as the government would set up under CAD. The late George Golding, himself a teacher and a downright collaborator, led those wishing to take part. He emerged as the leader of an organisation that stood for participation.

When the Nationalist government was established, they did not lose time dispatching the coloureds to the same end as the Africans. The National Party government removed the coloured voters from the common roll to a separate voters' roll. In parliament they were represented by whites. Within a matter of a few years the government had abolished even that and set up the Coloured Persons Representative Council. The National Party had accomplished its political objective: Afrikaner political domination.

In the early 1950s, SACPO (South African Coloured People's Organisation), later named the Coloured People's Congress, was established, and like other congresses in the Congress Alliance was party to the adoption of the Freedom Charter (FC). And more, it concentrated on organising the masses. True, it did not have much time before the National Party mounted its vicious onslaught against the Congress Alliance in the early 1960s. By this time the Non-European Unity Movement (NEUM) had largely disintegrated.

With the CRC remaining as the only statutory body, groups

committed to participation in such institutions vied for majority representation in the Council. The two main parties were the Federal Party which took over George Golding's mantle and the Labour Party. After the death of Tom Swartz, the Federal Party disintegrated and what was left of it ironically became the present Freedom Party led by Charles Julies. By the time the Nationalists dissolved the CRC, the LP was the only one of the participation parties that had any semblance of a nationally operated machinery. In the period since the dissolution of the CRC, it has maintained links with the Department of the Interior, of which Heunis was the minister until he assumed his present portfolio as Minister of Constitutional Affairs.

## The Indians

At the end of World War Two, the Smuts government passed the Asiatic Land Tenure and Indian Representation Act. As in the case of coloureds and Africans, some well-known individuals were prepared to play ball with the government. The best known of these were A.I. Kajee and P.R. Pather, who later formed the Natal Indian Organisation (NIO) in opposition to the Natal and Transvaal Indian Congresses led respectively by Dr Monty Naicker and Dr Yusuf Dadoo. The two congresses immediately launched the campaign for passive resistance of 1948. The call for passive resistance received the overwhelming support of the Indian population in the country. By the time the NP government came to power in 1948, the Smuts government had not even begun implementing the legislation.

The National Party government repealed the Act and adopted measures to repatriate Indians to India. As an incentive it offered to pay the fares for such Indian families as accepted repatriation. A few fell for it, but as the congresses campaigned against repatriation and the Indian government was unwilling to accept such repatriates, the Nationalists abandoned the scheme by the early 1960s. The government announced that it recognised that the Indians were citizens of South Africa and had made a contribution to its development. But it set up a separate Department of Asiatic Affairs as well as a Council through which matters dealing with Indians could be channelled to the government: this was the SAIC. There was no lack of elements which were prepared to participate in such a council, as was the case with the Africans and coloureds. When the government made the SAIC an electoral body, the forces opposed to participation in such council formed a united front, anti-SAIC, and called for a boycott of the elections. The poll was extremely low.

From this sketchy historical background we stress the following significant points:

(1) By the early 1960s the government had accomplished the task of making the highest law-making institution – parliament – the preserve of the whites, where the Afrikaner dominated.

(2) The separation of racial groups – geographically (group areas), politically (separate councils), educationally (separate ministries) and in provision of facilities and amenities in all spheres from the cradle to separate graveyards – became a key concern of government policy. And every racial group was bombarded with propaganda about the advantages of separation from others because they were outsiders.

(3) In setting up the councils the Nationalists did not take into account the feelings of the people for whose 'interests' they were purportedly established. The councils were there to serve and further the interests of the Nationalists. Invariably, to ensure that the scheme got off the ground, the government appointed its members.

*THE DILEMMA POSED BY CONSTITUTIONAL PROPOSALS*
A new dispensation! Power-sharing! Words. Words. What is in them? Given the programme of the National Party as from its inception – to organise and rally the Afrikaners as a group, to achieve two main objectives, viz to build a strong economic base for themselves as a group and, secondly, to take over political power, form a National Party government and use it as a battering ram to crush all opposition – has the National Party government abandoned its 'God-given' mission to rule this country along the path of apartheid?

In section II above we have attempted briefly to sketch how the Nationalists – in and out of government – have inexorably and with unwavering consistency pursued the path of Afrikaner domination of all non-Afrikaner groups, be they black or white.

Why, then, this new language they are now speaking? The answer is there for all to see who have eyes. The forces of progress led by the ANC have over the years been built into a powerful, irresistible force that draws its strength from the overwhelming masses of the people. The ANC offers the people of this country something to live and die for in the interim. The goals set out unambiguously in the Freedom Charter offer the only basis on which a just and peaceful society can be brought about in a country whose peoples have been exposed to paralysing oppression and apartheid propaganda for so long.

In the face of this threat, what does the NP government contrive to do in order to cling to power for as long as possible? It stretches a hand to coloureds and Indians and says: 'Come along, let us forge an apartheid-type democracy under which the stakes will be loaded 4:2:1 respectively for the dominant parties in each of the white, coloured and Indian separate chambers.' In accordance with this separate proportional arrangement, the three chambers will select a president who in turn will appoint a cabinet which need not necessarily contain members of any of the chambers. Here is a situation where the president is not accountable to anybody and a cabinet that is responsible to such a president. A classic example of a fascist dictatorship that has its roots in Afrikaner domination and its racist policies.

The Nationalists call upon the coloureds and Indians to give a helping hand, without which the establishment of such a fascist dictatorship would be shorn of any democratic trappings. There is no subtlety about the whole plan. The Nationalists have laid down clearly the conditions under which the coloureds and Indians must take them (the Nationalists) off the hook. They must accept that apartheid shall continue to be the guiding policy of the Afrikaner-dominated government. If the coloureds and Indians must therefore join the apartheid camp they cannot plead ignorance. In joining this camp they must accept in advance that there are certain apartheid holy cows which are non-negotiable, e.g. a unitary state, group areas, separate education et al.; they must accept that Africans are not citizens of South Africa, because even if the urban Africans were to be accommodated in the constitutional proposals there would be no democracy in this country. In short, the coloured and Indians must get into the apartheid camp to defend white domination by entrenching apartheid.

## Why the dilemma?

With the position so clearly set out, why should the LP and SAIC find themselves in a dilemma? All common sense points to the fact that their answer to the NP government should be out-

right rejection. Let us identify a couple or so factors that lie behind
the dilemma.

## Committal to participation

As from 1936 when the Hertzog government passed legislation
to keep Africans out of the common stream of South African
politics, all the three black groups have from year to year had to
fight one battle after another, either to defend what was still left
of rights they had enjoyed or to restore those they had lost over
years of unremitting struggle. In the course of the protracted
struggle there emerged two views on how best to meet the
onslaught to reduce them into a powerless sightless mass, completely under white domination. On the one hand, one view
crystallised around the Congress movement under the leadership
of the ANC, to marshal the forces of the masses of the oppressed
and exploited with a view to pitting their weight against white
supremacy; on the other hand there developed a view held by the
faint-hearted. Overawed by the apparent strength of the government they adopted the politics of pleading within the framework
of the law. It is those who cling to this view irrespective of any
change in conditions, who implemented the bantustan policy, who
manned the CRC, who prop up the SAIC. It is these, if not
stopped, who are going to drag the coloureds and Indians into the
apartheid camp under the NP constitutional proposals.

The fact that decades and decades of pleading have brought
nothing but have seen a grave deterioration of the plight of the
oppressed has little influence on them. Their problem is what they
will do if the government does not recognise them. Years of
collaboration have left them paralysed and their concern has now
become survival in that paralytic state. They would rather drag an
entire people into the vortex than face the fate of sinking alone.

Otherwise, what explanation can there be for the LP's decision
to join the apartheid camp? They have no confidence in the power
of the people they profess to be leading. They know their path has
come to a dead end – *die pad loop dood*. In the face of this stark fact,
what is their answer? Allan Hendrickse turns round to advise
coloureds: 'The Afrikaner and the coloureds share the same path
into the future, a path we will have to walk as fellow South
Africans. We share the same culture, the same language, the same
religion, the same habits.'

Curry, another collaborator, cries: 'I will not even answer to the coloured people. In my conscience I must be satisfied I am correct. I have decided that I will work for peaceful change and no one is going to dictate to us how we are going to play that game.'

And so the LP and the NP government must 'take each other's hand' (as Hendrickse said) to defend apartheid. That is all there is to it. The LP has opted for the apartheid camp.

*Just a beginning?*

Another factor which is being put forward as having influenced the LP and the SAIC to 'go in' is the belief that these proposals are just a beginning in the right direction. The hope is expressed that when the NP will have consolidated its position against the CP and Herstigte Nasionale Party (HNP) it will be in a position to make further concessions, whereas a rejection by the coloureds and Indians would result in a stillbirth of the National Party constitutional initiative.

This argument ignores the fact that the National Party has kept the coloureds and Indians out of the national political stream to eliminate any possibility of a combination by the forces of opposition. Left alone in the field with insignificant white (largely English-speaking liberal) opposition, it could build its apartheid structures and consolidate Afrikaner domination. That task has been accomplished and the Nationalists have done it without any assistance from either coloureds or Indians.

But, in the meanwhile, the forces of the liberation movement led by the ANC with the CP have launched the offensive against the apartheid regime on a multiplicity of fronts, nationally and internationally. It is in the face of this onslaught that the NP throws overboard all pretence of maintaining the façade of bourgeois democracy to set up a fascist dictatorship. And under cover of a smokescreen of high-sounding words with no meaning in reality, it lures the coloureds and Indians into the apartheid camp with but one purpose: to man the fascist war machine in defence of apartheid – of Afrikaner domination.

*Group salvation*

The Nationalists' race policies have wrought immeasurable damage to the peoples of this country. Separate residential areas, separate schools, separate everything right up to proposed separate parliaments. In making representation to the government through the respective state departments established for each group, the collaboration parties were led to seek the salvation of the separate groups. With these constitutional proposals and the practice of separateness in three chambers, the LP 'hopes' to further coloured interests, so do members of the SAIC, and the right to Afrikaner self-determination is assured in the white chamber.

It is not surprising that these political parties that have for years been committed to the politics of pleading within the framework of the law are propelled by the sheer force of logic to end up where they are – in the enemy camp. He who sups with the devil must have a long spoon if he is to keep out of reach of his clutches.

## The PFP stand

On the issue of the constitutional proposals by the Nationalists, the Progressive Federal Party (PFP) is in as much of a dilemma as the participating parties among the coloureds and Indians. The government claims it has embarked on a path of reforms. It is making a move which is unprecedented since Union in 1910. It is moving against a strong opposition from a sizeable section of the Afrikaners – their base – to bring coloureds and Indians into 'power-sharing' with whites at the highest level where decisions are made – in parliament. But in reality the Nationalists have so circumscribed the right of the coloureds and Indians to decision-making that their role in the tricameral parliament will be limited to endorsing the apartheid legislation programme.

The PFP sees all the flaws in the proposals, especially the refusal by the government to accommodate the Africans in the 'power-sharing' scheme. But to reject the proposals would be tantamount to throwing the bath water (flaws) out with the baby (reforms).

The PFP is in a dilemma because it is failing to face the crucial issue: that no one group has the right to decide on its own a constitution for all the people of this country. What right has the Nationalist government, representing as they do the Afrikaners; what right have they to ram down the throats of all the people of South Africa the race theories in terms of which the Afrikaners have a God-given right to rule this country? To allow them to translate these proposals into law is to assist them in hoodwinking the world into believing that the fascist dictatorship they are setting up under these proposals has the support of the peoples of South Africa. To bring Africans into the scheme by roping in some self-seekers would not make these constitutional proposals any more acceptable. It is not just this or that part of these proposals that is flawed. As conceived, the entire constitutional proposal is like a diseased foetus, and as such must be rejected.

## PROSPECTS FOR POPULAR COUNTER-STRATEGIES

The freedom forces have struck out. The people are on the march. Judged by any standard there can be no doubt that the National Liberation Movement (NLM) is entering a new era which may call for a departure from methods used in varying degrees in the course of the last forty years or so. In embarking on the concerted struggle which promises to be all-embracing in so far as it is going to bring together all progressive forces in the country to work to a common programme among all the oppressed groups, in particular, and freedom-loving people across the entire population spectrum in general. The Liberation Movement is poised for political action on a hitherto unprecedented scale. But it is just as well that it should be pointed out that the Nationalist government is going to react more viciously to try to smash the United Democratic Front as soon as it starts operating. The UDF poses the biggest threat to the Nationalists' plans to give the fascist dictatorship a democratic veneer. But we must be confident that the steering committee that is preparing the ground for the launching of the UDF and the executive that will guide it into action will build its defences in depth so that as the government bans or detains all trained leaders, others will come forward and replace them.

Bearing in mind that the purpose of this paper is to stimulate a healthy discussion of a topical problem in which we are vitally interested and not to suggest any guideline, let us start by restating the problem.

In essence the NP is determined to establish a fascist dictatorship dedicated to maintaining Afrikaner domination. And it covers its intention behind a smokescreen of high-sounding verbiage that it is introducing 'reforms' to move away from the orthodox apartheid or white supremacy by allowing coloureds and Indians to participate in 'power-sharing' and 'decision-making', under a tricameral system of government in which all of the three groups in their separate chambers will debate and legislate on matters affecting the group.

From the nature of the problem confronting the oppressed and freedom-loving people of the country, a counter-strategy would aim at achieving partly immediate or short-term objectives, and partly long-term objectives. Let us examine these in turn.

## The short-term objectives

The NP government is determined to push legislation during the current session of parliament to translate its constitutional proposals into law. It wants to do so at such a speed that forces opposed to them will not have sufficient time to rally the people against the proposals. They want to deliver a knock-out blow to such forces as the UDF. In the circumstances, the forces opposed to the proposals have only a few months within which to educate and rally opposition to the implementation of the first stage of the government proposals. The elections to the coloured and Indian chambers are scheduled to take place by October next (1983), i.e. in eight months' time. The immediate or short-term objective on the part of the anti-government, freedom-loving forces is to prevent the election of candidates to fill the coloured and Indian chambers. Alternatively, if the elections do occur, the task of the progressive forces would be to organise on a massive scale to rally the masses so that the poll would be marginal and thus to destroy any claims that those who have been elected are representative of the communities concerned.

This approach is a significant departure from the boycott calls of earlier years. Here we focus on organising the people to oppose these constitutional proposals; by running a massive campaign against them, the masses of the people will see clearly how the proposals are designed to further the interests of the oppressors. Hopefully the masses will themselves go out to dissuade the likes of the LP and disengage them from relations with the NP government.

Yet another important step before the elections take place is that the government must compile voters' rolls. The campaign against the proposals would call upon the people not to register.

The campaign has not yet gathered momentum but the forces of freedom have already chalked up some gains – COPE [Congress of the People] which was founded by Lofty Adams to collaborate with the government, has spat him out and reconstituted itself under the leadership of Marais and others into a force for the people's cause. And the Democratic Party under the leadership of J. B. Patel – one of the pillars of the politics of pleading in the SAIC – has rejected the government proposals. Now that the government has rejected, as expected, the request by the executive of the SAIC for the government to gauge the opinion of the Indian community by a referendum, we will not have to wait before Rajbansi and Co. finally take their stand.

## Why stop the elections?

The NP government has all along the line shown no scruples in their dealings with the oppressed and exploited. The government holds the popular views of the oppressed in contempt. All it wants are a few downright collaborators – the likes of [David] Thebehali – whom it parades as 'leaders' of their people and under the cover of whose name it perpetuates the fascist apartheid crimes against the people. We have seen how it uses the community councils like Soweto's, which is in office on a six per cent poll; how it declared that it regarded the members of the SAIC, which was returned on a poll of less than ten per cent, as a spokesman of the entire Indian community. Everything must be done to block the elections to these two chambers.

But we might as well reckon on the likely eventuality that, after the compilation of the voters' roll, mere nomination by registered voters is sufficient to send such a candidate to the chambers as elected unopposed. Once such men have taken their seats in parliament they will take decisions on behalf of their communities. The government has made it clear that 'power-sharing' and 'decision-making' at the highest level carries with it sharing responsibilities for the defence of a system that bestows on them power-sharing.

What then does this mean in effect? Among others it means that these 'parliamentarians' are going to be honey birds of apartheid, who will not only sing its praises but will enforce the Group Areas Act, separate education system, and all the evil laws of apartheid. Moreover, it means the coloureds and Indians must share in all measures to ensure the entrenchment of white domination, which is going to be enforced via a fascist dictatorship.

Everything has to be thrown in to ensure the short-term objective, viz the blocking of the elections, is achieved. If notwithstanding all efforts to block them, the government get the belly-creepers to fill the chambers, the freedom forces should have built massive popular support to move on to the long-term objective.

## The long-term objective

The campaign to attain the short-term objective is but the first step in the struggle that is going to be bitter and long. It should be expected that if the campaign succeeds the NP government would fall back on something – some other option like packing the chambers with appointees. It has not hesitated to do that in the past. When the Nationalist government lost the case in the Appellate Division, in the early 1950s, to throw the coloureds out of the common voters' roll, it packed the Senate with voting sheep (appointees) to ensure that it got the two-thirds majority required by the constitution to remove the coloureds from the common voters' roll and to have them represented in parliament indirectly by white members elected by the coloureds. When the LP executive council in the CRC failed to carry out its function, the NP government appointed Mrs Jansen. But what is important is that whatever options the government may resort to, they must be forced to do their own dirty work and not use sections of the oppressed and exploited to do it for them.

The era of the fascist dictatorship, with all the paraphernalia to assert its authority, is dawning; the jackboot is going to be used on a scale hitherto unknown to crush all open opposition. If the people are to regain their freedom which is their birthright, they must get rid of the fascist dictatorship and the sickly soil which gives it nourishment – racism and white domination based on the present mode of production. In short, the long-term objective of the popular struggle is the overthrow of the fascist dictatorship.

To avoid dissipation of effort and areas that may give rise to confusion in the course of the struggle, it is absolutely essential to set out clearly the nature of the problem as created by the oppressor and also the immediate or short-term and long-term objectives the popular forces of freedom aim to achieve. It is important in the first instance that the organised forces that join the UDF should have clarity on these issues so that they may in turn make the position clear to the vast masses of the people who are being pounded daily by incessant Nationalist propaganda. While bearing in mind that the danger posed by the rise of a fascist dictatorship affects all the oppressed and exploited, freedom-loving people in South Africa, for the purposes of this paper we concentrate on a sector of the UDF – the coloured and Indian – whom the NP government is seeking to lure into the apartheid camp.

## Realistic appraisal

It would be incorrect to underestimate the immensity of the task in hand. The time and financial resources are limited. These constraints force upon the UDF the need to draw a list of priorities and allocate work in certain areas to those organisations in the UDF best suited to organise locally. Let us examine prospects for mounting a popular counter-move against the proposals. The advantage in this approach is that we start off informed on the weak and strong areas within each of the communities, e.g. what is the current strength of political organisation, etc.

### Among Indians

By far the overwhelming majority of Indians are in the Durban region, which comprises Pietermaritzburg, South Coast, Durban complex, North Coast through to Stanger, northern Natal from Escourt through to Newcastle and Charlestown. The second large concentration of Indians is in the Transvaal, especially in the PWV area. In the Cape the numbers are smaller still. On the basis of the above distribution of the population it is clear that in terms of priority the Durban region is the most important. Greater resources will naturally be concentrated on this region. But it should be clear that important as the Durban region is, the campaign should be carried out as vigorously in the Natal area, if with a lesser allocation of resources.

Fortunately the NIC has through the years remained strong. What is now necessary – as they are doing – is to oil its machinery to gear it for the immediate and special task, firstly to prevent the election of Indians to the proposed chambers, and secondly to draw the masses into the struggle for the overthrow of the fascist dictatorship.

The state of organisation in the Transvaal has been at a low ebb. The decision to revive the TIC [Transvaal Indian Congress] in the face of the NP constitutional proposals is pragmatic. With assistance from the NIC and other progressive organisations, the TIC should be quickly back on its feet to carry the campaign to the smallest pockets of the Indian community in the Transvaal.

Already indications are that the political parties in the SAIC fear committing themselves to supporting the President's Council proposals, without a government referendum among the Indians. Even the NPP of Rajbansi fears to stick its neck out. As the campaign against the proposals gains momentum and spills over to the Cape, the short-term objective may be achieved.

*Among the coloureds*

The nearly 3 million coloured population is spread nation-wide. It is going to require considerable resources to reach out to people in the urban and rural areas and small villages scattered throughout South Africa. The highest concentration of the coloured population is in the Western Cape, which comprises in the main the Peninsula and surroundings, and Boland through to Worcester. The second largest concentration is in the Eastern Cape, from Port Elizabeth to Uitenhage. There are fairly big numbers in the towns in the hinterland in the Eastern and northern Cape as well as the Western and north-west Cape. Then there are sizeable numbers in Natal, OFS and the Transvaal. It is going to require considerable resources to carry the campaign to all those areas. There must be a careful listing of area priorities. If the LP fails to get support in the Western and Eastern Cape, the progressives will have netted enormous psychological gains as well as ensured the support of the highest concentration areas.

We must, however, reckon with the fact that there is no political organisation operating legally and nationally among the coloureds. This means there is no effective political machinery to co-ordinate activities country-wide. This is counterbalanced by the number of civic organisations of a progressive line and the many workers in the trade unions. It would appear one of the most vital steps is to form civic organisations in all important areas and to co-ordinate their activities and then bring them into the UDF. Also, to get the coloured trade unions affiliated to TUCSA to work even as individuals if they cannot bring their trade unions under the UDF.

Radio Freedom, it is hoped, will be broadcasting the message of the campaign into every home: Overthrow the Fascist Dictatorship. Set up a Democratic People's Republic.

## TRIMMING THE SAILS

The national liberation struggle has been on for a good many years now. But it goes through various phases as the oppressors come face to face with intensified resistance by the oppressed to liberate themselves. The significance of the new phase is that it does not occur after a lull. It is triggered off by defensive action the enemy is taking to shore up apartheid as the freedom forces under the leadership of the ANC — the guardian of the Freedom Charter — press on. Inevitably, the new phase of the birth of the UDF will fuse with the on-going politico-military struggle conducted under the ANC–SACP alliance. In seeking to bring the coloureds and Indians into the apartheid *laager*, the result is a backlash as the coloureds and Indians reject the government ruse in the proposals. The anti-government campaign on the proposals is awakening hundreds and thousands, nay millions, of the oppressed and exploited throughout South Africa, to the danger of being used by the Nationalist government.

The campaign, under the leadership of ANC, has not only to spread its sails to take full advantage of the situation but to trim its sails in such a way that the masses drawn into the campaign can see the direction of the struggle and, more importantly, the overthrow of the fascist dictatorship. The UDF must see the campaign as more than anti-President's Council proposals. A massive propaganda campaign must be mounted to alert the people that the campaign is but a phase of the struggle which has already developed to such an extent that the enemy is not being fought only in the field of ideas but also in the military field. The present upsurge must also be reflected in the swelling of MK ranks.

Another fact not to be lost sight of is that the imperialist stooges are seeking openly to influence the South African situation in favour of the fascists. Within hours of the LP Eshowe decision to join the apartheid camp, congratulations promptly came from the USA and UK governments. The struggle also assumes an international character more and more. It is well that the people know their friends.

From Part I through to Part II and now Part III, this paper has been completed over a period of three years. It is hoped that the reader will appreciate its unity.

The struggle in the country is becoming sharper, forcing the drawing of clear lines between those forces on the enemy side and those on the side of the people. The situation is not going to allow for any fence-sitting, and even the new groups that do not want to join the forces now forming the United Democratic Front will not have much time to play around with words as they did at a recent conference at Edendale near Pietermaritzburg.

The people are on the march!
*Amandla! Matla!*

[February 1983]

# PART THREE

# Good Organisation: The Key to Success

## A BIRD'S EYE VIEW

Most of us are familiar with an order which Jesus is reported to have given to his disciples on the eve of his 'ascent': 'Go ye into the wilderness and make the way of the Lord straight.'

But we who have to grapple with concrete socio-economic problems – problems of oppression and exploitation of man by man – have to adopt a more realistic approach to our problems. Oppression and exploitation are man-made by minority interests to the disadvantage of majority interests. What then must the oppressed and exploited majority do to turn things in their favour? In this paper we propose to find an answer to this vital question. And our starting point is to direct our attention and efforts to the source of our strength by saying: 'Go to the masses of the oppressed and exploited peoples of our land. Work among them; work with them to prepare the way for a take-over of power.'

Expressed briefly this is to say: 'Go. Organise.' Experience has taught, however, that a lot more requires to be known about organising if the product of our efforts and activities, i.e. organisation, is to be effective. And if the oppressed and exploited are to achieve their end, viz to take over power, they must build an effective organisational machinery. And to have such an organisational machinery there is no room for haphazard and half-hearted measures. The task has to be tackled seriously and systematically. In the following pages we propose to handle our material under the following broad headings: what to do to organise; the structure of an organisation; a question of survival; and closing remarks.

## WHAT TO DO TO ORGANISE

In seeking an answer to this question we shall be examining a number of closely related aspects, such as the purpose of an organisation (i.e. the cause justifying its existence), the functions of an organisation, etc. An organisation arises where there is an urge to solve a problem, and an urge, a burning desire, to solve a problem boils down to a desire to achieve something. As soon as that urge is there and has become so strong as to be irresistible, then the obvious thing to do is to take steps to bring about the desired end. In other words, to take steps to solve the problem, to work towards the achievement of what is desired. Let us look at a couple of examples in nature. In nature living things grapple with one major problem, to ensure survival. In a beehive or an ants' nest, the bees or ants operate as a group. They organise themselves in such a way that they achieve their goal, viz survival. To do so, a beehive sets up an organisation in which there is a strictly defined division of functions. The queen lays the eggs, the drones mate with the queen, the worker bees collect the nectar and pollen, build the honeycomb and defend the hive from enemies. But they are driven into these activities by blind instinct.

In this paper, however, we are concerned generally with human forms of organisation and in particular with Inqindi [ANC]. This is a much more complex situation which requires conscious effort. In the above paragraph we have seen how in the simple forms of life in nature, the problem of survival has called forth concerted effort. The bees or ants are driven by an in-built irresistible force – the instinct to adopt their type of organisation to ensure survival. Man faces an infinitely greater variety of problems which call for solutions. To find solutions he has to plan what to do to get out of a difficult situation. It is here that the Organisation, the ANC, fits in and points to a solution.

Let us assume a situation in an area in which the Inqindi does not exist. The people suffer in various ways but they are not organised in a way that points to a solution to their problems. The first task of an Inqindi cadre is to get the people to identify the problem and its cause. The people generally are poor: they find it difficult to find food, clothing and shelter, and a variety of other things. Starting on a small scale as necessarily one must do, one has to establish an underground organisational machinery. For a start the cadre carefully selects the individual to whom to introduce the ANC. Why are you and I and our families living in conditions of poverty? Do we want our children to go about in rags, to go the whole day without a good meal, and a host of other things we desire but cannot afford? No. Why are we not in a position to afford these things? Someone is holding them off from us: the National Party government – the ruling class. What must we do to rid ourselves of poverty? We must grab the power from the hands of those who deny us and our children the good things of life. How do we do it?

This is a key question, and the extent to which the Organisation receives the support of the oppressed people depends on how convincingly our cadres answer it. In answering it, it must be made clear that the oppressed people have themselves to become involved directly in efforts to take over power. Those who have common interests cling together to advance their common interests; those who have common fears must stand together to fight the common enemy. When they thus stand together they are organised to achieve a common goal. The organisation that embraces the efforts of all in our country who seek to take over power for the benefit of the oppressed is the ANC. Let us join it.

## The organisational machinery

We have now reached a stage when the Organisation is in existence in our area, i.e. in the area in which each cadre may be compelled by circumstances to reside. Before we examine how to go about the task of setting up the organisational machinery, let us observe that there may be areas in the country where Inqindi does not exist and the approach outlined in the foregoing paragraph may not be applicable. But on the other hand there are areas where Inqindi is organised underground. In such areas it should not take long before a new arrival is contacted and drawn into the machinery. In such a case the task of the cadre is to re-inforce the on-going organisational machinery. But whether one has to start from scratch or has to fit into an existing organisational scheme of things, the following discussion is intended as a framework for purposes of stimulating discussion on organisation.

The discussion rests on two closely related pillars, viz (a) building the organisational machinery, and (b) rallying mass support.

Let us examine these briefly in turn:

### Building the organisational machinery

At the beginning of a year a class teacher draws up a 'scheme of work' which indicates clearly and systematically what aspects of the syllabus he plans to cover from week to week, so that by the time his pupils have to write exams they will have covered the syllabus. Similarly in a factory the manager draws up a 'production schedule' which shows how much raw material he must have on hand to produce a certain quantity of the commodity, the time it will take to go through the various processes (stages) of production for the product to reach the market and to maintain the supply without a break. For the teacher or factory manager to meet his schedule he sets himself certain tasks and targets.

To take over power we must have a strong, closely knit organisational machinery consisting of a membership committed to the ANC's policy objectives as set out in the Freedom Charter. In the present underground conditions under which the Organisation operates, it is a hard and exacting exercise to recruit such membership. We must work to a time schedule, and the task and target method is a helpful aid. It consists of setting the organisers a certain target (goal) to attain over a given period of time, and then assigning certain tasks to perform in order to attain the target.

For instance, the Branch Executive decides that a new membership of a hundred should be raised in six months. That means in round figures seventeen new members per month. Now instead of casting the eyes over a big township, each organiser assigns himself the task of recruiting that membership quota in a given limited area bounded by four streets. He tackles that small area by approaching one individual at a time and convincing him about the need to become a member of Inqindi. It may be necessary to soak that individual thoroughly in what Inqindi stands for. Thereafter each of the two approaches two other individuals. The four are now a good number to operate as a unit: study the Freedom Charter; plan how to recruit the balance of the quota for the month; assign specific duties to each other, e.g. one to familiarise himself with the position of the families in the small area – the police houses, shebeens which invariably are frequented by the Security Branch; one to arrange a meeting place for the unit; one to find literature for the unit. Initially the work may appear to be very demanding. It is important to bear in mind that these organisers are working people and have to undertake this work in the evening. Thus most of their organisational work should not take them far from their homes. Then for the second month, another similarly small area is tackled and soon at the end of the six months the Executive which may consist of, say, three to five members carefully reviews the ground covered, pinpointing both failures and successes to find out what lessons may be learnt.

Step by step the branch membership increases until over a period of time the entire branch area has been covered. At this stage, depending on the size of the township, there should be several units operating under the leadership of the Branch Executive. The Executive draws up a plan of organisational activities for all the membership as comprised of all the units. To give an example: a programme of political education covering the policy of the Organisation as set out in the Freedom Charter.

To guide those who are to lead the classes it may be helpful to draw up speaker's notes. This also ensures uniformity of interpretation. It should be noted that at this stage we are still putting the organisational machinery on a sound footing before we tackle the major task below. The Executive will soon find that the amount of work it is called upon to handle increases in proportion to the membership of the branch. It must therefore develop arms – auxiliary organs – to help it carry out its functions more efficiently. It should set up a Secretariat consisting of members other than the Executive, except for the secretary of the branch. The Secretariat becomes a shadow cabinet in the event of the arrest of the Executive, or sets up a new Executive. One of the main functions of the Secretariat should be to prepare an all-embracing report based on reports from the contacts of the units, and any other work the Executive may allocate to it. Two other important auxiliary organs should be a youth and women's committee to advise the Executive on certain tasks that may be assigned to the youth and the women in the interests of the Organisation. Yet another important arm is a security committee to carry out the task of security for the whole branch as well as intelligence work, e.g. tracking down informers.

With our organisational machinery properly established and oiled, the Organisation is now in a position to undertake the very important task of marshalling as much support of the oppressed behind it as possible.

### Rallying mass support

The test of the effectiveness of our political machinery is the extent to which the influence of the Organisation is felt among the masses of the people who are not members of the Organisation. In other words, the second step after setting up the organisational machinery is to use it to rally mass support. Inqindi is seeking to give leadership to the oppressed people of South Africa in their fight against apartheid. And unless it enjoys their support, whom is it leading? We must now examine some of the nerve centres in the body politic which the Organisation must touch in order to get the desired mass support and launch the people into mass action when called upon. To do that means that the Organisation must set itself the task of assigning our cadres to operate in those nerve centres from which the entire community – from the branch to the national level – can be drawn into sustained activity under Inquindi's leadership. To mention but a few such nerve centres:

### The labour front

A concerted effort should be made to ensure that in all the key industries in the branch area a nucleus of Inqindi membership is created. For instance, two or more cadres who consistently perform the task of recruiting membership among the workers in a particular factory are preparing the ground for Inqindi policies to seep into the ranks of the workers. This does not conflict with the trade-union work in the factory. After all, the workers must be gradually led to realise that in the final analysis, it is the control of political power that will ensure freedom for them and their families and all who suffer as they do at the hands of the ruling class. In the various industries the workers are organised into trade unions, some of which are affiliated to umbrella bodies (federations) that discourage their unions from associating with the political struggle, e.g. unions affiliated to TUCSA.

If our cadres are properly guided they should be able to gain key positions from the factory floor through to the leadership of the trade unions in a number of industries. If this is done on a national scale, as Inqindi branches throughout the country should do, then we are a step nearer our goal of gaining mass support.

### At centres of learning

In dealing with the centres of learning it is important to bear in mind that these have an ever-shifting population. On average the period of stay by a student at both the secondary and tertiary levels of education covers five years. The setting up of an organisational machinery at these institutions should be done with an eye to continuity from one generation of students to another. Maybe it would help if before the year is out an executive should be brought into being to take over, with some of the outgoing executive to guide them. The Branch Executive should always keep its eye on ensuring that when a year begins a new school executive is in a position to function. A properly functioning organisational machinery in all the schools will ensure that the leadership of a students' movement at the secondary or tertiary level is correctly oriented, i.e. in the direction of Inqindi. During holidays the students may be drawn into the township's branch activities. This practice smooths the way for the students who leave school to fit into the branch organisational machinery. If this is not done the Organisation often loses contact with them after they have left school.

### Other nerve centres

Other important nerve centres within the area of the branch are the migrant labour hostels; sports' organisations; teachers' and nurses' associations; the churches, etc. We are seeking mass support and the masses are found in big concentrations in various walks of life. In whatever important groupings the masses are found, Inqindi cadres should set up a working organisational presence to extend the influence of the Organisation.

## THE STRUCTURE OF THE ORGANISATION

We must examine briefly the importance of the structure of the Organisation in seeking to attain its ends. Again, another look at nature will assist in underlining the point we are making. For instance, the structure of a fish enables it to adapt to and to survive in changing and sometimes very taxing conditions; to survive in the sea it has fins and gills. The frog, on the other hand, which spends part of its life in water and part on land, has webbed feet and lungs. Similarly adapted is the structure of the bird which is airborne most of the time. Depending on conditions, the Inqindi structure has had to change, and will continue to do so if it is to survive under changing conditions. It is very important that the membership appreciate this point. Otherwise insistence on getting it to do things as they were done before under a completely different set of conditions, or to do things for which it is not designed, may create difficulties that may not only retard progress but may also expose it to otherwise preventable enemy attacks. Now:

## The structure before banning

Before Inqindi was banned in March–April 1960 its structure provided for its operation at four levels:

(a) The National Executive was elected at annual conference, attended by delegates from branches operating in various parts of the country.

(b) The Provincial Executive was elected at annual conference, attended by delegates from branches in the particular province.

(c) The Regional Executive was elected at annual conference, attended by branches in the particular region.

(d) The Branch Executive was elected annually at a meeting attended by members of the branch. A significant departure and noteworthy development occurred in the Eastern Cape (1956–59), when meetings of more than ten Africans were made illegal in the Port Elizabeth and Humansdorp magisterial districts. The New Brighton branch adopted the parliamentary form of conducting an election. First, the Branch Executive issued papers to nominate candidates for the executive and thereafter papers (on a polling day) to elect the members of the Executive and office-bearers in the same manner that registered voters vote for parliamentary candidates.

At each of these levels were three corresponding semi-autonomous organisations: (i) the Youth League; (ii) the Women's League and (iii) the Volunteer Corps. Within this structure the membership enjoyed the highest measure of democratic rights. Everything was done openly and conference proceedings received as much publicity as the media cared to give. In addition the secretarial report covering the year's activities was a very valuable document which was sold to the public. This provided valuable reference and source material.

## The structure after banning

Three days before the three-day stayaway to mourn the Sharpeville massacre and a few days before the declaration of the state of emergency in 1961, the National Executive took a decision that the ANC would not disband if, as was anticipated, the government decided to ban it. It would operate underground. Accordingly it drew up a new structure which would enable the Organisation to operate under conditions of illegality. The new structure eliminated the Provincial Executive and modified considerably the relationship between the National Executive and the Regional and Branch executives. Thus

(a) The National Executive was to consist of seven cadres selected at that meeting. The decentralised structure was now to give way to a centralised machinery.

(b) An *ad hoc* committee to consist of seven members was appointed by the National Executive on a temporary basis to carry out the task of organising the branches and to introduce a plan to enable them to operate under illegal conditions. The task of organising rural areas (the 'Reserves') in each province was assigned to this temporary committee.

(c) The Regional Executive was to consist of seven, appointed by the National Executive, to co-ordinate the work of the branches in the region.

(d) The Branch Executive (to consist of seven members appointed by the National Executive) was to have the important function of establishing the organisational machinery in the branch area. The branch was the basic unit of the whole structure and was in direct contact with the people.

At that stage, and up to 1963, the National Executive was operating inside the country and therefore could direct the struggle from within the country.

The structure consisted of three levels, and the *ad hoc* committee was temporary and served as the lengthened arm of the National Executive.

The Youth and Women's Leagues, as semi-autonomous organs, were disbanded and replaced by committees of five each to advise the Executive, especially at the branch level, on special tasks for the youth and the women.

### The post-1964 period

The most significant feature of this period is that the National Executive operates from outside the borders of the country. As expected they have adopted a structure that enables them to guide the struggle within the country from outside the borders.

We may at this point pause to answer the question: under the structures adapted to underground operations, does the membership not lose the democratic rights they have enjoyed in the Organisation for so long? To a certain extent the exercise of free democratic rights such as participation in the electoral machinery of office-bearers within the country is suspended. But where conditions permit, as is the case outside the borders of the country, elections of the National Executive do take place in a free atmosphere. Within the country, discussions on issues which require the expression of views of the membership take place at unit level and such views are relayed to the Branch Executive through the contact system. Thus a two-way system of communication is established. In turn, the Branch Executive relays the decisions to the higher level. The membership therefore is still involved in decision-making.

## A QUESTION OF SURVIVAL

Operating under illegal conditions is beset with many risks. Our organisational machinery must be trimmed in such a way that the chances of being uncovered are reduced to a minimum, otherwise the very survival of the Organisation may be threatened. The arrest of one individual can lead to a chain reaction which may uncover a number of other members and their activities. Such information may give the police a lead to the arrest of other people by observing the movements of any person they suspect.

It must be obvious that the Organisation has to take some vital steps to ensure, as much as it is possible to do, not only its continued survival but also its ability to operate effectively. The two most important steps to take are: to tighten security and discipline. The Organisation must run a campaign to instil in the minds of every member security-consciousness. Even the smallest of its organisations, viz the unit which may consist of three to five members, must have one person entrusted with the task of looking after the security of the unit. For instance, any documents that have to be read at a unit meeting must end up with him to ensure their disposal; he must see to it that no two members of the unit walk together to the meeting place. Each must find his way. That does not mean that other members of the unit must relax. As breaches of security are reported from the units to the secretariat, it should in turn send out a reminder to all units. Discipline on the part of every member must be insisted upon. Observing such requirements as being at the appointed place on time, not carrying about in one's pockets incriminating documents such as a diary indicating dates, not touching liquor while on organisational duty, may appear elementary, yet failure to observe them is an indication of lack of discipline. In the course of the discussions, a lot more examples may be cited.

## CLOSING REMARKS

In this paper we have concentrated exclusively on the setting up of an underground organisational machinery in the industrial and other urban centres where the population is to be found in large concentrations, as in the urban townships. Since one of the main aims of the Organisation is to enlist mass support, this paper falls short of indicating guidelines for the setting up of organisational machinery to cover large sections of the oppressed people who live outside the urban areas: almost 50 per cent of the African population, 20–25 per cent of the coloureds and 15–20 per cent of the Indian population. It would require two separate papers to deal with the setting up of an organisational machinery for the 'Reserves', i.e. the bantustans, and for the large numbers of Africans and coloureds who work and live on the farms. These are spread throughout the farming areas in the country and number more than two million.

Another important aspect we have omitted in this paper is the cooperating role of the National Executive, especially in our situation where the National Executive has not only to coordinate the activities of the internal organisation machinery but also to synchronise that machinery with the military operations of MK. Bearing in mind this relationship should make our cadres realise the vital importance of security and discipline. For instance, take the question of giving reports. It is of vital importance that when a cadre gives a report, say to his unit, it should reflect the true situation about the matter on which he is reporting. Otherwise the Organisation may take decisions which are based on incorrect information, and as a result the decision may be wrong and cause costly damage. A report must not be coloured by the personal views of the cadre giving it. In the South African situation where the government itself is ever seeking to provoke riots in the townships in order to get an opportunity to shoot defenceless people in the name of 'law and order', the existence of an effective organisational machinery may reduce riot occurrences to a minimum. The mowing down of hundreds of defenceless people has a demoralising effect on them, and may be followed by a long period of apathy. But where the people are given good, effective leadership they know the goals they are seeking and how to achieve them. They will see police provocation for what it is, and resist the temptation of being drawn into their trap.

We bring our discussion on organisation to a close on the same note as we started it. Go to the masses of the oppressed and exploited peoples of our land. Work amongst them; work with them to prepare the way for a take-over of power.

Well may it be to draw inspiration from an injunction given, by S.E.K. Mqhayi at the end of World War Two, to the young men who had joined the South African army in the war against Nazism. On the eve of demobilisation he sounded a clarion call to them to return to fight for their freedom at home. His words, wrapped up in that famous couplet, rang true then and have a deeper significance for us today in the face of the grave situation created by apartheid:

'*Godukani ningalali*
*Nizothengiswa Ngooyihlo.'*
[Go home but don't fall asleep
For your fathers are going to sell you down the river.]

## APPENDIX A

1. Given a township which covers a wide area, the first step is to divide the township into zones or blocks bounded by, say, four streets.

(a) The Executive appoints one cadre (Chief Steward) to be in charge of all organisational activity in this zone or block.

(b) The zone consists of five horizontal streets and six vertical streets. The Executive appoints one street steward in charge of each street, i.e. eleven street stewards working and reporting to the Chief Steward.

(c) Let us say each of these streets has 20 houses, then let each group of 10 houses constitute a cell. That means each street has two cell stewards operating directly and reporting to the Street Steward, who reports to the Zone or Chief Steward, who reports to the Secretariat, who reports to the Branch Executive.

2. The procedure indicated above is followed in all the zones that make up the branch. Let us say that there are 25 zones in the branch, then there are 25 Chief Stewards. From their reports to the Secretariats, the Branch Executive knows about every activity in the township. In turn its directives find their way downward through the same channel to the membership. The directives or problems affecting the Organisation at the unit level, as shown in the main body of the essay, distinguish clearly between unit, cell and study group.

# Good Organisation:
# Carrying the Organisation to the Bantustans

## INTRODUCTION

It will be recalled that the previous paper under this title concentrated on organising the townships in the urban areas. We stated in that paper that organising the bantustans and the oppressed who work and live on the commercial farms would require separate papers. It will be seen therefore, that the title 'Good Organisation: Key to Success' is the main theme under which these papers are handled. Although they are separate papers they go to make up a unity. It must necessarily be so because the ANC aims at enlisting mass support for the struggle it is heading for the liberation of the oppressed and exploited in this country. The fact that these papers are separate does not mean they are independent of each other or that they are dealing with different, unrelated topics. Rather in dealing with these aspects of the Organisation we are taking into account the fact that the nature of the conditions in each area is such as to require a modification of organisational approach and methods to suit the prevailing conditions in each area.

According to the 1980 census the population of the bantustans into which the 'Native Reserves' have been divided is 10 467 000 million, i.e. nearly 10,5 million. This is more than double the white population, which is 4,5 million. The whole argument by the National Party government for the exclusion of Africans from any scheme purporting to accommodate the political aspirations of the Africans, lingers on. Their claim is that Africans have their own areas, viz the reserves, where they must exercise their political rights.

The purpose of this paper is to indicate broadly how to set up a political organisational machinery under the leadership of the ANC to rally the 10,5 million of the bantustans for the liberation struggle. If for no other reason, the figure of 10,5 million alone —

and there are other vital reasons – is enough to place the organisation of the bantustans high on the list of priorities to ensure mass support if the ANC is to succeed in its struggle to overthrow white supremacy.

The task of organising the bantustans is made more complicated than it is in the urban townships by certain locational factors regarding the population of the bantustans. To be clear, therefore, about how to go about the job of organising the bantustans we must first identify the location, and its nature, of sections of the bantustan population. Sections of the population of the bantustans are located thus:

(a) In the urban areas, migrant contract labour is housed in the hostels and compounds. At the seaports, the Railways operate their own compounds for dockworkers, e.g. in Cape Town a compound at the Docks, in Port Elizabeth a compound at New Brighton above the bridge, in Durban a compound at the sea point.

(b) Settlement in the bantustans. There are three types of such settlement: the peri-urban type, e.g. KwaMashu, Umlazi; the border area-type, e.g. Mdantsane, Madadeni near Newcastle, Zakheni near Ladysmith, Mabopane near Pretoria, Seshego near Pietersburg; and settlements not associated with any growth point, e.g. Sada and Kayalethu in the Ciskei, Limehill in northern Natal, Winterveld in the Transvaal.

(c) The areas under the administration of chiefs. In the following sections we shall attempt to relate the examination of the problem of organising the bantustans to these areas. It should be clear that this is not a blueprint for organising the bantustans. The purpose of the paper is to stimulate a serious discussion on one of the most vital areas for the Organisation and, if for different reasons, for the Nationalist government.

## ORGANISING THE HOSTELS AND COMPOUNDS

For the purposes of developing an organisational plan we shall treat hostels and compounds as areas in which the organisational machinery required to meet the care of one is equally applicable to the other. The migrant contract labour housed at the hostels has this distinguishing feature: that its life and interests are tied by leash both to urban and to bantustan conditions. For twelve months the contract labourer lives in the hostel situated in an urban area subjected to the same conditions at the work-place as the urban people, while his family is tied to the bantustans. After serving his contract (12 months) he is compelled by law to return to the bantustans, and may only return to the same employer in the urban area if his employer has issued him a 'call card' guaranteeing him employment upon return within a specified period of time. Thus there is always a constant shuttle movement of a large force of male labour. And it is important to note that this force is composed of able-bodied men between the ages of 18 and 50. The Organisation must catch them somewhere to bring them into the ranks of its membership or under its influence.

As most of the working life of migrant labour is spent in the places of work at the industrial centres, the obvious place to concentrate on is the hostel. Before we map out our plan of organising hostels we must be clear on the pattern of living adopted by migrants at the hostels. Generally they are cut off from the township and its activities. And this isolation engenders a feeling in the migrants that they are not part of the townships. Consequently they keep in touch with the distant bantustans where their families live, rather than with their immediate surroundings and the people in the townships. Within the hostel their living conditions are patterned like those in the mine compounds. People from a certain location under a certain chief live more closely together. Such a group leads a communal life and runs an insurance scheme of its own whereby if a death occurs, they raise among themselves money to pay for the transportation of the remains to the bantustans.

Now the task of organising the migrants in the hostels must necessarily fall upon the ANC branch in whose area of jurisdiction the hostel falls. The branch sets up a Rural Area Committee (RAC) of 5 to 7 members. Their main task is to form and establish organisational machinery within the hostel along the following lines:

*A hostel committee (HC).* The RAC first selects a few hostel inmates and gives them intensive training about the ANC and its policy, as well as forming and administering an organisational machinery in the hostel. In selecting the members of the Hostel Committee, the RAC should ensure that as far as possible the members of the HC represent a cross-section of the main regions or districts from which the hostel inmates are drawn. Such a more or less representative HC would be better placed to break down the barriers of tribe or locality that the authorities foster at the hostels and compounds.

In the course of training the RAC must give a clear exposition of the bantustan scheme: how it operates in the bantustans; what it seeks to achieve; how the problems encountered by the people in the bantustans are linked up with the problems of the people in the urban areas. As solution to these problems the RAC shows that the ANC is the only organisation that is in a position to give leadership to all the oppressed people of South Africa.

Then a Hostel Committee (HC) of 5 to 7 members is appointed (by the RAC) to set up an organisational machinery within the hostel to recruit members. Entry into the hostel premises is screened at the gate. In times of increased activity in the township (e.g. bus boycotts, stay-at-homes, strikes), only hostel inmates are allowed to enter the hostel, which is usually surrounded by a security fence with guarded points of entry. Meetings between the HC and the RAC should take place outside the hostel premises, i.e. in the township.

*The organisational structure* within the hostel will depend on the type of hostel structures, thus: (a) where the hostel is one giant structure divided into dormitories, the HC should set up small units of 4 to 5 members in the various dormitories; (b) where the hostel consists of separate blocks as is now the practice on the new mines and hostels, units should be set up in each block.

Migrant contract labour is an important link between the urban townships and the bantustans. Of what significance is this fact, on the one hand to the government, and on the other to the ANC? Realising the fact that the ANC would not only be strengthened in the urban areas but that it would gain a strong foothold in the bantustans if contract labour fell under its influences, the government does everything to reduce to the barest minimum the contact between the hostel inmates and the people in the township. On the other hand, the ANC cannot ignore the fact that on numerous occasions the government has used migrant labour to break popular political actions like stayaways and industrial strikes. Unless the ANC draws them into the political struggle under its own leadership, this big force would even do harm to the cause of liberation while floating between secluded hostels in the urban areas and in the bantustans, living in enforced periods of inactivity. Through planned and systematic organisation accompanied by political education, contract labour would carry the ANC and what it stands for to every bantustan in the country.

This is a backlash which the government can never stop as long as it maintains the migrant contract labour system.

## SETTLEMENTS IN THE BANTUSTANS

The three types of settlements listed in Section I above have one characteristic in common, viz that structurally they are similar to the urban townships. The organisational plan discussed in the previous paper on organising the urban townships applies to these settlements equally well. We must therefore address ourselves to the role which these settlements can play in the overall plan of organising the bantustans, i.e. those rural areas which fall under the direct administration of chiefs.

As the settlements are in the bantustans, there is unrestricted movement of people between the settlements and the areas under the direct administration of chiefs. This is a weakness in the bantustan structure which the Organisation must exploit to the full. It is easier to organise a more closely knit organisational machinery in the settlements than in those areas of the bantustans where people are sparsely scattered. But as the Organisation in the first two types of settlement, viz the peri-urban and the border areas, is in fact industrially orientated, it must be made to appreciate the need to organise the people in the bantustans and to bring them to a level of political understanding where they will realise that their problems are inextricably intertwined with those of all the oppressed people in the country. Given proper planning and direction the Organisation in the settlements should do a great deal of work to establish the ANC throughout the bantustans.

To illustrate how a properly directed, multi-pronged organisational onslaught can be mounted from these settlements, let us take the Natal–Zululand area. Nowhere else in the country have Africans been moved out of urban industrial centres onto the bantustan side of the border on such a scale as in Natal. The picture looks gloomy yet with careful planning and determined effort the ANC should turn the position to its advantage. Over weekends, organising teams could advance to the settlements of the neighbouring bantustans areas. For instance, from KwaMashu and Mlazi it should be easy to go to areas, e.g. Mbumbulu, Mzinto, Port Shepstone areas through to the borders of eastern Pondoland; from Mbali organising teams would cover areas like Harding, Ixopo, Ndaleni, etc.; from Zakheni settlement near Ladysmith organising teams would cover the areas from Umhlumayo; from the Limehill settlement organising teams would proceed into the heart of Zululand; while further north from the Madadeni settlement organising could cover the northern areas of KwaZulu to the borders of Swaziland and Mozambique.

## THE BANTUSTAN INTERNAL MACHINERY

In organising the bantustans the Organisation has two main aims in view, viz to achieve political and military ends. Owing to the vastness of the areas that have to be covered, the locational problems to be taken into account, and the scope of the security network the government has built in the bantustans, the task of organising the bantustans requires to be directed from a higher level that not only can muster bigger financial resources but is in a position to co-ordinate activites at various structural levels, and locational area, e.g. the urban branch and hostel, the settlement and the vast organisational machinery in the bantustan themselves. This is a task the National Executive Committee (NEC), especially that which operates from outside the borders, must delegate to the Ad Hoc Committee (AHC) for each province, which would then undertake to set up an internal organisational machinery in each bantustan thus:

*An Area Committee (AC)*. The size of the area committee would depend on the number of magisterial districts in the bantustan or alternatively on the number of Regional Bantu Authorities, which are made up of a given number of magisterial districts. Let us say the Ad Hoc Committee (AHC) appoints one member to the AC to represent two adjacent districts. If the bantustan consists of 14 magisterial districts, then the AHC would set up an AC of 7 members. On this basis the members of the AC would be drawn from various parts of the bantustan concerned. Their main task would be to organise the whole area of the bantustan under their jurisdiction. In small bantustans like the Ciskei, Qwa Qwa, KwaNgwane, Venda, Gazankulu and KwaNdebele, one member for each district is appointed to the AC. The AC should meet at regular intervals, say once every two months, to receive reports on the work done over the period in terms of their tasks and targets.

*District Committee (DC)*. The AC in its own turn appoints a District Committee of 5 to 7 members representative as far as possible of the wards into which the district is divided. As each ward is made up, more or less, of adjacent locations, a member of the DC charged with the responsibility of organising the locations in his area or ward would find it easy to cover the area by the cheapest means of transport, e.g. on horseback or bicycle. To determine the number of wards, let us suppose a magisterial district consists of 30 locations each administered by a chief. Divide 30 by 5. That will give 6 wards each made up of 5 locations. Thus in this case the DC would be composed of 6 members.

*Location Committee (LC)*. In each location the DC should set up a Location Committee of 3 to 4 members whose main task is to recruit membership and to organise into small units of 4 to 5 for political education and discussion. Such units can exercise tremendous influence at the location meetings convened by the chief. Without betraying organised opinion, they could sway the discussions in a manner that would enable them to carry the support of location inhabitants on issues that affect the community. Whenever important issues are brought up by the government, the Area Committee would meet to discuss and brief the District Committee who in turn would brief the locations on the line before the government proposals are brought to the people.

It is important to bear in mind that the government has built up a tight security network at the location level as well as an effective information system. Unless the Organisation devises a more efficient counter-plan to beat the government's, it will not be able to penetrate to the grassroots. And if the Organisation is to succeed in setting up an organisational machinery in the bantustans, it must penetrate the government's security network at the location level. Briefly the government security plan is as follows. At the head of the location administration is a paid chief or headman. In addition he gets a travelling allowance if he goes to see the Native Commissioner or the police station on official business. He gets a number of other fringe benefits and bribes. Through the emergency regulations that apply in all the bantustans the chief is armed with powers to break down opposition and to intimidate the people. See how in virtually all the bantustans a one-party system prevails. Each location is divided into small sections, each of which is headed by a sub-chief.

Note that all social activities, e.g. beer drinks, weddings or gatherings of any type, must have the approval of the Native Commissioner and the police. Note too that the kraalhead must report the arrival of a strange person at his home to the sub-headman or chief, who immediately must inform the location chief. In cases of urgency the chief must inform the nearest trader who has been appointed as a postal agency and had a telephone installed at his shop. The trader transmits such information to the police by phone. In the face of this it must be clear that organisers at the location level, i.e. the Location Committee, must be local people.

Elsewhere in this paper we pointed out that the Organisation's interest in extending its activities to the bantustans is twofold, viz to build a strong organisational machinery among the peasants, and secondly to prepare the ground for the recruitment and training of MK units. With a sound organisational machinery in the bantustans, MK should be able to establish itself in those vast open spaces and therefore extend its activities with the assistance, in a number of ways, of the local populace.

## THE CO-ORDINATING EXERCISE

In the foregoing sections we have dealt with various organisational threads but, as it were, left them dangling in the air, i.e. without weaving a coherent organisational pattern designed to achieve the Organisation's objectives in terms of a nation-wide plan to gain freedom from oppression and exploitation. This co-ordinating exercise is the task of the NEC, which in our circumstances it must delegate to the *ad hoc* committees. There should be four AHCs, i.e. one for each of the four Provinces. The headquarters for each of the AHCs should be at the main industrial regions, i.e. Jo'burg to cover the 6 Transvaal bantustans; Durban for the Natal–Zululand bantustans; Port Elizabeth for the Ciskei and the Transkei; and Bloemfontein for Qwa Qwa and the OFS.

The main instrument to use in the co-ordinating exercise is a news-sheet which should come out at given intervals. We suggest the title of the news-sheet should be *'Izwi lomzi/Lentsoe la Sechaba'* (The Voice of the Nation).

The news-sheet should be in the language predominant in the particular bantustan where it is to be distributed. In the first issue it is important that the meaning of *sechaba* [the nation], i.e. the way in which the ANC uses it, should be made clear. Decades of separation of one ethnic group from another by the government have narrowed the meaning of the word in the minds of the people to apply only to the ethnic group of the particular bantustan.

In each issue of the news-sheet an appeal should be made to the reader to pass it on to a friend in the way of a chain letter. Every issue must state that it is published and distributed by the ANC. Bearing in mind that the purpose of the news-sheet is to spread information on what the ANC stands for, the handling of the topics should be carefully and systematically treated stage by stage.

How does the AHC handle the distribution? Operating from its underground quarters, the AHC cyclostyles or prints each issue and distributes it as follows:

(a)  Each urban branch that has a hostel compound in its area is issued with sufficient copies to distribute the issue in such hostel or compound through the organisational machinery that the RAC has set up in the hostels.

Whenever the branch issues its own leaflets it should also distribute them through the hostel machinery to the contract labourers which must be drawn into the struggles of the urban people while they are in the urban areas. The hostels should be bombarded with leaflets from both ends.

(b)  All the settlements should be thoroughly covered through their own organisational machinery with every issue of the news-sheet. This would be in addition to any locally produced leaflets. Note: For purposes of security, if the urban branch and the settlements referred to in (a) and (b) above are far from the AHC seat of operations, they should be sent a copy each to reproduce in their own area.

(c)  In the bantustans themselves, how is the distribution to be done? Over time the AHC should compile a mailing list. It should be easy to obtain names and addresses from the contract labour through the organisational machinery at the hostels, from the organisational machinery in the settlements and from the Area Committee in the bantustans.

Armed with such a mailing list the AHC printing and despatch departments make up small parcels of half a dozen to a dozen copies and post to all the names on the mailing list. The advantage of this method of distribution is that even though some of the recipients get to be known by the police in the bantustans, they cannot be prosecuted simply because they do not know who sent them. Further, for lack of news the peasants will make each issue of the news-sheet a talking point so that one copy of the news-sheet will be talked about and discussed by a number of people at weddings, at beer-drinks, at dipping tanks – wherever people gather.

87

Note: (i) The AHC should collect as many calendars, catalogues, sales promotion bills, as they can lay their hands on. These are handy as wrappers.

(ii) The parcels should be posted at a number of post offices, ready-stamped.

(iii) Along the title at the top of the page each issue should carry the serial number thus: Vol. 1 No. 2 or 3 or . . . A/2/81 (i.e. February 1981 and AHC concerned).

(iv) A copy of each issue of the news-sheet should be sent to the NEC abroad for filing as well as to keep it informed of the work done.

## TO ROUND OFF

From the foregoing suggestions at organising the bantustans, it must be apparent that the task is not an easy one. It is a much bigger, much more extensive, probably more complex, and by far more costly undertaking than organising an urban township. Owing to the vast distances that members of the Area Committee and, to a lesser extent, members of the District Committee have to cover using various forms of transport, it must be accepted that they should be furnished with fairly liberal travelling allowances. Transport is far more costly in the rural areas than in the urban areas.

When the AHC arranges meetings with the members of the AC to brief them and to discuss general problems, it is safer to meet by arrangement with an urban branch in an urban township outside the bantustan.

The importance of setting up a working organisational machinery over as wide an area as possible in each bantustan is vital for the execution of the struggle. It is difficult to imagine how MK can even begin to operate there unless there is a political structure that can be relied upon to prepare the ground for MK operations of whatever nature. This is especially important in the case of those bantustans which lie along the borders of neighbouring states.

To show the immensity of the task, the AHC for the Transvaal would have to undertake the task of organising six separate bantustans as well as co-ordinating the work with hostels and mine compounds housing contract labour from all the bantustans in the country. Difficult? Yes. But if the job has to be done, it must be done.

*Amandla! Matla!*

# Notes on Leafletting and Pamphleteering

## INTRODUCTION

From prehistoric times man has had to contend with the problem of communicating ideas to those around him. For his survival it has been important for man throughout the ages to seek and harness the co-operation of his fellow men in order to overcome common problems and ensure not only continued survival but an improvement in the way of living. How in all the ages has man managed to maintain communication with his fellow men? Put differently, how has he been able to reach out in ideas to his fellow men? At simpler and lower levels of social development the spoken word was the main means of communication.

In spite of the great strides in technology since the emergence of capitalism, the formation of large urban communities, the growth of education and the development of mass media, the spoken word still holds its own. This is especially the case in the rural areas where the population is sparsely spread over wide areas, and the level of literacy is comparatively low.

In the subsequent sections we propose to examine the role of the written word in spreading ideas as widely as possible among people. We are not thinking of this in general terms but in a more limited sense. We are concerned here with advancing the cause of the ANC – our own organisation which has set itself the task of winning freedom from oppression and exploitation for the vast masses of the people of this country. For our purposes we are concerned with examining the best manner in which an outlawed ANC can set about the task of carrying its message to the masses of the people, whom it seeks to lead, in order to achieve its goals.

In concentrating on leafletting and pamphleteering, we are not claiming that these two forms of communicating the political message of our organisation are the only ones open to it. But we are seeking to highlight the role of these for a number of reasons which we shall examine below. What, however, we must emphasise at this stage is that the various means of communication open to our organisation complement one another. What is significant about the leaflet and the pamphlet is that unlike the other means of communication like the radio or the press, they are within the means of the Organisation even if it had to rely for its finances completely on funds raised by and from its membership. In the following pages we are going to examine the following aspects: the difference between the leaflet and the pamphlet; the role of the leaflet; the place of the pamphlet; and production and distribution.

## THE DIFFERENCE BETWEEN THE LEAFLET AND THE PAMPHLET

The difference between these two is largely determined by the use to which each is put in an organisation. A secondary factor to be taken into account in distinguishing between the two is the length and size of each. In dealing with these forms of communicating our ideas we hope that these two main differences will come out clearly as we deal with them under the respective sections.

## THE LEAFLET AND ITS ROLE

The conditions under which an organisation that is committed to a struggle against the government works, influence the choice of the media it may use. These conditions are either that the organisation operates legally, or the government bans the organisation so that it is unable to work openly. For 48 years the ANC operated legally. It recruited its membership openly; it held public meetings. During that period the main means of reaching out to the people was through the spoken word. By the early thirties it failed to keep alive its mouthpiece, *Abantu Batho*. Thus for thirty years (1930–60) it relied almost entirely on the spoken word to get its message across to the people. This has its advantages though very limited under conditions of illegality. The speaker is able in the course of his speech to observe the impact he has on the audience and to assess the response to his spoken word. But the spoken word reaches out only to those present at the meeting. And frequently those who attend regularly turn out to be members, so that from week to week the speakers are addressing themselves to the converted.

Depending on the impact the Organisation is making on the

politics of the country it may get publicity – sometimes openly hostile, sometimes slanted in such a way that it does not project a favourable image of the Organisation. It must be evident that the Organisation cannot rely on such incidental media to enhance its popularity among the people whose cause it seeks to advance. For instance, the ANC cannot count on the capitalist press in South Africa to project a favourable image for it, to say nothing of popularising its policies and defending its actions. What mention is made of the ANC in such press is only in connection with such of its activities as are essentially of news value, e.g. reporting court cases in which its members were arrested in the course of carrying out certain activities, like those of MK.

In the *Guardian* and its long chain of successors down to the last of these – the *Spark* – the ANC got very helpful coverage. But even these, good as they were, had serious limitations. They appeared in English and as such had a limited readership among the masses of the people. In the early 1960s attempts to operate an illegal radio were made, and after overcoming technical problems the ANC did go on the air from a radio operating illegally inside the country. This project had tremendous potential advantages. It went on the air at times convenient to the working man and woman throughout the country. It boosted the morale of the membership at a very difficult time when as a result of the banning in 1960 the Organisation was thrown into disarray because it had not then developed a fairly smooth-running organisational machinery for operating under illegal conditions. This takes time to develop and requires a high level of discipline on the part of the membership. An illegal radio operating within the country is, however, very vulnerable. The Post Office has developed techniques which enable it to track such a radio down.

A development that owed its birth to the banning of the ANC was the opening of offices abroad. The External Mission had a dual function. On the one hand, it had to launch a world-wide campaign to bring to the attention of the international community what the ANC stood for, as opposed to apartheid. On the other hand the Organisation was forced, as a result of the effective surveillance of the Nationalist government, to shift the executive function to the External Mission. This imposed on the Executive, now operating from outside the country, the added responsibility of building and maintaining an organisational machinery based and operating within the country where the masses of the oppressed people who must be activated and involved in the struggle are. But how was the Executive operating from such a disadvantageous position to reach out to the masses it sought to lead in their struggle for liberation? The Organisation was able to make arrangements to beam a concerted radio campaign to the country to set out its policy, to guide the people inside on how to organise and on what tasks to carry out. In addition it revived, outside the country, the publication of *Sechaba/Isizwe*.

These are important channels of communication. Radio Freedom especially came in handy during the 1976 upsurge and thereafter. In varying degrees these two media are making an important impact on an increasing scale on the people in the country. We must, however, face the fact that because of the distance between the seat of the Executive and the people at home, the effectiveness of these two media must necessarily be unfavourably affected by a lack of feedback. That is, they are unable to assess the reaction of the people and to adjust subsequent broadcasts on the basis of feedback information.

**What is our target?**

The ANC aims at influencing the people to accept its leadership in the struggle for freedom. The people are our target. In selecting the various media, by means of which we reach out to the people, we must be clear in our minds that the first step in that direction is to build a strong organisation capable of bringing to the attention of the oppressed masses the objectives set out to be achieved. The strength and effectiveness of the Organisation must be judged by the influence it wields over the oppressed masses whose interests it seeks to further. It is only when the millions of the oppressed and exploited people who live in the vast sprawling townships in South Africa's cities and towns, and yet other millions in the rural areas – the peasants in the bantustans and labourers on the white farms – accept the leadership of the ANC, that it can feel it has the support of the masses. Where are these townships? These are the African, coloured and Indian townships in the Pretoria–Witwatersrand–Vereeniging complex (PWV), in Durban–Pinetown, in Port Elizabeth–Uitenhage and in the Western Cape. It is vital to the success of the revolution that the ANC wields a controlling influence in Soweto, Mamelodi–Mabopane, Tembisa, Daveyton, Natalspruit; Sharpeville–Sebokeng, Lenasia, Carletonville; in KwaMashu, Chatsworth–Phoenix; in Schauderville–

Gelvandale–Bethelsdorp, New Brighton–Zakhele complex; Uitenhage African and coloured townships; in Mdantsane–Duncan Village; in Mitchells Plain–Athlone–Bonteheuwel–Steenberg, Guguletu–Nyanga, Langa. These townships do not complete the picture but they occupy a high position on the list of priorities. There are still big important concentrations in various parts of the country, e.g. eMadadeni, Limehill, Ladysmith, Seshego, Phalaborwa, and Kimberley area, to mention but a few. How do we reach out to our membership and the masses of the people in these townships, to the peasants in the bantustans and to the farm workers on the white farms?

## Through the leaflet

The leaflet as a vehicle for the spread of the message of the Organisation is of vital importance. In practice, a leaflet may cover one or two sides of a quarto size or foolscap size of duplicating paper. It takes one of two forms:

### Educational leaflet

The Organisation should embark on a carefully planned leafletting campaign in which it sets out clearly, simply and in an interesting manner what it stands for, and how its policies and programme are designed to protect and advance the cause of the people. To do this it should not only concern itself with problems of a national character such as striving to attain the goals set out in the Freedom Charter, but be quite prepared to take a full part in finding a solution for the more immediate local problems. What does this mean in practical terms? It means that in each township there should be a branch of the ANC whose task it is to strengthen first the organisational machinery. It is the township branch that is saddled with the task of activating the masses of the people, and by working among the people, attending to the day-to-day problems, the people develop confidence in the Organisation and accept its leadership. A few examples of such local issues suffice: badly run bus services, high bus fares, unpaved streets, poorly lit streets, police raids, increased rents, inadequate ambulance services, etc.

All these matters should receive attention in the educational leaflet as frequently as possible until the people associate the struggle against such hardships with the ANC both at the local and at the national level. The role of the leaflet becomes vital in projecting the image of the Organisation among the masses, most of whom are not even its members. Its appearance now and again assures them that it exists and operates among them rather than only from 'a safe distance outside the country'. If the organisational machinery is strong, the leaflet can be widely distributed in the township. One leaflet delivered in one household will be read by every member, or its contents will be discussed by the whole family. In turn the contents of the leaflet may be discussed by groups of people at places of work. In such discussions the one leaflet which sparked them off will have spread its message far beyond the one person who read it initially. Assuming a household consists of 5 people on average, one ream of 500 leaflets will have its contents brought to the attention of 2 500 people (500 x 5).

It is of great importance that the leaflet be presented in as attractive a manner as possible. The setting must be good: subheadings, underlining certain sentences, using capital letters for emphasis, the use of asterisks where a number of points are listed one after another. The length of the leaflet will be influenced by the nature of the topic dealt with. But it is preferable that it should appear on one face of the sheet to maintain the attention of the reader, especially if the leaflet is picked up at a bus terminus. If the leaflet covers both sides, greater care should be taken in running off the second page so that it comes out clearly without ink smudges. It is preferable to deliver leaflets of such length at households.

And the language: The language in which the leaflet appears must be determined by one consideration, and one consideration only, viz the language that is most commonly spoken in the particular township. The matter is easily settled for certain areas. For most African townships in the Cape, the leaflet must appear in Xhosa, but for townships in the north-eastern Cape (Kimberley), Choana is the dominant language; in coloured townships in the Eastern and Western Cape, English seems to be more widely read than Afrikaans; in African townships in Natal, Zulu is the language, while in all the Indian townships in Natal and the Transvaal English is the main language.

The position becomes a little more complicated when we consider the African townships in the Transvaal. But even in this area there are certain guidelines as to which language should be used. Take Soweto: parts of it are settled by and large on ethnic lines, e.g. for the Tladi–Naledi, Moroka areas, Choana is the dominant language. In the more mixed areas – Orlando East and

West, Emdeni, Zola, etc. – Zulu would be read with understanding by most people, but if there should be the slightest doubt
about this, then the one face of the leaflet should be in Zulu and the
other in Southern Sotho. For the other townships in the PWV area
the branch leadership, who are more familiar with the local
conditions, should have no difficulty in deciding on the language
in which leaflets in those townships should appear.

The guiding principle is that we are aiming at reaching out to
the greatest number of people in the various townships in which
the ANC should be operating. And if our message is to make the
maximum impact, then it must be conveyed to them in the
language spoken by the majority of the people in the area.

### The leaflet for rural areas

In considering the best means of reaching out to the rural areas,
we should distinguish between the peasants, now confined to the
bantustans, and farm labourers (African and coloured) employed
on the white-owned farms. Let us deal with these in turn:

(a) *The peasant areas.* There are the peasants who are settled in
the bantustans. The Nationalist government has contrived efficient
machinery in these areas with a view to sealing the people in these
areas off from outside influences. The administrative structure of
Territorial Authorities, Regional Authorities, chiefs, headmen
and subheadmen is designed to regiment the peasants. In these
areas public meetings and even social gatherings are not allowed
without permission of the police. These conditions have reduced
the use of the spoken word for political purposes as a means of
reaching out to the people, to the barest minimum. Illegal
meetings are the only answer for those who do not support the
apartheid scheme of things. In such circumstances the message of
the ANC must be spread through the written word, i.e. the leaflet.
In addition, the peasants must be encouraged to know that they
have friends outside their ghetto – friends, nay allies, who are
engaged in the struggle for their freedom as well.

There are also the big peri-urban settlements which for purposes of administration are on the bantustan side of the border but
service the labour requirements of capitalist enterprises on the
white side of the border. A few examples of these are Mdantsane,
Dimbaza, Madadeni settlement near Ladysmith, Mlazi, Kwa-
Mashu, Mabopane, Garankuwa, Seshego, etc. For all practical
purposes the branch organisational machinery in these areas will

be similar to that in the urban townships. But in addition these settlements should serve as a convenient channel for the relay and spread of ideas to the peasants. The leaflet in these settlements must also play as important a role as in the urban townships but with this notable approach: although the leaflets for the various settlements will basically be putting across the ANC policies and offering the Freedom Charter as the goal, the leaflets in these settlements will draw their propaganda material from the conditions in the border industries which draw their labour from such settlements.

Yet a large force of the peasants is contracted out by the bantustan administration as dirt cheap migrant labour in the industrial areas. They live in compounds (hostels) in the urban townships. These people should be bombarded with leaflets dealing with their peculiar position in the urban areas where they spend the greater part of their working lives. They should also be bombarded with leaflets which deal with conditions in the bantustans because their families are there, and as such are branded as bantustan citizens. They should in addition be asked to post leaflets to the peasants in the bantustans.

(b) *Farm labour.* Before the organisation was banned it had hardly penetrated the white farms. Branches had been established in the Sundays River Valley (Kirkwood) in the Eastern Cape, and some important organisational work was being done in the Bethal area in the eastern Transvaal. It would appear that at this stage leafletting among the two million-odd farm workers is out of the question.

### The action leaflet

This form of leaflet is necessarily short and to the point. It is intended partly to pep up the morale of people involved in some form of action, e.g. during a strike, or a bus boycott, and partly to sound a clarion call to action. It sets out, in bold type and double spaced, a few points to urge people into action, in solidarity, e.g. calling upon people who are not directly affected by the cause of the action elsewhere, to embark on similar sympathy action in support. An extreme example of this was when action leaflets were issued in the Eastern Cape to boycott buses there in solidarity with the people of Alexandra township in the 1950s. The people in the Eastern Cape responded to the call immediately. It must be clear from the nature of these two forms of the leaflet that the educational leaflet requires to be produced and distributed as frequently as is feasible, taking into account security under conditions of illegality.

## THE PLACE OF THE PAMPHLET

In Section 2 above we have attempted to draw a line between a leaflet and a pamphlet. Unlike the leaflet – the most commonly used medium for the dissemination of ideas on a mass scale by a political organisation representative of the interests of the poor and with very limited financial resources – the pamphlet is intended for mass consumption, especially where it is issued by an outlawed organisation. The ANC is such an organisation. With its branches in the various townships relying on funds largely generated from its membership, it cannot mount a sustained and ambitious propaganda campaign. Thus with its very limited financial resources it must fall back on the leaflet for the dissemination of its message. A ream of duplicating paper has about 500 sheets and from it can be produced 500 leaflets.

However, on occasions when the Organisation requires to deal in greater depth with some aspect, it uses the pamphlet. For instance, on average the length of the essays we are accustomed to here would take a few quarto-sized sheets of duplicating paper stapled together. In running an organisation with a large membership the allocation of work gives rise to the development of leadership levels. These leading members are by the very nature of their functions required to have a very clear understanding of the policies and programme of the Organisation. They must be equipped with such a high degree of political education as the average member does not find the time or the facilities to acquire. The pamphlet provides a ready answer to the problem of finding the means of enlightening the leading cadres on a wide range of issues, some of them specialised. Under illegal conditions it is not easy to hold even executive meetings at whatever level of organisation. Pamphlets distributed among the leading cadres have the very important advantage of providing a uniform interpretation of policies or understanding of certain issues of political significance to the Organisation. This helps to equip the leadership at various levels with material to enable them to clarify certain questions to the membership in such a way that there is no conflict within the Organisation on its broad goals and policies. Also, both our leadership and membership are armed theoretically to meet external hostile attacks against the Organisation.

Some of the issues discussed in these pamphlets need not necessarily stem from the policy document of the Organisation. Now and again a series of pamphlets should deal with the general political situation at home and internationally, and relate this to the overall strategy and tactics of the Organisation for the attainment of its own goals. Under conditions of illegality pamphleteering assumes a role which can improve the quality of our leading cadres in a manner that will be infused among and reflected in the confidence of our entire membership, simply because it sees clearly the direction in which the Organisation is moving. In addition, the individual member becomes conscious of how he forms a part of a giant machine which can only run smoothly if every component part is where it is, doing what it should do. As a matter of interest we may add that in the early 1960s a few pamphlets were published by the Bureau of Social and Political Studies. This was an independent body that dealt with topical issues which assisted our cadres to meet the attacks from Impama [PAC] and its associates. The advantage of using an independent body was that the pamphlets were distributed openly.

## PRODUCTION AND DISTRIBUTION

In dealing with leafletting and pamphleteering, production and distribution are very important aspects. Both of these are achieved in the face of police surveillance. If the Organisation is unable to solve the problem of production and distribution, there are no leaflets. And accordingly the ability of the Organisation to reach out with its message to the masses of the people and thus spread its influence is seriously hampered. At the price of repetition, let us emphasise that our study takes into account all along the line that the Organisation is operating under illegal conditions. Our production and distribution must be planned with a view to overcoming problems associated with this reality. Now let us deal with these two aspects in turn.

### Production

The basic equipment for the production of leaflets and pamphlets is a duplicator (preferably a 3-speed duplicator) and a good, (preferably) portable typewriter. The materials used in the production of leaflets consist of: means of duplicating paper (quarto-size or foolscap as the case may be), stencils and ink, and correcting ink for the typist when he cuts the stencil. Although each township has its own branch, it may be expedient to central-ise production for a number of branches. A Regional Executive would in this case undertake production for the branches in its areas. Whether the production is undertaken by the Regional Executive or the Branch Executive, strict security measures must be observed. Some of these are: the duplicator and typewriter should preferably not be kept at one place. If the police should pounce on the production centre they should not find all the equipment there. Even more strict measures should be taken to reduce the chances of the typewriter falling into the hands of the police. Police experts are able to say after examination that the type appearing on a number of leaflets in their possession was made by the typewriter they have impounded. Secondly, it is safer that the Organisation service its own duplicator to avoid taking it to the suppliers where the SB [Security Branch] have planted their informers. To overcome this problem the Organisation should train a couple or so of its own cadres to service its equipment. Thirdly, at the point of production one or two operators are sufficient. The fewer the people who know where the production takes place, the better. If the production centre is located within the branch area the distributors should not collect their leaflets there. If the production centre falls in some other area, say in a white suburb, it is advisable that the production cadres make up parcels. The instructions on parcelling should be set out clearly, and secondly, the man who takes the leaflets out to the distributors should find the loaded car at some pre-arranged spot and not at the point of production. Fourthly, under no circumstances must the typewriter used for illegal work be used for general purposes, e.g. typing letters.

**Distribution**

Even in the days when the ANC operated legally, the effective distribution of leaflets was always a taxing task. Under conditions of illegality the distribution of every series requires careful planning. Every leaflet ends thus: Issued by – The ANC (Bonte-heuwel/Langa/Tembisa, as the case may be). If a distributor is caught red-handed he is immediately arrested. The police will want to obtain as much information as possible about the chain of command. This knowledge is more important to them than obtain-ing a conviction against one individual. In planning distribution it is important that the chain is broken at occasional intervals so that a person who is caught can give information up to a point simply because he genuinely does not know beyond this point.

In spite of the risks involved, the ANC must reach out to the people, and the leaflet, in our situation, is one of the main means towards that end. By banning the ANC, the government is aiming to cut it off from contact with the people and thus to destroy what influence it has over them. The ANC, on the other hand, strives not only to maintain contact with the people but at increasing the points of contact and multiplying its influence. It cannot and shall not therefore allow itself to be strangled and stifled to death by severing its lines of communication with the people. And the leaflet is one of the most vital media, under conditions of illegality, to inspire them with confidence that the Organisation is alive, working amongst them and as committed as ever to the struggle for liberation.

We do not here wish to suggest the various means the Organisation will adopt to ensure as effective a distribution as possible. But the early evening hours while the streets are still full of people can be effectively used to deliver from house to house. If things are properly organised school boys (12–16) under proper direction can do a lot of work. House-to-house distribution is most effective but it must be varied so that the police are kept guessing.

We may now briefly refer to distribution in the sparsely populated peasant areas. It is important to compile a mailing list, over time, of addresses in the bantustans to which to post leaflets. The addressees need not necessarily be members. In addition, some of these leaflets should be given to the Organisation's contacts in the urban compounds with instructions to post to certain addresses in the reserves.

## CONCLUSION

From the foregoing it will have become clear that effective leafletting implies the existence of a well-oiled organisational machinery. But as the purpose of this paper is to focus attention on the importance and role of the leaflet in propagandising, the existence of a good organisational machinery is taken as given. If the organisation is to survive as the ANC is determined to do, and to lead the people of this country to freedom, then it must devise all manner of means to keep in contact with the people, especially where there are springing up legally operating organisations that are staking claims as the leaders. It must mobilise the people to fight for freedom — not just a vague concept — but as set out in the Freedom Charter.

We have concentrated on the leaflet as the main means of keeping contact with the masses of the people. From a financial point of view, the leaflet is within the means of the Organisation. Its production and distribution gives the cadres confidence and a sense of achievement. Above all, the people are reassured that the ANC is there, determined to lead them into the field of battle to gain freedom. Complemented by other media at the disposal of the Organisation, e.g. Radio Freedom and the operations of MK units, the leaflet as a channel of communication plays a formidable role.

*Amandla! Matla!*

# PART FOUR

# Notes on the Business Cycle, Unemployment, Inflation and Gold

## THE GENERAL APPROACH

The issues dealt with in the following sections are of more than just theoretical interest. They are burning issues here and now of both international and national or domestic social significance. We propose laying greater emphasis on the national effects of these, and sketching briefly the international links. We are not going to follow strictly the terms of reference. Instead of dealing with just two aspects, viz recession and depression, we suggest that we handle these in proper perspective, by briefly outlining the business cycle which consists of four phases, the upturn or upswing, the boom, the downturn or downswing or recession, and finally the slump or depression.

It will be observed in the course of the discussion of the business cycle that the first two phases show increasing business activity whereas the last two phases show decreasing business activity in the cycle. Although we deal with unemployment in a section of its own, employment or unemployment is closely linked with these phases of the business cycle.

## THE BUSINESS CYCLE

A capitalist economy has an inherent weakness. This is that like an epileptic, it suffers from occasional fits. Sometimes the fits are mild and sometimes they can be violent. In terms of the business cycle the capitalist economy is subject to business fluctuations, i.e. ups and downs in economic or business activity.

The fluctuations in business activity take on the nature of a periodic character. That is, like seasons of the year they occur at certain intervals, though not necessarily so regularly. In other words, they go through a cyclical character, and when a business cycle has spent itself a new cycle begins. Hence we talk of an inherent weakness within the capitalist system. These cycles are known as business or trade cycles.

Business cycles are associated with the rise of industrialism. They were first noted in England after the end of the Napoleonic wars. In other words, we see that they came after the start of the Industrial Revolution. Where the economy was still largely agricultural, as was the case in countries like France, Germany, Japan, America, what disturbances took place in agricultural production did not take the nature of a cycle. Such disturbances were due rather to natural phenomena such as good rains one year, drought another year, hailstorm or similar changes. A question may arise: what lies behind a cycle? In other words, what are its causes? Two main causes have been identified, in a general sort of way; those causes which come from outside the system itself, known as exogenous forces, such as changes in business activity brought about by an outbreak of war, discoveries of natural resources, new inventions and the development of new techniques like the steam engine. On the other hand, there are causative factors that arise from within the operation of the system itself. These are called endogenous factors, i.e. those arising out of responses by the economy to certain stimuli. In an open economy – where there is trade across national boundaries, in other words international trade – any disturbance in the economy of the trading partners is sure to affect the others. And today, all countries are involved, to a greater or lesser extent, in international trade.

At this stage we are in a position to deal in turn with the phases of a business cycle. We would suggest strongly that the reader should observe how the employment of labour is affected during the various phases of the cycle.

## The upturn or upswing

Assume that we start from the position of very low business activity and some stimulus occurs. (A stimulus may occur, for instance, if the wool farmers, because of an increased demand abroad, get a high price for their wool. Now the farmers have to spend that to acquire consumption goods. This immediately stimulates the producers of the goods which the farmers now want, to produce more.) The entrepreneurs will start investing to increase the scope of production in anticipation of rising profits. They order raw materials, employ more people to man the machines. The atmosphere, psychologically, is one of expectation. The demand for raw materials and semi-finished ones means that supply of such materials initiates activities intended to increase that supply as demanded. The whole process now assumes the nature of a chain reaction. The workers who get employment as a result of the initial investment on the part of the entrepreneurs, themselves receive incomes which they spend to acquire such essentials as food, clothes and other things like furniture and so on. The expenditure by the workers gives employment to other workers in the factories where the goods they want are produced. In other words, an increased demand calls for an increased supply; consequently the whole economy becomes activated. But the costs of production are still low as at this stage there is no need to buy machines since the old ones which were not used to their full extent during the period of low business activity are still there. As more and more people are drawn into employment, the production of goods does not keep pace with the demand, and this has the effect of forcing up prices. Thus, the expansion phase is invariably accompanied by an increase in prices and profits.

**The boom**

In the early stages the costs of production are relatively low as during the period of slack business activity the machines were producing well below capacity. The profits are therefore high. In this climate of high profits there is general optimism and even light-headedness. New entrepreneurs are attracted by high profits and decide to jump on the bandwagon to make hay while the sun shines. Those who are already in business decide to put into production new machines to increase their production capacity and meet the growing demand. In anticipation of new orders, factories build their inventories, i.e. stocks. The wholesale firms do likewise and so do the retailers. The piling up of such stocks results in increased insurance costs. At the same time as the prices go up, the trade unions press for wage increases to counteract the rising prices. Thus the costs of production, which are low in the upswing phase while prices and profits were increasing, catch up, and the rate of profit begins to decline. In the meanwhile the banks, seeing improved business prospects, extend credit – give out loans – especially short-term credit on a big scale. In a typically capitalist atmosphere of 'business is good', the climate is ideal when people believe in 'everyone for himself'. In such a situation, not all keep their heads sufficiently to realise that the expansionary forces are weakening.

## The boom levels off

The expansion of business in the boom period meets with a series of limiting forces which act as a brake on continued expansion. There occurs a period when it levels off. That is, while there is no further upward expansion business activity continues to be quite brisk but at a declining rate. It is like a body that is carried forward by its momentum even though the primary force that propelled it into motion has long spent itself. The momentum is slowed down by countervailing forces until the body comes to a stop.

In the case of a boom the limiting forces impinge, and not only does the boom lose its momentum but business activity starts declining. This does not take place all at once across all the sectors of the economy. Among the forces that work against further expansion are increasing costs, such as rising prices of raw materials and of labour, and interest rates, i.e. interest percentages paid to banks etc. for loans. As the productive resources become fully stretched, less efficient management and labour are drawn into the production process as well as the distribution channels, thus affecting efficiency and increasing costs. The margin of profit becomes narrower. As prices continue to rise, consumption declines. An accumulation of inventories against a background of declining consumption leads to a cut-back in production.

## The recession or downswing

During this phase, the forces that make for contraction of economic activity become pronounced. When orders for consumption goods are cut down, the first sector of the economy to be affected is that of production of capital goods, e.g. machines. As economic activity declines in this sector and workers are laid off, the steel industry is immediately affected. The downswing is first noticeable among the weaker business concerns. The banks tighten up loans and insist on repayment of old loans. With accumulated stocks moving slowly, a number of firms are unable to meet their financial commitments. There is nothing left to them but to face liquidation. The recession is now biting deep into the economy. And not only the weaker firms are in trouble but large ones too in almost all sectors of the economy and they have to make adjustments in one way or another, by cutting back on their activities.

In a country that is largely dependent on international trade as South Africa is, a recession among its trading partners further aggravates the position as the balance of payments also gets into difficulties. Exports like minerals decline, owing to the lack of demand for them abroad. The loss of export markets results in loss of employment for workers in the exporting sectors of the economy. Thus, the main characteristics of the recession are a sharp decline in orders for equipment for the production of consumer goods as the demand for such goods contracts; a significant decline in business activity in sectors that employ large numbers of workers like construction, which further reduces the demand over a wide range of sectors linked up with construction. Banks become stricter with credit and interest rates rise; liquidation becomes a common feature; and unemployment reaches alarming proportions, especially in the industrialised economies. For instance, unemployment is running into millions in all the imperialist countries. If the downward slide is not curbed, then the economy plunges into the worst and final phase of the cycle.

## The depression

At this stage there is a collapse of confidence. This is a crisis which breeds panic. A bank or a big corporation announces its inability to meet its debts. This sets off a wave of fright. Depositors at banks are seized by panic and start withdrawing their savings, to invest them in other banks – usually foreign, as in the case of Mexico recently.

In this climate there is a general curtailment of productive activity and there is no growth; instead the economy slumps into stagnation. Unemployment reaches a peak. The main characteristic of this phase is a notable fall in production of goods and services, and unemployment. In manufacturing, mining, construction and transport the cut-back is substantial. In pre-Second World War conditions, the accumulation of inventories and a decline in the purchasing power led to a fall in prices. Not so under monopoly capitalism. Inflation sweeps upwards along with a contraction of economic activity.

The general upsurge of costs and fall in the margin of profits are followed by losses. These induce a mood of pessimism and a reluctance to invest. Under the influence of falling profits comes a wave of reduction of output with further unemployment, further reduction of purchasing power, further accumulation of stocks, and a further fall in bank credit. And so the cumulative troubles feed upon themselves until the cycle has run its full course. When business activity reaches its lowest ebb, the economy begins to pick up again.

## UNEMPLOYMENT
We must first single out the causes of unemployment. They are:

### The main cause
The factor that plays the major role in the production of commodities and services is the human factor. If there is an increasing, effective demand there must necessarily be an increase in the rate of employment of workers to produce commodities to meet that demand. In a capitalist economy demand represents the ability to pay. The productive forces are harnessed to produce not what the society needs but that for which those who have an income are in a position to pay. When the ability to command an income declines, the demand for commodities and services drops. If the overall demand drops, the production of commodities must accordingly drop. Since the main factor in the production of commodities is human labour, it follows that if demand declines less labour will be employed. In other words, workers will be laid off.

Now, as we have seen in our discussion of the business cycle above, fluctuations in business activity are inherent in the capitalist system.

Thus the main cause of unemployment is a decline of effective demand during certain phases of the business cycle. At the best of times, i.e. at the peak of a boom, full employment or anything approximating it is hardly ever realised. This is especially so in South Africa where discriminating unemployment is a matter of policy as we shall see below.

On the other hand, in the mature capitalist economies, full employment, especially after World War Two has become a goal of economic policy. But the question is whether it can be anything other than an unrealizable ideal as long as capitalism remains capitalist.

### Subsidiary causes of unemployment
(1) *Structural unemployment.* When a firm embarks on adjustments that affect the structure of the firm, the adjustment brings

about a reduction of employment in the volume of employment. For instance, if a firm, for one reason or another, switches over from labour-intensive to capital-intensive operations a number of workers are laid off. This happens especially as the economy attains higher levels of industrialisation. A glaring example of this switch-over is most noticeable in construction. In the early days large numbers of unskilled workers were employed to use pick and shovel in the construction of roads or railway lines. But today much of that is done by giant earthmoving machines – one such machine operated by one man does, in a relatively short period of time, what used to be done by scores of manual workers.

(2) *Seasonal unemployment.* A most common example of this type of unemployment occurs in food-processing industries. During the deciduous fruit season, for instance, food and canning factories employ thousands of workers, while off-season they keep in employment a small, largely maintenance, force.

(3) *Discriminatory unemployment.* This form of unemployment is usually found in countries where racist practices occur, as in the USA and South Africa. But in South Africa the position is made worse in that racism is government policy. As a result, discriminatory legislation based on such a policy has as one of its main objectives to throw Africans out of employment.

The creation of bantustans and the implementation of influx control measures through the *dompas* ensure mass unemployment of Africans irrespective of the prevailing state of economic activity. We are all familiar with the daily scene of long queues of workers seeking employment at the labour bureaux the whole year round. Millions more – like dirt swept and pushed behind the door – are shunted to the bantustans, away from public view. Even if the economic conditions are at a low ebb, as they are presently in the country, with unemployment estimated at 2,5 to 3 million, government spokesmen boast that unemployment among whites is less than one per cent. However inconvenient unemployment as caused by the first two of the subsidiary causes is, it is usually of short duration and affects workers in selected firms.

### The social effects of unemployment

Unemployment has a demoralising effect, firstly on those who love their jobs and secondly on their dependants. The worker, however lowly paid, has to maintain some standard for himself and his family. And the standard he aims at is influenced by the general standard of outward appearances which is generally accepted in his environment. The wife should dress passably well. The children's standards of dressing at school should not fall visibly short of that of other children. Children who lack these may develop psychological complexes which dog their steps through to adulthood. The worker and his family strive always to furnish their houses nearly as well as their neighbours. To attain these goals the worker has to adopt a longish-term plan. He buys goods like furniture on a pay-as-you-use basis. If he falls behind in the payment of the rent the whole family is thrown onto the street.

The impact of such dreadful consequences of unemployment has been softened by unemployment insurance for registered workers. Until very recently the bulk of the country's workforce did not qualify for such benefits. Even now that they are included in such pension and unemployment benefit schemes, those workers who have for so long been excluded are reluctant to join either because their wage is so low that they prefer to use it all today rather than put a bit away for a rainy day or because, through insecurity of unemployment, they fear losing it.

But even in the countries of western Europe where such unemployment benefits are well established, to stand in dole queues and live in a city without anything to do can be a very unsettling factor.

## Political effects of unemployment

The success in 1917 of a working-class revolution under the leadership of the Communist Party in the USSR shocked the capitalists as nothing else had done before. The first step they took towards reducing discontent among the working class was to devise means to cushion the impact of unemployment. After the Depression (1929–33) during which tens if not scores of millions of workers in Western Europe and the USA were walking the streets in search of work, not only were leading economists of the capitalists called upon to find ways of minimizing the cyclical fluctuations in business activity, but they developed schemes like public works which were intended to absorb as much unemployment as possible. The aim was to keep the men in some activity even if what they were doing would never have been tackled otherwise; for instance in France men would be hired to dig trenches which they were subsequently to refill or build unnecessary roads which would never have been undertaken. The

end of World War Two and the establishment of socialist governments in eastern Europe further shattered the arguments among
imperialists that the 1917 working class take-over in the USSR
was but a flash in the pan. Nor does glib talk such as appeared in a
recent statement by Reagan that 'Communism is a temporary
aberration' give any comfort to capitalists including Reagan
himself. The fear that grips capitalists as unemployment figures
approach the level of the Great Depression years was expressed by
Anthony Sampson during October last. In a serious vein he warns
the imperialist: 'However authoritarian, inefficient and unattractive the eastern European countries, they can honestly boast that
they offer one benefit which western Europe does not, a guarantee
of a job . . . if the west cannot face up to the problem of creating
jobs, this promise from the east will inevitably begin to look more
attractive to young people who see no likelihood of work in their
own country in their life time.'

## TRADE UNIONS IN CAPITALIST COUNTRIES

This is a crisis for capitalism, but given time capitalism will come
out of it – although weakened. This then raises the question: are
the recurrent crises into which the capitalist economy plunges
sufficient by themselves to make capitalism grind to a halt or to
bring about a change in the capitalist system? We pose this
question because quite often a statement is made of 'a deepening
crisis'. Statements of this nature should not lull us into a false sense
of security or create exaggerated expectations that such crises
may bring about a change in the state of the oppressed and
exploited. As we pointed out in section two above, the capitalist
system has been bedevilled by these cyclical crises in the course of
the last two centuries.

By and large, however, as the trade union movement developed
and became accepted both by the working class and by the employers in the industrialized countries, i.e. western Europe, a
correlated tendency has emerged which has taken on the character
of a live-and-let-live relationship between the trade unions representing the working class in the production process and the
employers representing the capitalist. The issue has become the
size of the share of the cake, i.e. profits, each side must take.

When periods of unemployment occur on a big scale as during
these cyclical crises, the trade unions concentrate on looking after
the interests of those in employment while the unemployed have

to fend for themselves as best they can on unemployment benefits.

In other words, the trade unions in the industrialised countries are applying neither their thinking nor their energies to the problems of eliminating the cause of the misery to which the working class are ever exposed under capitalism. Nay, they have instead come to terms with capitalism.

## The role of the non-privileged working class

With the spread of imperialist wings over the greater part of the world, industrial outposts have sprung up, notably in South Africa, Canada, and Australia. The traditional pattern of the role of trade unions in western Europe and the USA has been transplanted to these developing countries. TUCSA, for example, in South Africa is playing this role, which suits the privileged white working class. Now that the vast majority of the oppressed working class, whose unions were not recognised until very recently (two years ago) have a legal right to become members of recognised trade unions, TUCSA and even the [South African] Confederation [of Labour] are working overtime to draw the non-privileged workers into the old-time pattern of trade unionism.

In the South African situation, what role must the non-privileged oppressed and exploited working class play? Unemployment in this country is hitting hardest this section of the working class, especially the Africans. The estimate of 2,5 to 3 million unemployed in SA refers mainly to Africans.

Discriminatory unemployment accounts for a high percentage of this estimate.

Unemployment resulting from fluctuations in business activity in the course of a business cycle aggravates a situation where discriminatory laws prevail. What further distinguishes the South African situation is that even those who become unemployed as a result of such fluctuations are thrown out of urban areas – once unemployed – to the bantustans. That is where the overwhelming numbers of the 2,5–3 million unemployed are presently vegetating.

The problem of what to do in the circumstances takes on a dual character: organising the workers in the work place into trade unions. The role which progressive trade unions like SAAWU [South African Allied Workers' Union] are playing is invaluable. The keen awareness of the distinctive conditions under which trade unions have to operate in South Africa is reflected in the manner in which SAAWU links trade unions with community problems. This relationship has been most clearly set out in recent statements by leading and progressive unionists such as Qaqawuli Godolozi and Government Zini, amongst others.

It is, however, important to bear in mind that as most of the unemployed are dumped in the bantustans, the task of reaching out to them is beyond the ability, as well as the resources, of the trade unions. It is a political task – the task of Inqindi, which calls for urgent and immediate attention. Left to themselves the plight of these millions of unemployed is far worse than that of workers who draw unemployment benefit. From the moment they are dumped in the bantustans they face starvation. If nothing is done to offer them something to live for they become demoralised and apathetic. How often have we seen children suffering from malnutrition, both in the urban townships and in the bantustans, sit listlessly and watch with watery eyes the children from better-fed families at play. Adults in similar straits fare no better.

While Inqindi cannot feed the unemployed workers who have been dumped in the bantustans, it should organise them to fight for their survival. As many as can be absorbed in MK should be drawn there. Others should be drawn into active political work in the rural areas on a scale that will bring about unsettled conditions in those areas. This is a task which falls to Inqindi. Now probably as never before, the need to co-ordinate the organisational work in the industrial and rural areas is crucial to the furtherance of the revolution.

## Inflation

One of the major problems – especially of our age – of a capitalist economy is inflation, i.e. a general upward movement of prices. While we do not propose to go into a detailed study of the problem, we hope, however, to touch on its main features.

### What is inflation?

When the total effective demand for goods and services exceeds the domestic output, then there is inflation. From observation and on a small scale, we know that if there are a few boxes of tomatoes at the local market those who have the means will compete with one another to have the tomatoes. The competition takes the form of offering to pay a higher price than the next man. In this way the box of tomatoes will be sold at a price far above what the producer would have realised per box if he had brought to the market enough to meet the demand; that is, to enable those who have the money to buy and take the tomatoes home.

In this example, one fact stands out clearly, viz that the total supply of money in the hands of the people at the market who want tomatoes exceeds the available output of tomatoes. Stated more dramatically and on a wide front across the whole economy, and not just in respect of a local or regional market or a single product, inflation is present in a situation where 'money chases goods' – 'more money chasing few goods'. In other words, when the supply of money exceeds the stocks of available goods, prices are pushed up as consumers scramble for the limited output.

A significant feature of our age, especially in the post-Second World War era, is that prices are always rising whereas in earlier periods prices did fall or were held fairly stable for some long periods of time. Today inflation has become a feature of economic life in capitalist society so that when governments and economists speak of fighting inflation they are not thinking of reducing prices but of reducing the rate of the rise of prices. Now let us examine briefly a few causes of inflation.

## CAUSES OF INFLATION

The causative factors which lie behind inflation may be divided into two broad classes, viz external and internal sources of inflation.

### Imported inflation

All countries that are engaged in international trade are affected by price movements in countries from which they import. High prices in the exporting countries will be reflected in even higher prices of such imported commodities in the importing country. For instance, the price structure of a country like South Africa which does a considerable amount of foreign trade – both in exports and imports –in exports and imports – is necessarily affected by high prices in its trading partners. In addition, the receipts from abroad from the sale of exported products at inflated prices introduces a flood of money in the country which increases the supply of money in the country relative to domestic output. Yet another source of large inflow of money – hundreds of millions – is foreign capital that seeks opportunities for investment while the profits and interest rates are high.

Although imported inflation plays some substantial role,

internal causes of inflation generate by far the most powerful forces that feed the inflationary prices. Now for a few of the internal causes:

(1)  *The supply of money.* The biggest culprits in the country – and in any capitalist country for that matter – are the government and the banks. According to strict accounting rules one can only spend what one has received if books have to balance. Common sense isn't it? If an individual lives beyond his means he gets in trouble. On an infinitely bigger scale, if government expenditure exceeds its revenue, the government must find the money elsewhere in order to make up the difference. Since the government has the authority to print paper money, it does not hesitate to use that power if and when it is in difficulty. Government activities are increasing on a tremendous scale. Take the Department of Native Affairs – a giant machine which grows bigger by the year to cope with a mass of oppressive legislation. It has increased its non-productive personnel to scores of thousands. Similarly other departments like Justice (i.e. police and prisons) and Defence are making increasingly substantial demands on the state's financial resources. The government just cannot meet such demands from taxation. Instead it resorts to printing paper money, which floods the economy. This flood of money is thrown into the hands of people – about 40 per cent of the economically active white population – who produce no goods and services. The result is an increasing supply of money far in excess of available goods. The net result is that with so much money competing for limited goods, prices are pushed up on a wide front. The excessive supply of money is a very important cause of inflation.

Side by side with the government in causing inflation are the banks through bank credit. During the expansionary phase of the business cycle (i.e. the upswing and the boom) the banks extend credit quite liberally, thus increasing the supply of money via credit.

(2)  *Administered prices.* Under the conditions of monopoly capitalism, the producers set the price and the consumer becomes the price-taker. The producers who have become bigger and fewer in almost all product lines not only set the price of the product but use coercive measures to make distribution channels fall into line. They use such practices as Re-sale Price Maintenance, thus prescribing the price at which the retail trade should sell their product. To avoid contravening the provisions of the Monopolies

Act, they claim that they only 'recommend the price'. And the agreement between the producers is informal in so far as it may be discussed at the golf course and by such 'gentlemen's agreements' they 'recommend' to the retail trade. Failure to comply on the part of the retail trade may lead to some punitive measures, such as curtailment of credit. The result is that the prices are always going up from year to year.

One of the most notorious examples of the ever upward movement of prices, irrespective of whether there is overproduction or not, is the Agricultural Control Board system in South Africa. Farmers who are producers of particular products dominate the control board for their products. Every year they find an excuse to raise the price, which the government in turn backs with the force of the law. An upward movement, for instance, in the price of maize affects prices across a wide range of other products directly or indirectly connected with the maize product, e.g. milk, cheese, butter, beef, poultry, etc. In other brutal cases farmers hoard their over-produced stocks or simply dump their surplus so as to maintain their high prices – hence further contributing to an upward movement of prices.

(3) *Collective bargaining.* The system of collective bargaining between the trade unions and the employers has, in one important respect, turned to the advantage of the workers. The power of the employers to lower wages in the face of a decline in business activity (during the downswing phase of a business cycle), as was the case in the earlier periods, has been largely neutralised where workers are organised. But each time a wage agreement is signed, the producers pass the increase in wages on to the consumers by way of increased prices. In a country like South Africa where the standard of living of a white worker is protected even if he shows no increase in productivity, wage agreements arising out of collective bargaining are a cause of inflation. Bearing in mind that such agreements cover comparatively short periods of time before they are re-negotiated, prices right across the economy are ever moving upward.

And because the producers, under the conditions of monopoly capitalism, are the price setters for their products, they hardly resist wage demands by white workers. In the first place they pass such an increase on to the consumer, and secondly, while they readily concede the wage demands of white workers, they keep those of the black workers (Africans, coloureds and Indians) at barely subsistence level. In this way the capitalists not only keep the white working class contented but ensure their support for the exploitative and repressive machinery.

## Who benefits from inflation?

From the amount of storm that is raised in the media, one would think that all sections of the population stand to lose by inflation. Not so. Some of those who make such noises are just crying crocodile tears. If anything, they are reaping a rich harvest from the inflationary conditions.

At a two-day conference of the Economic Society of South Africa a number of papers on various aspects of inflation were read. These were followed by extensive discussions. Invariably the Afrikaner economists favoured a certain amount of inflation for economic growth. This was in the later part of the 1960s – a period when Afrikaner capital was seeking to establish itself in the manufacturing and mining industries as well as in commerce. During a period of rising prices profits also rise. On this basis the spokesmen of Afrikaner capital were justifying inflation, and it would be a mistake to think that the capitalists are – everything taken into consideration – not reaping some substantial benefits from inflation. But true to the idiom: What is food for the capitalist class is poison for the working class, especially the non-privileged working class in South Africa. Now to this aspect.

## The damaging effect of inflation

Although inflation is, in varying degrees, a world-wide problem, we must try to keep our study as close as possible to the domestic scene. In doing so it is important that both unemployment and inflation are closely related to the phase of the business cycle. They must therefore not be studied in isolation. We propose that persistent inflation may give rise to:

(1) *Speculation*. When inflation runs high, those who have funds which in normal circumstances they would have put in savings, begin to look around for real assets in which to invest. Rather than looking on while their money savings lose value they buy land, for instance. This starts speculation in land by people who are not interested in developing it, but in keeping it as a store of (wealth-) value. Soon a scramble to purchase land or gold starts, and this pushes up the price of land. But the process does not stop there.

The farmers re-evaluate their farms on the basis of the current
land prices and add this increase to their cost of production. This in
turn leads to further increases of prices of all agricultural
products. Not only that, but rents for housing shoots up.

(2) *Desperation.* With rampant inflation, i.e. where prices rise so
fast that as soon as people get their income they hurry, for
instance, to buy food because by the next day the amount of
money which can buy a kilogram of a certain product today may
not be enough to purchase half a kilo in a matter of days, then
desperation sets in. It was such circumstances in post-World War
One Germany when the German mark was hardly worth anything, that Nazism reared its head. In such a climate the will of the
people, especially the privileged classes, is eroded. It becomes
comparatively easy for a 'strong man', promising to right the
situation, to rise to power. After Hitler, the Latin American
dictators have ridden to power on a wave of discontent arising out
of deteriorating economic conditions, especially rampant inflation.

Mounting discontent here at home rising out of crushing
economic business is perceived by the privileged whites as a threat
to their position. Already there are clear indications that the
overwhelming majority of whites are resigned to the establishment of a fascist dictatorship or a dictatorial executive president
to be ushered in under the auspices of an Afrikaner-dominated
National Party.

(3) *Grinding poverty.* Taking into account that at the best of
times, by far the overwhelming majority of the non-privileged
section of the South African population (four-fifths) barely earns a
subsistence income, what must be the effect of such a high rate of
inflation as presently prevails? Even those who are still in employment are working short-time, and it must be a struggle to make
ends meet. As for the millions of unemployed, they and their
families are facing disaster. When the rate of inflation in the 1960s
was 3 per cent, the average family of a working man in the
townships could only afford tripe or an ox skull once or twice a
week or one meal of white bread and tea. At today's prices, with
inflation running at five times what it was in the 1960s, the burden
of poverty must be crushing. The net result is that poverty diseases
such as malnutrition, TB, etc. must be taking an increasingly
heavy toll of life. How much worse must the position be in the
rural areas where the millions of unemployed are dumped? In
better times, frequently one has listened to a mother as she asks for

a couple of kilograms of mealies, describe the position: *'Abantwana balala ngamanzi / Bana ba Robala ka metsi . . .'*

## Control of inflation

If the causes of inflation and the factors that bring about such causes can be identified, there seems to be no reason why inflation cannot be curbed or at least controlled. But before we seek ways of controlling inflation, it must first be determined whether those in a position to implement such control measures see inflation as an evil or not. The government always has the means to check inflation, or to control it in such a way that its damaging effects are kept as low as possible.

It is not our intention to go into the technicalities of controlling inflation. What we should consider is if the government is prepared to apply seriously such technicalities, why can't it apply them through the banking system as well as through taxation? But the government only applies them half-heartedly because as one leading South African economist (now dead) put it: Inflation allows for 'The temporary sectional advantages which may and do accrue to certain population groups.'

What must be stressed is that the National Party government is ruling in the interests of those groups, and it could not care less what happens to the vast non-privileged masses. If anything, apartheid is achieving via inflation what Nazism accomplished crudely in such camps of death as Buchenwald, Belsen, Lublin, etc.

Bearing in mind the apartheid policy, one must agree unreservedly with the view expressed by the economist cited in a preceding paragraph that 'In essence inflation is frustration, fraud and theft'. And the way out? We must intensify the struggle to destroy apartheid and the foundations on which it is built.

*Amandla! Matla!*

# Economic History: South Africa

1. A careful study of the two views represented by X. and O.V.P. shows the area of agreement between the two views is much wider than that of disagreement. After a proper examination of the points of difference it is comparatively easy to resolve the differences. The two representative views agree on three very important aspects of the circumstances of the birth, development and nature of the struggle for liberation in our country. They agree (a) that in the era of capitalism the basic contradiction is the class struggle; (b) that the starting point in the study of the movement for national liberation in South Africa, after 1910, is a study of the composition of the society in this country with special reference to Africans; and (c) that the epoch of Imperialism brought with it a complementary contradiction to that mentioned in (a) above, namely national exploitation and oppression.

2. The two views refer to what we call the 'basic contradiction' as 'primary contradiction' and what we call 'complementary contradiction' in (c) as 'secondary contradiction'. In our view this classification can easily create confusion in thought. The tendency may easily develop in the mind to place primary in relation to secondary in the same position as one in relation to two in a numerical table. One comes first and two follows and two can never take the place of one.

The advantage of our classification into basic and complementary contradictions may be illustrated by the following analogy. The sinking of a shaft to mine gold or any mineral is the basic project, but to be able to get to the area of the basic project roads and railways must be constructed. These are complementary projects and, depending on circumstances, it may be necessary to provide these first in order to facilitate work on the basic project. How much of the resources at their disposal the planners of these projects will devote to one or the other of the projects will be influenced by practical requirements of the situation at the particular stage of development.

3. In the light of our remarks in 1 and 2 above we accept as incontestable the view of both X. and O.V.P. that the basic contradiction in the era of capitalism is an irreconcilable struggle between the bourgeoisie and the proletariat. For conditions where the basic contradiction was not complicated by the existence of a complementary contradiction, the conflict took on the nature of a direct confrontation between two antipodes. It took on the nature of a class struggle. Examples of this are ready at hand in the history of the countries of Western Europe.

The development of capitalism to a higher stage, viz Imperialism, gave rise to a complementary contradiction – complementary in the sense that in order to intensify exploitation the Imperialists reduced entire peoples and not just a class to a substandard of living. In other words, an entire people was degraded. An important condition of intensifying exploitation was to create an inexhaustible supply of labour from the colonial countries on the one hand, and on the other to secure the express or tacit co-operation of skilled labour, in the imperial countries, to introduce the techniques of capitalist production and supervise the application of those techniques in the colonial countries. We see therefore that in the epoch of Imperialism an enclave of representatives of the capitalist mode of production in the imperialist countries is physically located in the colonial country and completely subjugates the indigenous people.

In the light of the observations made above, we are now in a position to examine the conditions in South Africa prior to the formation of Union and the Inqindi.

4. In the following paragraphs we are going to set out to show (a) that by 1900 the process of class formation in South Africa had been completed; (b) that structurally the capitalist class consisted of whites as landowners, whereas capital for development came from abroad; (c) that the middle class among Africans had already developed and engaged in activities as teachers, interpreters, clerks, the clergy, writers, etc.; (d) that the working class amongst Africans had been developed. Superimposed on this capitalist class structure, characterised as we have seen above by the basic contradiction of a class struggle, was the Imperialist enclave, characterised by the fact that it thrives on national exploitation and oppression – a complementary contradiction. We shall also show

(e) that a section of the African population lived in the subsistence economy on which it depended for its livelihood.

The subsistence economy or dual economy is not only a feature of South Africa but characterises all underdeveloped countries, with this exception that the process of development is not tailored to perpetuate the existence of a dual economy as is the case in South Africa.

5. The first private commercial bank, viz the Cape of Good Hope Bank, was established in 1837. By 1860 there were no less than 28 banks mainly in the Cape (Hobart Houghton, p. 14). The establishment of banks is a feature of capitalism, although this period up to 1860 was marked largely by the existence of one sector of the economy, viz agriculture. The mode of production in this sector was capitalist. It employed labour, both KhoiKhoi and African. The Imperial banks made their first appearance in the early 1860s e.g. the Standard Bank. The earlier small banks were finally swallowed up by the Imperial banks, but for the one example which has lived down to the present day, viz the Stellenbosch and District Bank.

The discovery of diamonds, gold and coal and their mining gave an impetus to the commercialisation of agriculture in order to meet the ever-increasing demand for agricultural production around the mining centres, where towns developed, and the ports. The result was increased employment of non-white labour on the farms. In addition to producing for this market, farming was producing before 1900 for export ostrich feathers, wool, wine. In 1899 the value of livestock alone was 85 million pounds while by 1909 it had gone up to 95 million (Franzsen & Willers). For the farmers who were scattered over a wide area, to maintain such huge investments required a lot of labour. In addition, after the cattle-killing episode in 1857 the Xhosa population was reduced from 150 000 to 37 000. It is said that what enabled the 37 000 to survive was taking up employment on white farms.

6. The discovery of diamonds and gold brought about a big structural change in the economy of the country; from an essentially agricultural economy the country became an agricultural–mining economy. A flood of capital flowed into the country and this is the advent of Imperialism in South Africa. In 1881 capital of 17 diamond companies was £16 million while between 1887 and 1905 capital invested in gold mining amounted to £8 million (Houghton, p. 81). In the decade 1890–99, the capital assets on the

gold mines amounted to 21 million pounds and in the decade 1900–09 to 31 million pounds (Franzsen & Willers).

7. The main lessons which flow from these big investments in mining are that

(a) As a result of mining operations there developed towns at the mining centres. This gave rise to a building boom and construction of streets and other facilities. Thus in addition to the workers required for mining purposes, workers were required for the building and construction industry.

(b) Roads, railways and telegraphic communications had to be laid between the mining centres and the ports. In those days there was no heavy earth-moving equipment, and consequently a lot of labour was employed to work with pick and shovel.

(c) Tertiary activites, e.g. shops, and complementary industries to mining, e.g. tannery, engineering and clothing factories, developed in mining centres and required labour.

(d) Diamond and coal mining are labour-intensive industries and therefore required a lot of African labour.

It is important to note that by 1899 gold mining alone already employed more than 100 000 Africans, and by 1910 nearly 200 000.

8. Railway construction over the period 1861–1911 increased from virtually nil to 7 548 miles. By 1900 the assets of the South African Railways and Harbours were 43 million pounds (Franzsen & Willers). Most of the labour employed to dig with pick and shovel on the railroads was African: they provided the majority of unskilled labour in the construction of fixed capital assets.

The first census taken simultaneously in the four provinces occurred in 1904. A study of the geographical distribution of the population disclosed the number of people living in urban areas per group:

| Year | Whites | Africans | Coloureds | Asians | Total |
|------|--------|----------|-----------|--------|-------|
| 1904 | 600 000 | 300 000 | 200 000 | 40 000 | 1 200 000 |

These figures represented the following percentages of the total population in respect of each group in urban areas:

| Year | Whites | Africans | Coloureds | Asians | Total |
|------|--------|----------|-----------|--------|-------|
| 1904 | 53,6% | 10,4% | 49,2% | 36,5% | 23,6% |

(Rynders: Table D, p. 21 and these statistics coincide with those of Brand and Tomlinson: Table 3)

Basing our assumption on a commonly observed trend in a capitalist economy that one third of the population is economically active, this would mean that of Africans who were living in urban areas, 100 000 were working people, i.e. they earned their living by the sale of their labour power, either in secondary or in tertiary economic activities.

Although the manufacturing industry in the country was still at its early stages of development in 1904, it already employed 75 000 people. If we base our estimates of the ratio of African labour to the other racial groups today, viz 65 per cent, the majority of these workers should have been African. The book value of buildings and machinery in the manufacturing industry was 12 million pounds in 1904, and by 1909 had increased to 22 million pounds (Franzsen & Willers).

The first census after the formation of Union took place in 1911 and showed the following state of urbanisation:

| Year | Whites | Africans | Coloureds | Asians | Total |
|------|--------|----------|-----------|--------|-------|
| 1911 | 1 276 000 | 4 019 000 | 525 000 | 152 000 | 5 973 000 |
|      | 51,6% | 12,6% | 46% | 46% | 24,7% |

(Houghton, Table 1, Statistical Appendix)

10. Let us now direct our attention to a brief study of the formation of the middle class amongst Africans in the period before 1900 and up to 1910. The first educational institution in the country established to cater largely for African education was Lovedale in 1848. As a matter of interest we may observe that Lovedale like other institutions of its kind admitted white students, who studied side by side with their fellow African students. The primary school syllabus in the Cape was the same for all schools until 1921.

At the outset Lovedale and many other institutions that were established in keen competition by missionary bodies provided the following courses: teacher training, building trade, carpentry, printing, blacksmithing, tailoring and dressmaking. Not long after Lovedale, Healdtown, St Matthew's, Blythswood, St John's, Kilnerton, Indaleni, Adams College and Mariannhill were established, some years before 1900. On the completion of their courses, students from these institutions became teachers, interpreter-clerks, ministers of religion, writers and artisans.

11. During this period two developments which were subsequently of importance took place. In the Ciskei and seven districts in the Transkei, the Cape government provided an alternative individual land tenure which was valid for the title-deed holder on condition he paid his quit-rent regularly. This was done after the final boundaries of what came to be known as Native Reserve Areas had been drawn. By 1900 these boundaries were fixed, and they served to mark the outer extremities of the areas which under the Land Act of 1913 came to be known as Scheduled Areas. Side by side with this development, a number of Africans, much fewer than the holders of title deeds, on pain of payment of quit-rent had bought landed property on an individual freehold tenure basis in the Cape. A number of such properties were acquired by Africans in urban areas between Port Elizabeth and Umzimkulu. Moreover, farms ranging from several hundred morgen to over a thousand morgen were acquired in a number of districts between Peddie and Umzimkulu. In the northern provinces a few such properties were bought by Africans, e.g. New Scotland and Edendale in Maritzburg; Ladysmith; Sophiatown in Johannesburg. Farms, however, in these provinces were largely bought on a collective tribal basis, e.g. Ekuphumuleni in Ladysmith, Dinokana in Zeerust, and others excepting those in Thaba'Nchu.

With regard to the first form of land tenure, it is important to note that succession was based on primogeniture. As a result, from the time when the allocation of land took place on this basis not an additional acre of land became available for arable purposes. An increasing rate of landlessness was consequently aggravated by the increase of population over a period of more than 100 years. We raise this point to forestall an argument that migrant labourers partly subsist on the produce of their land and as such do not strictly qualify as part of the working class. Migrant labour has always, and more particularly in the post-1900 era, depended almost entirely on their wages. During the period of forced retirement they constitute the disguised unemployed in the rural areas, i.e. where their marginal productivity in subsistence farming is zero.

The position therefore by 1900 is that a capitalist class structure was in existence in this country and that the Africans formed the majority of the working class; there was also a middle class. The capitalist class amongst Africans, however, had not been formed, and the ownership of large farms which, unthwarted, would have led to the emergence of a capitalist class was frustrated by the passing of the Land Act of 1913 and subsequent legislation aimed at complete dispossession of Africans. We may add in conclusion that where we have not given the numbers of Africans employed we have indicated investment, and capital must have labour to co-operate with.

12. We proceed to correct a view which gives the impression that since the laying down of arms by the Africans no political struggle for liberation took place until the formation of the ANC in 1912.

In 1853 the British government gave representative government to the Cape. As a corollary of this constitutional development, the franchise was granted to all males in the Cape irrespective of race or colour on condition that certain qualifications were fulfilled, e.g. the attainment of the age of 21, ability to read and write, ownership or occupation of landed property valued at 75 pounds, or receipt of an annual income of 50 pounds.

Realising that the armed struggle was lost, the African middle class led by the intellectuals conducted the struggle for liberation in the electoral field. They helped thousands of adult Africans to learn to read and write in order to qualify for the franchise; they convinced the less advanced of their communities who had the means to build properties which would enable them to qualify for the franchise. In general, a massive campaign was embarked upon to educate the African people about the value of the vote. School songs were composed: *'Yilweleni ivote; lilungelo lenu'* ('Fight for the franchise, it is your right'). They believed that if they got a bigger number of their representatives in parliament they would restore their rights as citizens of the country. The result of such a campaign was that in some constituencies in the Eastern Cape, the majority of registered voters were Africans, e.g. St Mark's, and other constituencies like Aliwal North and Tembuland were largely African. It was as a result of the rallying of African voters that Dr Rubusana was returned to the Cape Provincial Council. When this vote was split as a result of Tengo Jabavu contesting the same constituency, Rubusana lost to Payne.

It was after the return of Rubusana and Jabavu from Britain where they put the case for the protection of the right of the African to the franchise, and the realisation of the fact that the British government would do nothing about it, that the then leading class of the African people – the middle class – led by intellectuals decided that the struggle for the liberation of their people was no longer to be sought in parliament, as was proposed by the white representatives at the 1909 National Convention.

The Africans had seen this coming in the efforts of the Bond Party to eliminate the African right to the franchise and Rhodes' trick to neutralise the power of the African vote by passing the Glen Grey Act of 1894 to provide for the establishment of the Bunga system.

The decision by the leaders of those days to form the ANC belies the argument that they sought to protect the 'status quo'.

13. A word about the role of the chiefs prior to 1900. Up to the end of the last wars in the 1880s, the chiefs had led their people in wars against dispossession for a period of 100 years. The incident at King William's Town when Sir Harry Smith demonstrated to the chiefs what he would do to them if they continued to engage in wars against the British forces, showed the important role they played in those days and for some time after. Harry Smith placed a charge of dynamite under a wagon and ordered that it should be ignited, whereupon the wagon was blown into splinters. By 1854 Sir George Grey had been convinced that the Africans could not be defeated by arms and sent dispatches to England recommending a change of policy.

Although by 1910 most of the chiefs were employed by the government, they were still regarded by the people as their traditional leaders. When, therefore, they attended conferences with their *amaphakathi* [councillors] it was because that position was accepted by their tribes, and reports of the proceedings and decisions of such deliberations were given on their return at the *inkundla* [clan meeting]. It must be said that at that stage the chiefs were themselves not satisfied with their subservient state and would have seized any opportunity to turn against their subjugators. This was the picture in 1910, which however has largely changed today.

14. When Inqindi was formed, all strata of African society took part: the middle class led by the intellectuals, the peasantry represented by chiefs and their *amaphakathi*, and the working class consisting of the then urbanised Africans. In the period before 1920, in the campaigns against passes, and against laws which made it a criminal offence for an African to travel in railway coaches, or to walk on the pavement in the streets of Johannesburg, the working class took an active part. The presence, for

instance, of men like Letanka, who was arrested in a workers' strike in 1917, in the executive of Inqindi cannot be ignored. Ordinary rank and file took part in these campaigns; e.g. for an article in the first issue of *Spark*, I wrote a main feature article with a photograph of Isaac Ruba. This told the story, obtained from him, of the role of the working people in these campaigns before 1920. The campaigns in the Western Cape waged by working-class leaders like Elliot Tonjeni who died in the late fifties, are on record (Eddie R[oux]). Elliot had to be dressed in women's frocks to avoid arrest and brutal assault by the police in the Worcester location. By 1923, as a schoolboy, I personally was attending meetings and concerts of the South African Native Congress (SANC) among peasants in the southern Transkei.

The above examples are cited to show that in fact Inqindi was from the very word go representative of all the classes in existence in African society when it was formed. The leadership, however, was largely provided by the intellectuals. In so far, then, as it was representative of all the strata of African society, it was a people's movement and has continued to be so to this day. We must not allow weaknesses of organisation to obscure this fact. Such weaknesses could only be corrected on the basis of experience, e.g. individual membership and improvements that have been made in the constitution (1943 and 1957).

15. In his document, X lays down the conditions that must be fulfilled before a national liberatory movement can qualify as a people's movement: 'it is necessary that it should embrace the working class and the peasantry, the middle class and the national bourgeoisie . . . and must contain a programme that provides for the transfer of Imperialist concerns into the hands of the people . . .'

On this showing Inqindi is not yet a people's movement since an important condition remains unfulfilled in its present programme – the Freedom Charter – namely, the socialisation of imperialist concerns.

Strangely, towards the end of his documents X concedes that Inqindi today is a people's movement. If, then, this is the view, what is the quarrel all about? Inqindi should be allowed to accomplish its task.

After a careful study of the situation in our country, the Party arrives at the conclusion that the National Liberation Movement should rally all its resources to remove, as priority number one, the complementary contradiction, and in its programme it exhorts its own membership to give unstinted support to the National Liberation Movement as spearheaded by Inqindi to achieve this goal. This is the correct approach, and to attempt to force the Inqindi to carry out functions of the Party will bring failure to both the Party and Inqindi. The understanding that has existed both in the Party and Inqindi of the respective roles of the two has enabled the struggle for liberation to be carried to the high level at which it is now.

# Monopoly Capitalism in South Africa: Its Role and Extent

### INTRODUCTION

The purpose of this paper is to consider to what extent monopoly capitalism is a feature of the South African economy. Towards this end we propose to follow, as systematically as possible, steps which will assist us to lay bare the development of monopoly capitalism in South Africa. We would like, however, to sound a warning that while the study may be fairly extensive it may fall short of the necessary depth. This can be achieved by the compilation of empirical data. Bourgeois economists here as in other parts of the world have deliberately and understandably circumvented the study of this problem, which has emerged in the course of the development of capitalism. The problem in the advanced countries has only been examined by Marxist economists. It is to be hoped that now the South African economy is reaching a high level of development, the younger cadres with the necessary training (and the liberation movement has already produced a sizeable number) will be able to produce a well-documented, systematised study on monopoly capitalism in South Africa and the effects of its operation on the masses of the people.

For the preparation of this survey of the problem in South Africa, we have had to rely on data gleaned from scanty and piecemeal sources of bourgeois origin, but nonetheless useful for those who seek to study the problem with a view to assessing its extent and role in the country's economy.

Inasmuch as monopoly capitalism in South Africa is largely a recent development especially in the secondary and tertiary sectors (i.e. industry and commerce respectively), we must precede the study of the problem in South Africa with an outline of monopoly capitalism as a phenomenon that emerges at some stage in the development of capitalism. In other words, we shall deal in broad outline with the historical development of monopoly capitalism as well as some theoretical aspects. It is intended therefore that this section should form a point of reference for our main study, which is covered later in the paper.

In dealing with our main topic we shall necessarily consider the structure of the South African economy and the manner in which economic concentration (i.e. monopolistic condition) has built up over a relatively short period of time. Without burdening the paper with statistical data we shall, however, include in our study a few tables to lend support to our analysis. Such tables will be designed in a straightforward manner and they are absolutely necessary for an appreciation of certain important aspects of our study.

Even if briefly, we propose to refer to the current campaign by the capitalist countries to highlight the importance of 'free enterprise' as if it is a new idea.

## THE GENERAL PROBLEM IN OUTLINE

We take Adam Smith's *Wealth of Nations*, first published in 1776, as the foundation of a suitable beginning for a study of 'free competition', which became the very kernel of capitalist economic theory. As Adam Smith saw the position, the individual in his economic activities set out to advance his personal interests and only incidentally did he serve the interests of society. Thus he started from the premise that: 'The sum of individual interests, although some individuals might not recognise it, equalled the national interest.'

Proceeding along this line of thinking, according to which the individual sought his self-interest, he emphasised: 'Every individual is continually exerting himself to find out the most advantageous employment of whatever capital he can command. It is his own advantage, indeed, and not that of society, which he has in view.'

In explaining why the individual supports the domestic (i.e. national) industry instead of foreign industry he has this to say: 'By preferring the support of domestic to that of foreign industry (the individual) intends only his own security; and by directing that industry (i.e. domestic industry) in such a manner as its produce may be of the greatest value, he intends only his own gain, and he is in this, as in many other cases, led by an invisible hand to promote an end which was no part of his invention.'

Thus Adam Smith laid the foundations firmly and clearly for

competitive capitalism, and lest anyone be still in doubt, he further elaborated: 'Every man, as long as he does not violate the laws of justice, is left perfectly free to pursue his own interest his own way, and to bring both his industry and capital into competition with those of any other man, or order of man.'

This attitude to the role every individual was entitled to play to advance his self-interest, in the process of which he found himself 'led by an invisible hand' to promote the interests of society, explains Smith's uncompromising objection to state interference, i.e. in the form of mercantilism in his day. To him 'that government governs best which governs least'. Free competition in which the strong survived came to be accepted by successive generations in the course of the political economy. And Adam Smith was accorded a place of honour as the father of political economy.

According to Adam Smith any number of firms, all engaged in the production of a homogeneous product, could compete against one another. Realising the chaotic situation which could arise from such unbridled competition, his successors set about building a body of economic theory which sought to provide a national framework within which 'free competition' could operate. In pursuance of this notion, other sweet-sounding catchwords with which we are all to familiar have been developed, and are being peddled freely by bourgeois scribes and their media in the face of reality. These are: free enterprise, market mechanism, the free world's way of life . . . All these boil down to one thing, viz the development of a price theory according to which the primary objective is maximisation of profit. In so far as the price theory must operate within the framework of competition, bourgeois economists had to lay down conditions, or principles, necessary for the existence of pure competition. We set out briefly these conditions or principles as follows:

(a) *Homogeneity of the product.* That all sellers of a particular product sell homogeneous units of the product. The outcome of this would be that the buyers would have no reason to prefer the product of some seller to those of another.

(b) *Smallness of each buyer or seller.* That each buyer or seller of the product involved is so small in relation to the market for the product that he cannot influence the price of that product he is buying or selling. That is, whether an individual supplier withheld his product from the market or an individual buyer did not buy would not cause any change – up or down – in the price of the product.

(c) *Absence of artificial restraints.* No artificial restraints must be placed on the demand for, supply of, and prices of goods and resources (i.e. labour, raw materials, capital, or managerial skills). In other words, prices must be free to move in an upward or downward direction in response to changing conditions of demand and supply. In other words, there must be no governmental price fixing, administering of prices by producers' associations, or labour unions (trade unions).

(d) *Mobility.* There must be mobility of goods and services, and of resources in the economy. In other words, new firms must be free to enter any desired industry, and resources (the most important of which is labour) must be free to move among alternative uses.

(e) *Knowledge of the economy.* That all 'economic units possess complete knowledge of the economy'. In other words, any discrepancies in prices quoted by the sellers will be known immediately and buyers will buy at the lowest price. If, on the other hand, buyers offer different prices for whatever they purchase, sellers will know this immediately and will sell to the highest bidder. Thus in the market for any particular product or resource, a single price will prevail.

According to this reasoning, the price will be determined at that point where supply corresponds to demand. The downward-sloping demand curve and the upward-sloping supply curve intersect. Very neat! Sound logic!

In spite of the passage of time and changes in competitive capitalism, bourgeois economists continued to treat economies in terms of 'free competition'. The realities of life which had emerged in the course of the development of competitive capitalism were brushed aside, while the conditions for the existence of free competition were still put forward under conditions in which to talk of pure or perfect or free competition was just unrealistic. Even an outstanding bourgeois economist, Alfred Marshall, the founder of the Cambridge school of economics, the influence of whose teachings was widely spread in Europe, would not face up to the new realities that took shape before his eyes. The most he could say to acknowledge the changes, in a statement made in 1881, was: 'The work I have set myself is this: how to get rid of the evils of competition while retaining its advantages.'

And so he, together with his former students who by 1883 were said to have occupied 50 per cent of the economics chairs at universities in the United Kingdom, merrily carried on expounding economic theory within the framework of free competition. Born in 1842, he had already established his professional career as an economist when Karl Marx published his *Das Kapital* in 1867. At the time of his death in 1924 when his *Principles of Economics* (first published in 1890) was the standard book for the teaching of economics in the United Kingdom as well as Europe, bourgeois economists had still hardly taken notice of the changes that the competitive capitalist system had undergone.

It was not until 1933 that Joan Robinson and Edward H. Chamberlin published their respective books: *The Economics of Imperfect Competition* and *The Theory of Monopolistic Competition*, that bourgeois economists came to accept what was already long a fact of life, namely that competition was neither that perfect nor that free. Shortly thereafter, Keynes published in 1936 his *General Theory of Employment, Interest and Money*.

It is this book which made such an enormous impact on the whole capitalist world, largely because it addressed itself to current problems following the Great Depression. To this day it forms the pivot around which bourgeois economic theory revolves. But although Keynes was very critical of certain aspects of the classical theory, he conducted his own analysis on the groundwork of free competition, thus ignoring the extent to which the abstract foundations on which it was built had been eroded by developments which limited competition to a minimum area of the capitalist economy.

We are now in a position to examine the development of monopoly capitalism. The emergence of significant social phenomena cannot, with any precision, be given a date simply because they are a development in the course of a process after an accumulation over time of a variety of social forces. Be that as it may, monopoly capitalism emerged at about the same time as imperialism. Let us examine in outline the build-up of forces that ultimately burst onto the stage in the development of capitalism, which Marxists characterised as monopoly capitalism as distinct from competitive capitalism.

In the course of the development of competition, the individual capitalist accumulated a quantity of capital under his own ownership and control. Marx called this process 'concentration of capital'. The increase in the concentration of capital was immediately followed by another process which Marx called the 'centralisation of capital', i.e. a combining of capitals, e.g. in two or more firms. The combined capitals grew and developed into a huge concern under single control. With the combined accumulated capital it was but a short step to an increase in the capital-labour ratio (i.e. organic composition of capital), thus leading to mass production. As Marx put it in the preface to the first edition of *Das Kapital*: 'The battle of competition is fought by cheapening commodities. The cheapness of commodities depends . . . on the productiveness of labour, and this again on the scale of production. Therefore the larger capitals beat the smaller.'

In the unequal struggle the individually owned and therefore smaller firms are either squeezed out of the market or swallowed by the bigger and more efficient concerns. In this way, 'the competitive struggle itself is an agent of centralisation'. Once the process of centralisation had begun there could be no reversing the process of history to fit with competitive capitalism based on theories of free competition as envisaged by Adam Smith, and further elaborated by his successors.

The rise of corporations, i.e. stock companies, did not have far-reaching implications for the character and functioning of capitalist production, only in so far as technical changes leading to mass production were involved, but it led to a progressive replacement of competition among a large number of small individual producers by control of the market by a small number of giant corporations which sought to eliminate competition in prices among themselves. A further reinforcing factor that became harnessed to the advantage of centralised capital was the credit system. The credit system – through the banks – drew the money resources from all levels of society and fed them into the hands of the capitalists. The availability of credit soon became a 'formidable weapon in the competitive struggle'. As would be expected, the centralised firms attracted more credit than individually owned firms and this further weakened the hold of the small business on its share of the market. It is of interest to note that recently Anton Rupert announced a scheme for the formation of a development fund to make credit available to small businesses – all this in the newly aroused public welfare spirit to revive free enterprise! The lion proposes to make small handouts to the smaller and weaker beasts of prey so that it should not alone be singled out as being tainted with the blood of its victims.

Although Marx saw in his day the enormous power which the stock company (centralised capital) would be in a position to wield vis-à-vis the private individual capitalist, it was not until Rudolf Hilferding published, in 1910, his studies of this phase of the development of capitalism that new light was thrown on the role of corporations (i.e. stock companies). As a matter of interest, when Hitler rose to power Hilferding fled to France. But when the Vichy government prepared to deport him back to Germany he committed suicide. In his *Finance Capital*, he sought to bring Marx's analysis up to date. He was quick to warn that the formation of the giant corporations was not a step towards socialism. On the contrary he saw the formation of such corporations as leading to the development of a 'new aristocracy of finance'. With the rise of the stock company the owners of the means of production, i.e. the stockholders, were progressively divorced from management and control. The shareholders did not have to direct production like the old individual capitalist. Instead the shareholder came to resemble a lender of money who can regain possession of his money by selling his shares on the market (the stock exchange).

The rise of the stock companies gave rise to a new function unknown in the era of the individual private capitalist. The new function was that of an agent (a promoter) to sell shares to those who had large funds for which on their own they could not find paying avenues of investment. The stock companies became more and more impersonal. The capitalist who bought shares in an enterprise did so not because he was interested in it, but because he was interested in the yield of his capital held in shares in the particular enterprise, and when he wished he felt he might sell at a profit. For instance, those who bought gold shares in South Africa, say twelve months ago, must be realising a windfall at today's gold share prices. In Germany the function of promoting was undertaken by the commercial banks. But as the corporations became stronger they were able to amass vast sums of money, and thus became less and less dependent on banks for credit. Today commercial banks provide mostly short-term credit in the form of overdrafts.

With their own vastly accumulated capital the corporations, dominated by a small number of capitalists, were able to extend control from one corporation to another by buying shares in other corporations. As a result, representatives of concentrated economic power would sit on the boards of directors of a number of corporations. This gave rise to interlocking directorates – a practice which in turn gave rise to a community of interests, not of the majority of shareholders but of the small 'leading echelon of the property-owning class' that controls the giant corporations which are able to adapt and follow common market policies. This community of interests has led to the formation of cartels, trusts, mergers and other forms of combination and collusion all aimed at monopolistic control of the market. This is capitalism at its monopoly stage in which it seeks to eliminate competition. The specific characteristic of this organised form is that it is designed to increase profits by monopolistic market control. This stage became apparent in the 1880s. Of it, Engels in editing Volume II of *Capital* had this to say: 'The long cherished freedom of competition has reached the end of its tether and is compelled to announce its own bankruptcy.' Yet bourgeois economists did not begin to face up to this reality until 1933 (in the persons of Joan Robinson and Edward Chamberlin).

Now with the development of giant corporations, what pattern of behaviour can be expected from these huge management-controlled and financially independent corporations? True, in the big corporations management has become separated from the stockholder control. But in practice the managers are among the biggest owners, and because of the strategic position they occupy, they function as the protectors and spokesmen for all large-scale property. They are not just interested in the income they receive as part of the management but have a vested interest in the corporation form of business organisation because of the powerful position these corporations have come to occupy in the whole economy. Today it is largely the initiative of the corporations which 'sets the economy in motion, their power that keeps it moving, their policies that get it into difficulties and crises'. It must necessarily be so because they control by far the greatest part of the market. In relation to the big corporations small business is 'without effective power to counter them and still less to exercise an independent initiative of its own'. Hence: 'Smaller business should properly be treated as part of the environment within which big business operates rather than as an actor on the stage.'

Under monopoly capitalism the giant corporations, occupying as they do a dominant position in the economy, protect their position by resorting to a variety of restrictive business practices, all of which in one way or another are aimed at either dominating competition or reducing its effectiveness to a minimum.

So far we have been dealing with monopoly. It has been aptly said that: 'The crucial difference between competitive capitalism and monopoly capitalism is that under the former the individual enterprise is a "price-taker" while under the latter the big corporation is a "price-maker".' Thus under monopoly capitalism a corporation aims at controlling the market for the sale of its product at a price which will maximise profits for the one producer (monopoly) or a few producers (oligopoly). But we should mention also a market situation in which producers of a homogeneous product combine for the purpose of purchasing a certain resource. As opposed to monopoly, this is called monopsony. This is of special interest in South Africa. For instance, the gold mining companies have combined to form the WNLA, which is the sole employer of African labour. The gold mining companies do not compete among themselves for African labour, and in this way are able to keep wages at a depressed level largely by restricting the mobility of labour. The labour bureau system is designed to extend a monopsonistic labour-market situation to all sectors of the economy in so far as an African worker is tied to a specific industry. For instance, if he loses his job in a certain textile factory he is generally not permitted to take up a job outside the textile industry. The formation of regional boards is designed to streamline the working of this monopsonistic market situation and to ensure that all employers, including farmers, however unattractive their working conditions, get a fair allocation of their requirements of African labour.

The outline we have given in this section is intended to serve as a backdrop against which to study the development of monopoly capitalism in South Africa.

## THE SOUTH AFRICAN SCENE
### Background
The economic development of South Africa is divided into distinct phases:

(a) *1652–1870:* Agriculture was the dominant form of economic activity.

(b) *1870–1909:* Mining became, next to agriculture, the second most important sector of the economy. Although the discovery and mining of diamonds preceded the discovery of gold, within a short period of time thereafter it gave rise to a great influx into the area of capital speculators and artisans from Europe, especially the United Kingdom.

(c) *1910 to date:* The outbreak of World War One scarcely four years after the formation of Union, and the problems of transport from Britain to the British forces fighting in various parts of Africa, stimulated the establishment of certain processing industries to supply the forces. In 1923 the government passed the Board of Trade and Industries Act, under which was formed the Board of Trade and Industries (BTI) to advise the government on ways and means to stimulate industrial development and growth.

But it was not until the government passed in 1955 the Customs Act that a definite policy was adopted to foster the development of the manufacturing industry. In terms of this legislation, the government armed itself with powers to raise tariff walls to protect infant industries in the country. In this way considerable stimulus was given to the establishment of manufacturing industry under protective cover from competition of imported goods. No sooner, however, had industrial development started, especially during World War Two, than complaints of malpractices were lodged with the Minister of Commerce and Industries. As a result of these complaints the government re-enacted the BTI Act in 1944. In terms of the new Act the government ordered the BTI to inquire into and advise the government on 'Combinations, trusts and monopolies and restraint of trading tending to the detriment of the general interest, especially by restricting production or maintaining or raising prices and the prevention thereof'.

From the above we see that before two decades had elapsed after legislation to stimulate the development of industry, complaints of centralisation of capital and monopolistic practices flowing therefrom indicated – all within such a short period of time – the rise of monopoly capitalism in the country. Or should we say: once given the conditions such as industrial development, monopoly capitalism extended its influence to South Africa, much in the same way that capitalism, whether competitive or monopolistic, struck root in the country.

The 1944 legislation did not, however, confer administrative powers on the BTI, nor did it make any provision for sanctions, but it was an 'important advance in so far as it provided for a study by the BTI of monopolistic situations which interfered with competitive policy'. Thus, acting on a directive by the Minister, the BTI undertook a series of investigations into specific industries for monopolistic tendencies. Following on the report of the BTI submitted in 1951, the government scrapped all previous legislation relating to monopoly, and passed in 1955 the Regulation of Monopolistic Conditions Act. It is in the light of this legislation and its application that much of our study will be brought to bear on monopoly capitalism in South Africa. We now turn to monopoly capital.

## The mining sector

Mining in general involves a heavy demand for capital and expertise to make mining measurably safe for labour and to extract minerals economically. Further, there is considerable risk involved in mining. These conditions call for vast capital outlays starting from exploration operations to the time when the shaft is sunk. It is estimated that a gold mine of average size requires an investment of about R60 million to get it into production. It may take a few years before any profit is shown. These conditions make mining unsuitable for small-scale operations. Small mining firms cannot command sufficient capital or attract science-based skills which mining operations under modern conditions call for. And consequently by the close of the nineteenth century, the small mining firms were fast disappearing. Either they merged into the big, but few, mining groups that dominate the mining sector today, or else they completely disappeared from the scene.

As these groups accumulated capital, especially financial resources, they established finance houses specialising in finding new channels of investment for the enormous funds at their disposal. Extensive as the mining activities are in the country, ranging over a number of minerals, the area of investment in mining is limited, and, what is more, mining is a wasting asset. The more intensively a given mineral is exploited the more and more are its deposits reduced. Haunted by the nagging fear of the exhaustion of mineral resources, the giant mining houses have diversified and branched out into other sectors of the economy besides mining. With their enormous financial resources they have tended to dominate any sector or industry to which their interests have extended.

By the early 1960s mining interests in the country had been reduced to only eight mining houses. With the wide range of mining operations, it means that the economic power concentrated in the hands of the few mining houses must be tremendous. Taking Anglo American Corporation alone we see the large number of gold mines under its control, then the coal mines. As for diamond mining it has virtually a monopoly over a vast area from Tanzania down. As far as the marketing of diamonds is concerned De Beers has a world monopoly. A large number of other mining activities of other minerals, e.g. copper and nickel, iron ore, manganese, etc. is under Anglo American control. There is also the diversification into activities other than mining, plus others which Anglo American set up in the late 1960s and during the 1970s such as the Vanadium and Steel Corporation near Phalaborwa. In those areas of the economy in which Anglo American Corporation has shown interest, smaller business enterprises will not dare enter. Among these are African Explosives and Chemical Industries, Forest Industries and Veneers. In recent years Anglo American has extended its interests to farming on a large scale.

The other mining houses are Anglo-Transvaal Consolidated Investments, Central Mining, Federale Mynbou, General Mining and Finance Corporation, Johannesburg Consolidated Investment Co. (JCI), Gold Fields of South Africa and Union Corporation. These highly centralised capital corporations are financed from foreign sources, e.g. West Europe.

Among themselves these mining houses have forged links that strengthen community of interests, e.g. Federale Mynbou linked up with General Mining while recently General Mining has linked up with Union Corporation. By forming such links the mining houses strengthen their position vis-à-vis the others. Thus in this sector centralisation of capital has taken place on such a huge scale that the mining operations in southern Africa are in the hands of an oligopoly, at the head of which stands, head and shoulders above all others, the Anglo American Corporation with its world-wide interests. Not only is monopoly capitalism in this one sector of the economy a firmly established matter, but by diversifying into manufacturing and farming, they open in these sectors on a scale that gives them a monopolistic advantage partly by virtue of the scale on which they operate (which derives from the vast financial resources from which they draw), and partly by deliberate policies and practices to corner the market for themselves.

We should mention here even if in passing the share of the

workers in the economic surplus. Until 1974 the Chamber of Mines released annually figures reflecting their operation. But after 1974 figures relating to employment of Africans and Europeans have been omitted. This period coincides with the marked rise of the price of gold.

However, the following figures for 1973 and 1974 tell a tale.

**Table 1. Wages and dividends of gold mines.**

|      | No. of Europeans | Wages | No. of Africans | Wages | Dividend declared |
|------|------------------|-------|-----------------|-------|-------------------|
| 1973 | 36 911 | R217 710 000 | 372 384 | R134 850 000 | R320 204 683 |
| 1974 | 37 255 | R247 331 000 | 318 242 | R202 875 000 | R565 830 000 |

The most striking features shown by these figures are the comparative numbers of Africans and Europeans employed on the gold mines, and their respective wages. The gap is really wide. Now compare the total wage bill, consisting of both African and European wages, with the amount of dividend declared for the shareholders. Actually for 1974 the dividend exceeded the combined wage bill. Recently the chairman of the Chamber of Mines stated that the average wage of an African mine worker is R153 per month. And with the rapidly increasing price of gold, the government has lost no time in letting it be known that the increases in the price of gold will not be passed on to the workers by way of increased wages. This decision was taken to avoid feeding the fires of inflation, but no damper is put on increasing dividends.

In recent years African mineworkers have made some gallant efforts to fight for increases in their wages, but the effect of the monopsony powers which the gold mines exercise over the employment of African labour will continue to influence the movement of wages to the great disadvantage of the African mineworkers.

**The secondary and tertiary sector**

Following the complaints (referred to previously) concerning increasing monopolistic practices, the Minister directed the BTI to investigate these complaints and to recommend legislation to deal with them. The BTI produced a comprehensive survey in its report no. 327, which it drew up after it had visited Europe and the USA to study modern thinking there on monopolies and monopolistic tendencies. On the basis of this information the BTI drew up guiding principles and objectives on which legislation was to be based, taking into account conditions peculiar to South Africa. It indicated the following guidelines.

(a)  The wholesale condemnation of monopolistic tendencies is unrealistic and not justified. The policy should distinguish between harmful monopolistic tendencies and those which are innocuous, depending on what is regarded as the public interest.

(b)  The size of the firm does not necessarily suggest a monopolistic conditon.

(c)  Restrictive agreements should be controlled, not prohibited.

(d)  Large businesses or groups should be subject to dissolution. But any legislation aimed at doing so should not be related to size, but to abuse of power, judged by its economic effect.

The outcome was the passing of the Regulation of Monopolistic Conditions Act in 1955. The approach of this legislation is that it is not the extent of economic power, i.e. size of the firm, but its abuse that is important. Thus economic concentration does not constitute 'an element of the definition of a monopolistic condition, whereas restriction of competition is an essential prerequisite'. Thus the approach of government policy is such that in practice centralisation of capital is encouraged, and even restrictive business practices are connived at unless they are too glaring. But economic power does in reality involve the use of restrictive business practices whether by design or not. By increasing the size of the firm the purpose is to control a larger share of the market. But even assuming that the firm did not aim at doing so at the expense of its competitors, its presence in any industry scares the smaller competitors away simply because they realise they are not in a position to compete with the giant. Under monopoly capitalism, increasing the size of the firm is not an altruistic exercise. Its purpose is to smother competition and place the firm where it can dictate the price and thus maximise profit.

In terms of the Act, the function of the BTI is to investigate, upon being directed by the Minister, the existence or otherwise of monopolistic conditions. If the investigation reveals the existence of a monopolistic condition, the BTI is required to ascertain whether there are circumstances which justify such a condition in the public interest. But the Act does not define the 'public interest'. If the BTI has established the existence of a monopolistic condition, the responsibility rests on the firm concerned to advance extenuating circumstances which justify such a condition in the public interest. If the firm fails to advance convincing argument, the BTI advises the Minister to take suitable remedial measures. In practice, the attitude of the law in South Africa is one of acceptance of monopoly capitalism as a fact of life. All that the law is concerned with is its control. That is the right climate for monopoly capitalism to flourish.

At this stage it will be helpful to refer briefly to the forms which economic concentration has taken in the country, i.e. we are going to refer to those forms of centralisation of capital which came about as a result of deliberate action. These forms occur as a result of mergers, take-overs and other actions. For our purposes we distinguish here three main types of mergers and take-overs that have contributed to much of the economic concentration that exists in the country.

(a) *Horizontal combinations.* These take place between enterprises that are engaged in the production of a similar product, in other words between firms that operate in the same industry and market. A recent example is the merger between SA Breweries and the Cape Wine Distillers.

(b) *Vertical combinations.* These take place between enterprises responsible for successive stages in the supply and production of a product. Such a combination can occur between suppliers of iron ore, a steel producer and a firm that specialises in the production of steel products, e.g. farm implements.

(c) *Conglomerates.* This type of merger or take-over consists of a combination of enterprises with unrelated activities, in other words firms that are engaged in the production of products which have nothing in common. A typical example is the mining houses and the number of enterprises under them that fall outside mining activities. For instance, JCI owns SA Breweries, which has in turn entered into a horizontal combination with Cape Wine Distillers but has formed a conglomerate by taking over OK Bazaars.

These forms of economic concentration are a common feature of the South African economy. Financial journals report almost weekly various combinations of the more commonly known types mentioned above and yet more subtle ones with which we need not deal here. In addition, certain financial institutions specialise in providing expertise to advise on the formation of mergers and take-overs, as well as encourage firms to merge. Merchant banks specialise in this service. Monopoly capitalism has become the order of the day in South Africa. Our problem is to decide on a criterion to determine to what extent the phase of monopoly capitalism is operative in South Africa, or posed differently, how concentration has taken place and how is it using the power that goes with such concentration. We are going to use two methods of measuring economic concentration. These are:

(a) *Absolute measures.* These measures indicate the percentage of dominance in an industry by a given number of firms. For our purposes we are going to show how much of the total turnover in a given industry is controlled by three or five larger firms.

(b) *Summary measures.* These indicate the numbers of firms responsible for a given percentage of dominance, say 10 per cent or more of the turnover for the industry. We shall use the two measures in conjunction. Reference to the following tables will make the position clear. In Table 2 we select twenty subgroups in the manufacturing sector to show that at least 70 per cent of the total turnover in the particular industry is controlled by three or less firms. We have selected mostly industrial subgroups which manufacture products of immediate interest to the average man.

In Table 2 the first striking feature is the small number of firms in each of the 20 industries studied in the table; the second is the very high percentage of the total turnover in each subgroup by three or less firms of those in the subgroup; and third the number of firms holding at least 70 per cent of the total turnover shows that each of the twenty industries on Table 2 is either monopolistic, duopolistic or oligopolistic in structure. An industrial structure of this kind shows a high degree of monopoly (as Michael Kalecki described it).

Further we propose to follow the classification of industries adopted internationally, viz the Standard Industrial Classification (SIC). We are going to show in Table 3 how the total turnover is distributed in four major sectors of the South African economy, viz in the manufacturing, wholesale and retail, construction, and transport sectors. The table is so arranged that it shows the four major sectors. As of 1972 the total number of manufacturing establishments (foreign and domestic) nears 12 568, wholesale and retail nears 53 623, construction nears 7 845, and transport 9 307.

**Table 2. Industrial sub-groups where 70 per cent of total turnover is controlled by three or less firms.**

| Industrial sub-group | No. of firms in sub-group | Percentage of total turnover held by 3/less firms | No. of firms holding at least 70% of total turnover |
|---|---|---|---|
| 1. Condensed milk, milk powder, etc. | 14 | 81,8 | 2 |
| 2. Sausage casings, dripping and lard | 4 | 92,0 | 2 |
| 3. Dried-fruit packing | 2 | 100 | 1 |
| 4. Instant breakfast food | 5 | 90,2 | 1 |
| 5. Macaroni, spaghetti | 4 | 99,7 | 1 |
| 6. Vinegar | 7 | 73,6 | 3 |
| 7. Breweries | 3 | 100 | 1 |
| 8. African beer | 12 | 84,9 | 3 |
| 9. Cigarettes, tobacco, cigars, snuff | 15 | 98,4 | 2 |
| 10. Blankets | 10 | 78,8 | 3 |
| 11. Linoleum | 8 | 88,7 | 2 |
| 12. Pulp, paper, paperboards | 13 | 74,3 | 3 |
| 13. Fertilizers | 15 | 90,6 | 2 |
| 14. Matches | 2 | 100 | 1 |
| 15. Explosives and ammunition | 4 | 99,4 | 1 |
| 16. Tyres and tubes | 5 | 85,8 | 3 |
| 17. Dry cell batteries | 4 | 97,7 | 1 |
| 18. Electric bulbs and fluorescent tubes | 6 | 91,3 | 2 |
| 19. Motorcycles, scooters, bicycles | 10 | 96,0 | 1 |
| 20. Crayons, chalk, pens and pencils | 5 | 81,2 | 3 |

For each sector the table gives the following information: the first column shows the percentage of firms at intervals of 5 per cent and its multiples up to 100; the second column shows the number of firms out of the grand total (as given above) corresponding to the percentage in the first column, e.g. 628 firms in the manufacturing sector, 2 679 firms in wholesale and retail, 392 in construction, and 465 in transport. Column 3 shows the percentage of the turnover controlled by the relevant number of firms in column 2, which constitute the corresponding percentage of the total number of firms in each sector.

**Table 3. Distribution of turnover in four major sectors in the South African economy, 1972.**

| Percentage of firms | Manufacturing | | Wholesale and retail | | Construction | | Transport | |
|---|---|---|---|---|---|---|---|---|
| | No. of firms | % of turnover | No. of firms | % of turnover | No. of firms | % of turnover | No. of firms | % of turnover |
| 5 | 628 | 63,1 | 2 679 | 68,5 | 392 | 63,2 | 465 | 72,6 |
| 10 | 1 257 | 75,7 | 5 360 | 77,0 | 785 | 74,6 | 931 | 81,5 |
| 15 | 1 885 | 82,7 | 8 041 | 81,8 | 1 177 | 80,8 | 1 396 | 85,9 |
| 20 | 2 513 | 87,1 | 10 722 | 85,2 | 1 569 | 84,9 | 1 861 | 88,9 |
| 25 | 3 142 | 90,3 | 13 404 | 87,8 | 1 961 | 87,9 | 2 327 | 91,0 |
| 30 | 3 770 | 92,6 | 16 085 | 89,9 | 2 354 | 90,3 | 2 792 | 92,7 |
| 35 | 4 399 | 94,3 | 18 766 | 91,6 | 2 746 | 92,2 | 3 257 | 94,1 |
| 40 | 5 027 | 95,6 | 21 447 | 93,1 | 3 138 | 93,7 | 3 723 | 95,2 |

In Table 3 we show, only up to 40 per cent (column 1) of the firms in the sector, the corresponding numbers of firms and the turnover they control. From the information thus given it is clear the market is controlled by a few, thus leaving the smaller business competitors very little of the market to share among themselves. In short, the prevalence of economic concentration shown in these four major sectors of the economy as well as in mining reveals to what extent monopoly capitalism determines the character of the South African economy, and it is reasonable to infer that the other sectors of the economy will be no exception to the rule. The effect of so much economic concentration is probably felt in a direct way in the retail trade in the main industrial centres, where giant distribution business organisations have sprung up in recent years. The emergence of hypermarkets with daily takings which the 'corner shop' could not make in a generation indicates the power of economic concentration. Commenting on the performance of a hypermarket in Jo'burg's Norwood suburb, the general manager had this to say: 'On the opening day which was a Wednesday the takings amounted to R300 000, and at the close of business — midday Saturday — three-and-a-half days' sales of more than R1 million had been recorded . . . it is claimed that these giant emporiums have forced the small trader out of business.' He went further to observe: 'Lacking the hypermarket's bargaining power traders in the black townships buy their goods at higher prices and therefore charge black consumers more.'

## Foreign investment

From the time when diamonds and gold were discovered in the country, foreign investment was the first to set the wheels of industrial development moving, and later discoveries of a wide range of minerals increased the demand for foreign investment. The development of the manufacturing sector opened up new opportunities for foreign investment as well as a new and lucrative market for foreign manufacturers. The government policy, after 1925, to raise tariffs to protect infant industries raised the prices of such imported goods, as were produced by South Africa's protected industries, so high that foreign exporters had to find ways and means of circumventing the problem. The most acceptable way out is to produce the goods in the market area where they are not subject to any discriminatory treatment, as imported finished goods are. The obvious thing to do was, therefore, to establish subsidiary plants. In the course of years, especially after World War Two, giant manufacturing corporations in Europe and America which have the title of 'multinational' firms set up subsidiary plants in various countries, including South Africa. It is not always easy to identify all the foreign subsidiaries, except in a few outstanding cases like automobile assembly plants, tyre manufacturing plants, Siemens, etc. For our purpose we shall identify foreign investments by the number of subsidiaries individual foreign countries have established in South Africa. As of 1977 the position was as follows:

| Source | Number of firms |
| --- | --- |
| United Kingdom | 1 200 |
| West Germany | 350 |
| USA | 335 |
| France | 50 |
| Australia | 35 |
| Belgium | 20 |
| Netherlands | 20 |
| Italy | 21 |
| Switzerland | 12 |

The value of American investments then were about $2 billion, British £5 000 million. The estimated value of all foreign investments was more than $10 000 million. By any standard that is something to defend. It is worth noting that these subsidiaries themselves were very big, e.g. General Motors, Ford, Firestone, etc. and are branches of monopoly capital in the metropolitan countries. In those sectors of the economy in which the subsidiaries of the foreign giant corporations operate, they constitute monopoly capital and control the market for their product.

In some cases, foreign monopoly capital firms are controlling the market in South Africa from supply sources in the metropolitan countries. This is particularly the position in the case of science-based industries. The pharmaceutical industry is a case in point. A considerable amount of research and development (R&D) takes place in developing medicines, and South Africa with its small, but not insignificant, market has not been able to become independent of foreign supplies of medicines. As of 1975, foreign-owned concerns accounted for 85,7 per cent of the South African market for prescription medicines. In the lead are the USA, Britain, Switzerland and West Germany. Thus the industry shows a monopolistic structure dominated by a few foreign-owned firms.

The development of a pharmaceutical industry goes through five stages, and the South African industry has only reached the third stage, which is still concerned, as with the first two, with packaging the finished products from imported final products ordered in bulk. The multinational firms have been streamlined to meet supply requirements under conditions of monopoly capitalism and wherever they establish themselves outside the metropolitan countries, they strive to capture the lion's share of the market. That is the way of things under monopoly capitalism.

## Financial institutions

Financial institutions are a very important aspect of the monetary system. Their function is to provide the main channel through which finance, i.e. credit, passes from the lender to the borrower. The real functioning of the capitalist production system is unthinkable without a properly functioning monetary system with its wide range of financial institutions. The various types of financial institution channel credit on terms which suit the various types of business activity. Their growth has kept step with the development of capitalism. In the epoch of monopoly capitalism they have become highly centralised in order to muster loanable funds on a scale big enough to meet the credit requirements of business concerns that operate on a large scale.

We do not propose to give anything near a comprehensive survey of the nature of these institutions, other than to note their functions and their character under conditions of monopoly capitalism. The sophistication in the types of financial institution depends on the market for the finance provided by such institutions. In South Africa we distinguish the following financial institutions:

(a) *The South African Reserve Bank.* As in all countries whose economies have got off the ground level, at the centre of the financial structure stands the Central Bank. This position in South Africa is held by the Reserve Bank. The main function of the Reserve Bank is to control the country's monetary system so as to ensure its economic development. Its other functions are to issue bank notes, and to keep the country's gold and foreign exchange resources, and also the cash reserves of the commercial banks; it supplies credit to commercial banks and other financial institutions. In short, the Reserve Bank is the pivot around which the entire monetary system revolves. As such the Reserve Bank keeps a close surveillance on all the financial institutions in the country, especially the commercial banks. The Reserve Bank uses various measures to influence the policies of commercial banks with regard to limiting or extending credit.

(b) *Commercial banks.* Commercial banks, as distinct from other banking institutions, not only accept money deposits but provide for payments by depositors by cheque. There are at present five commercial banks in the country, viz Barclays, Standard, Nedbank, Volkskas and Trust Bank. These banks collect vast sums of money, which they lend out in various ways, e.g. by way of overdraft, at interest, on current account, medium-term loans, discounting bills, etc. They render a wide range of services we need not list here. As dealers in money they occupy a very important position in the financial structure. And in keeping with developments under monopoly capitalism, they are highly centralised capital structures. They strive to capture as much of the funds in the hands of individuals and businesses as possible to enable them to extend credit to their clients.

(c) *Merchant banks.* Merchant banking has significant features which distinguish it from commercial banking. Whereas commercial banks take even very small amounts for deposit, merchant banks usually will not accept anything less than R10 000 per unit of deposit, and for advances the minimum unit of loan is R100 000. Thus they have earned themselves the reputation of being engaged in 'wholesale banking' to banking institutions. Commercial banks engage in 'retail banking'. As a specialised banking institution and because of the small number of deposits and advances it handles, it conducts its business with a small staff who are mainly specialists.

(d) *Hire purchase houses.* These are an important channel for funds to finance the purchase of durable consumer goods, like motor cars, furniture and household equipment such as refrigerators and electric stoves. Without the services of hire purchase houses, products of monopoly capital would largely be out of reach of the classes that have a limited income.

(e) *Building societies.* The building society, like all other financial institutions, accepts deposits. But its field of investment is strictly limited. It provides funds to those who wish to acquire a home. The house is held as security, and thus the loans are much less than the value of the property financed. One of the conditions of the loan is that the owner of the property must contribute an initial sum toward the cost of development or building.

(f) *Insurance companies.* One of the most important sources of long-term funds is the insurance companies. The two giants in this field in South Africa are the Old Mutual and Sanlam.

(g) *Pension funds.* It is a generally accepted practice in the large firm to run pension schemes for its employees. The employers and employees usually contribute to such pension fund on a 50–50 basis. There are large public pension funds which represent a number of business organisations. These have large funds at their command, which they invest in various ways approved under legislation controlling the use of such funds. The amount due to an employee is not paid to him in a lump sum on retirement but as a pension for the rest of his life. The accumulation of these contributions over the working life of the employee and the spread of the payments, in relatively small amounts, in the years of retirement enable the pension fund always to have huge funds, which grow by the year.

In recent years private pension funds confined to a particular firm have become common, and are turned to good use by way of investment in the firm concerned under legally approved conditions. Thus pension funds today provide one of the most important sources of loanable funds for investment.

(h) *Discount houses and accepting houses.* These are specialised financial institutions which have been established since the latter 1950s to meet the increasing demand of a growing industrial economy for various types of credit.

The financial institutions we have so briefly sketched above are, except for the Reserve Bank, all in the private sector. As will have been observed, each group of financial institutions exercises a monopolistic control of the category of credit it caters for. The huge business combinations that characterise the phase of monopoly capitalism require finance on a scale that measures up to their vast operations, and it is only if the financial institutions themselves corner the market for their type of financing activity that they can survive. This explains the anaemic condition of the small individual entrepreneur. He is starved of credit, and therefore hardly grows. If he has to survive he moves away from the central business district (CBD), i.e. the heart of the business in a city, to the residential areas of the depressed classes, i.e. the areas of the low-income working classes, where he supplies elemental needs. Alternatively, he moves to the outskirts of the CBD to the residential areas of the low-income classes.

## The public sector

To close this section without making reference, even if in passing, to the state's activities in the country's economy would fall short of a complete picture. The government's activities in the country's economy are varied and extend over a number of sectors. In whatever business activity it engages, it has a virtual if not a complete monopoly. As far as what are called public utilities it enjoys a monopoly control. If there should be any threatening competition it does not hesitate to resort to the use of restrictive business practices to bar entry of competitors or to hamper their activities by monitoring or harassing them. The effect of such competition is thus minimal. The state runs the railways, the airways, communications, education, shipping, postal services, radio broadcasting, etc. To complement the railways it runs a road transport service (passenger and goods buses) on the trunk roads.

On such roads it bars entry of private business services, such as taxis, and private cartage of goods.

The state's activities in the manufacturing sector have been increasing at a fast rate and penetrating a wide range of manufacturing industries, such as SASOL and ISCOR.

In these ventures as well as in many others, some of which are in the border industries, the state has either a monopoly control or has joined hands with private monopoly capital to control the market for the product of such a joint venture.

To ensure that there is a regular source of finance for the business activities in which the state has an interest, it established a number of development corporations. To mention but a few, even though some of these have recently changed their original names, they are: the Industrial Development Corporation, the Fisheries Development Corporation, the Bantu Investment Corporation, with its ethnic-based subsidiaries, and the Coloured Development Corporation.

It is not easy today to indicate definitely the size of the public sector, with its widely spread ramifications in the South African economy. In the early 1960s it was estimated that the public sector accounted for 42 per cent of gross investment as against 58 per cent by the private sector. We have thus a situation in which the private and public sector share the major part of the market under conditions which are monopolistic in character.


## THE BIG TALK ABOUT FREE ENTERPRISE

There has been revived in capitalist countries a campaign about free competition now under a new catchphrase, free enterprise. It has been turned into a slogan that has a magic effect on some sections of the oppressed petit bourgeoisie and the emergent middle class. Old, now threadbare arguments that were advanced in the heyday of competitive capitalism, and shelved with the advance and consolidation of monopoly capitalism, are being dusted, given a new veneer and promoted under high-pressure salesmanship as a newly discovered cure-all of a socio-economic nature. Its protagonists state that the 'primary objective of a competition policy . . . should be the promotion of effective competition in the economy'. This belief, they state, derives from the 'philosophy of competition policy' which sets out the following two basic principles: (a) 'that the efficient utilisation of the country's limited resources is promoted by the free play of competitive market forces'; and (b) 'that competition is the most effective form of social control over all economic activities in a country and consequently limits the application of other forms of control for the protection of the public to a minimum'.

Who are the authors of and profound thinkers behind this philosophy? Strange to say! It's the captains of industry themselves, it is the monopolists, the top 10 per cent in the manufacturing industry, in commerce and all the main sectors of the economy who have under their firm control more than three-quarters of the market; it is the 'price-makers' who determine what the price of their product or service will be, they who smother competition by keeping would-be competitors out of their economic sphere by all means, fair or foul. Today they turn round to preach the philosophy of free enterprise to those whom they have denied all opportunities to get their due share of the economic surplus.

Should the ordinary man not understand, the protagonists of the philosophy of competition set out to explain what the concept of 'effective competition' is all about. The term, they say, denotes a market situation: 'in which no trader is so powerful that he is able to impose his own terms on his customers unilaterally or coerce his competitors; new entrants are not restricted by any handicap other than the fact that others are already established; there is no preferential status for any important participant on the basis of law, politics or commercial alliances'. Effective competition, it is said, means a market situation which works in practice and which is not irreconcilable with the public interest.

All these points are no departure, in fact, from the principles and assumptions on which the case for free competition was based in the phase of competitive capitalism as outlined earlier. Are the protagonists being honest in putting forward these arguments in support of their campaign for free enterprise in a situation where the market structure is either monopolistic or duopolistic, or at least oligopolistic as shown in Table 2? Or are they just being unashamedly and downright dishonest? After carving up the vastly greater share of the marketing among monopolies and insulating their market shares, they turn round to declare in sanctimonious tones that the next entrants are restricted from entering their market spheres only by the fact that the monopolies themselves have already occupied those positions. What poor consolation is that for those who have, for one reason or another, come late into the business scene!

The question arises and calls for an urgent answer. Who are the protagonists of free enterprise and why do they press forward with this campaign in such haste? It is not the working class throughout the capitalist world, least of all the nationally oppressed and exploited working class and peasants in the colonial and semi-colonial areas. True, the petit bourgeoisie may entertain hopes of blazing a path for themselves into the business world, but the area of the market available for their products and services is limited to 20–25 per cent at best. Who then blows the free enterprise trumpet the loudest? It is the top 10 per cent who in practice have no use for free competition among themselves but have a lease of life to gain for monopoly capital if they can arouse in sections of the underprivileged classes a strong enough desire to follow the capitalist path under the banner of free enterprise.

In a survey conducted a couple of years back among Africans in some of the main industrial areas, including Africans in the southern Transvaal complex and the Durban–Pinetown complex, it was found that a sizeable percentage preferred socialism to free enterprise. But an even more forthright report on the feelings of the oppressed was that described by Louw (over the radio recently). He reports that when a question was put to Africans in Zimbabwe as to what they preferred, socialism or free enterprise, the answer was: 'If what we have been under is free enterprise, we prefer the opposite – socialism.'

Singing the praises of free enterprise Dr H.J.J. Reynders, executive director of the Federated Chambers of Industry (FCI), says that one of the main truths of free enterprise 'is equality of opportunity for all – regardless of race, colour or creed – to participate in economic endeavour and to be part of the process of the creation of wealth, and to share in the rewards of such participation'. But he is quick to ask: 'But what of our black compatriots? Do they feel themselves as part of this system? . . . It would not be surprising if there were a wide feeling among some blacks that they do not feel themselves as part of this system.' This leads him to the unhappy feeling, such as to bemoan: 'This is a tragedy, and a further deterioration in black attitudes towards the free enterprise system might well result in its disintegration in the only part of southern Africa in which the system is soundly based.' There you have it! The answer to the question why do the representatives of monopoly capital preach free enterprise in and out of hours to the oppressed.

## CONCLUSION

The most recent investigations show that monopoly capital plays a very important part, if not a dominant part, in South Africa. Among some of the reasons advanced to explain this development is the smallness of the market. As a result, in some industries only one or two modern plants can supply the needs of the available market. This, however, does not explain the general trend towards monopolistic tendencies in the whole economy.

Even in a sector where there is a large number of producers and free competition could be a feasible proposition, i.e. in agriculture, the government has stepped in to establish a one-channel marketing system through which prices are administered, rather than leaving them to take their level under the competitive market mechanism. The various Marketing Boards for agricultural products fix prices which the consumer may take or leave. After taking into account the views of those who support the trend towards monopoly capital and those who call for the strengthening of South Africa's free enterprise system, a semi-official view is: 'This problem should be approached with the utmost circumspection in view of the fact that economic concentration is often an important dynamic factor in the development of a young industrial country like South Africa.' Monopoly capitalism as a phase in the development of capitalism cannot be reversed. It may only be replaced by socialism, where there is a determined working-class party to spearhead the revolutionary struggle to effect that change.

# Movements in African Real Wages
# 1939–1969

## INTRODUCTION

In recent years, and more particularly since the late fifties, there has been an increasing clamour to establish a national minimum wage, and to ensure that such a minimum wage will in fact be paid.

Surveys have been conducted on the cost of living of unskilled African labour, and the average earnings of such labour have been compared with the bare requirements necessary to maintain an African urban worker at a minimum subsistence level with his family. The list of such items was drawn up by the Department of Nutrition and includes the following items: meat, bread, vegetables, fat, margarine, mealie meal or other maize substitute like samp, salt, fruit juice, and transport. The best known of these surveys are that prepared by Mrs Joy de Gruchy of the Institute of Race Relations in 1958 and more recently that prepared by Miss Sheila Suttner (1966) on the cost of living in Soweto, also under the auspices of the Institute. Yet other surveys which have thrown light on the subject are those of UNISA in Pretoria and of the University of Natal in Durban.

All these surveys reveal that the average real wages of unskilled African labour fall short of the poverty datum line, based on the minimum nutrition requirements compiled by the Department of Nutrition. Let us examine the movements of African real wages in the last thirty years as well as factors influencing such movements.

### The Second World War Years: 1939–1945

During the war years, the wages (real) of African workers increased by 50 per cent. During this period scores of thousands of workers — black and white — left their employment to join the war effort. On the other hand, a number of substitute industries were established to make up for imports which had become virtually impossible to obtain from overseas. Consequently there was a keen demand in the secondary and tertiary labour sectors. To attract labour from the other sectors wages were increased, particularly in the Cape Peninsula.

But the more important reason for the general rise was the fact that the government passed the Cost of Living Allowance regulations, which were loaded more in favour of lower-income groups than of the higher-income ones. The government insisted on the payment of such cost of living allowances.

## The Post-Second World War Period: 1945–1956

The real wages of unskilled African workers during this period tended to stagnate in spite of the fact that there was great economic activity. On the contrary, the wages of white workers were increasing during the whole of this period. Those of unskilled African workers did not only stagnate on the whole, but between 1953 and 1957 there was even a negative increase in some years amounting to as much as -1,5 per cent, according to Table II of Steenkamp's article 'Bantu wages in South Africa', in *SAJE*, June 1962.

What explanation could there be for this phenomenon? As a general rule wages tend to lag behind prices. This tendency becomes worse in cases where workers are not in a position to exercise pressure on employers to increase wages. In the case of white workers, the lag does not last long because white workers are able, through their trade unions, to get frequent revisions of their wage agreement. Because African trade unions are not legally recognised, African workers are denied this most effective weapon for the adjustment of their wages. As a result, during this period of price rises following on the release of the pent-up demand after the war years, African real wages stagnated. Where they were organised and they resorted to strike action to back up their demand for higher wages, the police broke up such strikes. This reassured the employers and consequently they kept the wage levels down, while profits increased with the increase in prices.

Even the Wage Act, in terms of which wages could be revised by the Wage Board in certain trades, could not be invoked to ensure that wage determinations were revised or new ones fixed. The intervals between old wage determinations and new ones were very long. The Wage Act provided for revisions to take place over a period of ten to eighteen years. Most of the ruling determinations were made during the war years and these had to run their allotted span before they were revised.

Although some registered trade unions do take up the question of an increase in wages of African workers belonging to their trade at Industrial Council negotiations, by and large African workers do not benefit much from this source.

## The Second Decade: 1958–1969

1. As from 1957 onwards, the Wage Board was given the responsibility by the government to raise the real wages of African workers. Further, the government provided for a review of determinations much more frequently than had been the case in the past. In fact, after 1958, reviews occurred at intervals of about five years. Also two Wage Boards operated.

2. Substantial increases in the real earnings of Africans were made largely as a result of recommendations by Wage Boards.

3. For purposes of assessing the impact of wage determinations on real wages of Africans, we may deal with the trades investigated under four groups:

(a) *Manufacturing and related trades.* The manufacturing industries were subdivided into four groups as per Table I of the *SAJE*, June 1968, in an article by Donald Pursell. The highest increases took place in Group A, whereas virtually no increases were recommended for Group D. Only moderate increases were made in Groups B and C. Considerable increases in Group A ranged up to 30 per cent.

(b) *Distributive trade.* The commercial distributive trade benefited considerably in all the main centres which were investigated by the Wage Board. Increases ranged from 0,4 per cent in Cape Town to 28,1 per cent in Maritzburg. The baking and meat trade received only modest increases.

(c) *Hotel trade.* The Wage Board reviewed the position in the hotel trade in the main centres in 1959 and 1964. However, only small increases were made, as the employers pointed out that increases in wages could not be compensated by higher productivity, but would have to be passed on to users of the service in the form of higher prices.

(d) *Unskilled determinations.* A number of new wage determinations were made for unskilled workers in a number of centres in 1958–60 and again in 1965–66.

In the first determination the Wage Board appears to have

159

made a concerted effort to increase real wages, and the benefit was widespread.

The Wage Board was not alone, however, in increasing the real earnings of African workers. Some employers did so voluntarily, and this was always more liberal than the meagre increases recommended by the Wage Board by and large.

## Conclusion

(1) Between 1957 and 1966 in a number of trades covered by the Wage Board, real wages were increased, and we may therefore say that compared with the previous decade there were definite indications of an advancement in real earnings as from the late fifties onwards.

(2) The Wage Board was responsible for most of the increases, which in certain cases ranged upwards of 30 per cent. Wage determinations made between 1959 and 1962 were much higher than those of subsequent years.

(3) Private employers also increased wages voluntarily and have often acted ahead of the Wage Board, e.g. in the case of sales tax in 1969.

(4) The increases in real wages of Africans seem to have had an unfavourable effect on African employment in the manufacturing sector.

# PART FIVE

# Who Benefits from Apartheid?

At long last here comes my skimpy answer to your searching questions.

1. The opening quotation in your note reminds me of a statement made by my principal in the course of a sermon one Sunday evening during my secondary school days in the latter half of the 1920s. He said: 'The battle of "if" has never been won.' He was commenting on some historian's reference to the outcome of the Battle of Waterloo, in reference to which he observed: 'Had it not rained that day, the history of Europe would have been otherwise.'

Unable to explain why at times the course of history took a different direction from that which it had been following, bourgeois historians have so often stood puzzled at what they regarded as the crossroads of history. But history has no crossroads. Yes, its course is marked by what we might liken to bends in the road when as a result of the interaction of forces which are beyond the control of individuals, things, as colloquially we say, take a different turn. It is amazing how bourgeois historians often lose sight of historical perspective and thus behave like a child whose milk tooth falls out while he is chewing some food and in despair and disappointment moans, 'If I had not eaten this meal I would not have lost my tooth.'

It is needless to say that the rain on that one day had very little or nothing to do with Napoleon's defeat, any more than the child lost its sweet tooth because it was chewing something. No, it was not lack of foresight or negligence on the part of the Russian bourgeoisie which opened the way for a victorious proletarian revolution.

To answer the question, Are the Imperialists and the national and petty bourgeoisie capable of solving the apartheid question?, let us examine, if in passing, the circumstances which led up to the

stage when apartheid came to mark a particular stage in the course
of our development.

2. With the discovery of diamonds and gold in the area now
known as the RSA began the influx of foreign capital and human
resources from the metropolitan countries. As a result of this
happening, two important developments took place as a corollary
that shaped the future social relations in the country.

Firstly, class stratification as it already existed then in Europe
was transplanted to the area: the capitalist class and the working
class came with the imported capital. Secondly, the African and
Afrikaner farming societies could not avoid or escape the disintegrating impact of an industrial economy. The process of
proletarianisation among them developed over time. Bourgeois
and petit bourgeois developed among them too.

As has been the practice in the vast areas of the world to which
capital was exported as Imperialism spread its tentacles, the
economy was divided roughly into two categories, viz the modern
money or market sector, and the subsistence section. By a combination of factors arising out of the Wars of Dispossession (with
which we need not deal here), the Africans were driven into the
subsistence sector. In spite of the fact that the Africans were
drawn in increasing numbers into the market section as wage-
earners and therefore as part of the working class, the capitalists
projected an image of the African as an undifferentiated mass that
belonged to the subsistence sector of the economy.

By this device they drew a line between black and white. The
white working class was led to believe that its living standards
were threatened by the competition of black labour, which was
satisfied with wages that kept its standard of living at the level
present in the subsistence economy. To perpetuate the practice of
paying a subsistence wage, bourgeois economists built the myth of
Africans working for short spells at a time if they earned a high
wage, and all this was wrapped up in technical language that lent a
professional touch and justification for some of the worst forms of
exploitation.

To ensure that their freedom to exploit the Africans was un-
interrupted, the capitalists erected a wall (the industrial colour
bar) between the black and white working class and raised it so
high that the white working class was virtually completely
alienated from the black working class. The capitalists entered
into agreements that placed the white working class on a separate

footing from the black working class. Consider as a typical example of this the agreement arrived at between the Chamber of Mines and the Mine Workers' Union from the time the Union of South Africa was formed in 1910.

The capitalists lost no time in ensuring that the bar erected in industry and accepted by the white working class was erected in all spheres where black and white could possibly have common interests: in politics, in religion, in social life and so on. Thus the relations between black and white came generally to be regulated under a policy of segregation. Under this policy the capitalists gained a free hand to employ masses of black labour in labour-intensive forms of production at bed-rock levels of wages and with the highest level of return to capital, i.e. of profit.

At various times, as a result of the struggle by the oppressed and exploited people, the segregation policy, under which both the Imperialists and the white* national bourgeoisie have waxed fat, has gone under different names according to the various stages of the struggle. The new names were often intended to hoodwink the oppressed into believing that the new name meant a change of policy for the better: now segregation, now separation or development along their own lines, now trusteeship, now apartheid, now separate development. Apartheid was the notable exception in that it did not seek to disguise what the National Party government intended to carry out under that policy, as was spelt out from time to time by the leading exponents of the policy. But each name represents a stage in the development of a policy designed to enable the Imperialists and the national bourgeoisie to batten onto the backs of the oppressed and exploited masses.

Who are the engineers of this ingenious plan? The Imperialists and the national bourgeoisie. Are they capable of solving the apartheid question? The answer must be sought in answering the question: is it rational to expect them to commit suicide for the sake of those whom they oppress and exploit?

3. From the foregoing section it will already be apparent what the nature of apartheid is. Apartheid, as a stage in the development

---

*It should be noted that in our reference to the national bourgeoisie we mean the white national bourgeoisie. It is necessarily so because for all practical purposes there is no bourgeoisie among Africans and coloureds and only an insignificant number is beginning to emerge among Indians. A clear understanding of this fact is very important to the Liberation Movement for the shaping of correct strategy and tactics in the fight against oppression and exploitation.

of a policy by means of which the ruling class has been tightening the screw of oppression, was first given expression after the end of World War Two. At first most people regarded it merely as an election slogan of the National Party, i.e. as being in the same category as others around which the National Party had before sought to rally the support of the white and especially the Afrikaner electorate, such as 'swartgevaar'.

But the South African public did not have long to wait before they realised that apartheid was not just another name in the course of the implementation of the policy of segregation, i.e. a name intended to sound sweet in the ears of the oppressed. Although historically it is a stage in the development of policies which had been pursued by previous governments, it marked the highest stage in that development and qualitatively a departure from the trodden path.

The war years had seen an upsurge in the demands of the oppressed for equal rights. In the face of this, as well as the unfavourable development in the conduct of the war, Smuts had declared that 'Segregation had fallen on evil days', and in the light of such developments he announced his intention to arm 'the natives' in defence of their common heritage. Furthermore, the Smuts government appointed a commission – the Fagan Commission – to inquire into the operation of pass laws with a view to recommending legislation to relax such laws. The commission came out with a report which held out a firm promise of the first steps towards a phasing out of racial oppression. But when the National Party came into power it declared apartheid, which many had regarded as merely an election slogan, as its basic policy. It therefore lost no time in giving it concrete form in a series of legislative measures that opened with the Suppression of Communism Act and the Bantu Authorities Act. Racism, as in Nazi Germany, assumed the importance of a philosophy; to wit, according to Strijdom: 'die wit man moet altyd baas wees' ['the white man must always be master']; and according to Verwoerd: 'The Bantu must not be led to believe that they can graze on the green pastures of the white man.' Thus, with the passing of the Suppression of Communism Act, apartheid represented a rallying point for its upholders against the working class. As the implementation of the National Party programme unfolded, the hideous face of fascism under the local label of apartheid came into view.

But we must yet briefly probe into the circumstances that gave rise to this short-circuiting move into fascism (which is by common consent regarded as the highest stage of capitalism), when in reality the South African economy only reached the 'take-off' stage during the World War Two years. That is, the local economy only then entered the stage of sustained growth marked by industrialisation on a broad front.

Before and up to the beginning of World War Two, the bourgeois class had largely been drawn from the English and Jewish minority sections of the whites. The Afrikaners who constituted the overwhelming majority of the whites had largely been confined to farming or had swelled the ranks of the working class. Although some of the leading Afrikaner intelligentsia had set up the Sanlam Insurance Co. in 1918 and Volkskas Commercial Bank in 1934, it was not until the war years that the Afrikaner working class rose in large numbers to the level of skilled workers and thus began to command high incomes. Taking advantage of this, both Sanlam and Volkskas embarked on a sustained campaign to collar the savings of the Afrikaner working class. And to do so they appealed to the nationalist sentiments of the Afrikaner working class, farmers and white-collar workers, to insure themselves in their own Sanlam, and to ensure the safety of their savings by depositing their savings in their own bank, Volkskas.

The huge funds which these two accumulated during the war years were quickly channelled into Afrikaner-owned enterprises: Federale Volksbeleggings, Bonuskor, Federale Mynbou (with varied interests on a wide front in the industrial, commercial and finance sections of the economy), the Rembrandt group, and a number of others that took advantage of the industrial decentralisation policy, e.g. in border areas like Rosslyn, Newcastle and elsewhere.

Thus the Afrikaner bourgeoisie had emerged, but to compete with the long-established English and Jewish interests was a tough proposition. To succeed required, among other things, that they should get control of certain areas where the Afrikaner bourgeoisie could operate with minimum competition. It was this desire which basically lay behind the National Party boycott campaigns in the late 1940s of Indian traders in the Transvaal countryside areas, and of Jewish traders in the Free State. But more important to them was control of state machinery, which they succeeded in doing with the return of the National Party to power in 1948.

Once in power, the National Party set out systematically to clear the decks for the advancement of Afrikaner bourgeois interests. The main source of labour, the Africans, had to be firmly controlled and regimented by the National Party government, which in the first instance used the state machinery to serve and advance the interest of the Afrikaner bourgeoisie. What African worker does not know the significance of 'Permitted to remain in the urban area of . . . while employed by . . .'? This appears in the *Dom Boek*. To ensure that absolute control, the Nationalist government used the Bantu Authorities Act, and subsequent legislation flowing from its implementation, to cut Africans from the body politic. Similar legislation was enacted for the coloured and Indian groups. It made a clear enunciation of its intentions in November 1955 when after a special session of the Transkei Bunga the government got that body to accept the Bantu Authorities Act, and all that that acceptance implied.

Analysing, in a series of articles in *Liberation* in 1957, the situation that had thus developed, the writer arrived at the conclusion that the Nationalist government had under the Bantu Authorities Act established an 'introverted colonialism'. In its programme adopted at the October 1962 conference, the SACP characterised the situation as 'colonialism of a special type'. If we bear in mind that the main export from such 'colonies' – the bantustans – was under complete control, what could the government do but to ensure that Afrikaner vested interests got the labour they required at the lowest rates? The Afrikaner bourgeoisie did not have to compete for this. Thus for the African the fight against apartheid is a struggle for physical survival. In turn the government employed its racist policies to hit coloureds and Indians in a variety of ways, e.g. the removal of coloureds from the common voters' roll, and their ultimate removal from the body politic; and the Group Areas Act. It also awarded fat contracts to Afrikaner interests; it used a big stick to silence all opposition from whatever source, black or white. All who did not approve of apartheid had to face the secret police – the SB – or keep quiet.

It is these shock tactics so similar to those used by the SS in Nazi Germany that Brian Bunting wrote about in his book *The Rise of the South African Reich*. Thus for those who value freedom, the fight against apartheid is in essence a struggle against fascism.

4. Are foreign investors behind the move to scrap apartheid? Let us throw the whole question into proper perspective. In

1958–59, the ANC took a decision firstly to call for an international boycott of South African products and, secondly, to call on foreign investors to discontinue investing in the country, and at the same time issued a warning that any foreign investment entering the country after that date would be nationalised outright and without compensation when the ANC took over government. The ANC took this decision after a careful study of the role foreign capital played in boosting the country's economy and therefore creating conditions which amounted to aiding the Nationalist government to carry out the implementation of apartheid. The importance of the role foreign capital played, and also how sensitive it is to any destabilising conditions, was shown in the early 1960s. Fearing an uprising after Sharpeville and Langa, foreign capital fled by the hundreds of millions. Subsequent exchange control measures taken to stem the outflow of capital have considerably shaken the confidence of foreign investors, and because South Africa relies heavily on foreign trade, anything that disrupts it and the movement of capital creates favourable conditions for discontent internally.

The emigration from this country in the 1960s of large numbers of people, who were persecuted by the Nationalist government, resulted mainly in the formation of the Anti-Apartheid Movement abroad, in which we play a leading role. The concerted campaigning by this movement over the years has awakened the peace-loving people throughout the world, and especially in the Imperialist camp in the countries of Western Europe, to the apartheid threat to peace internally and to the rest of the world. With their memories still fresh of the disastrous consequences of the failure to stem fascism in time, the working class in Europe are bringing pressure to bear on their governments and big foreign investors to disinvest in South Africa.

As would be expected, rather than succumb to these pressures, foreign investors are looking for ways to dampen revolutionary enthusiasm here at home by pressurising the national bourgeoisie to move towards the granting of some concessions which hopefully some sections among the oppressed would see as a move in the right direction. One of the ways adopted by foreign firms operating in the country has been to issue a general guide to their local managements to increase the wages of blacks at least to the effective minimum level, to promote them to the skilled work positions, and to relax discriminatory practices based on race in the work situation. As far as the question of investment is concerned, we see therefore that the answer of the national bourgeoisie operates in the same direction as the wishes of foreign investors. 'To beat apartheid, maintain a high level of investment to ensure a high level of economic activity,' says H.O. [Harry Oppenheimer], whose voice in this respect we may regard as representative of the point of view of the national bourgeoisie.

True, no government in the Imperialist camp can come out openly in support of apartheid today, and in fact they have expressed condemnation of it. Indeed, we owe a great deal, especially to the governments and people of the Netherlands (R21 million), Sweden (R6 million), Denmark and Norway (investments are shown in brackets behind ëach country). But what do the governments of big foreign investors say?

| | |
|---|---:|
| UK | R1 200 million |
| West Germany | R350 million |
| USA | R335 million |
| France | R50 million |
| Australia | R35 million |

Are they calling for a scrapping of apartheid, and to what extent is there a contradiction between foreign investors and the national bourgeoisie? To answer these questions, we must consider the factors that influence the decisions of the bourgeoisie in the Imperialist countries on important issues. This applies especially to the countries of Western Europe, West Germany, France and Italy, and in varying degrees to the UK and the US. The bourgeoisie who are the main force behind foreign investments have, since the end of World War Two, balanced uneasily on a tightrope. They live between two mortal fears: the fear of an uprising by the working class in their respective countries, on the one hand, and on the other, the fear of the spread of Communism and its gaining control in various areas of the world, especially in the developing countries.

It is therefore rational to expect that foreign investors would like to see, in the countries in which they invest, governments that welcome foreign investment and create favourable conditions in which such investments prosper. Such conditions include stable labour, i.e. where labour disputes are settled with the least disruption in production. In this respect South Africa is one of the most reliable and profitable investment areas. It is unlikely therefore that foreign investors and their governments would hastily do anything to undermine the authority of such a government.

But in so far as this government pursues the apartheid policy (which, throughout the world, is regarded as fascist with a strong accent on white race superiority), the Imperialists will seek to find solutions to remove this stigma. They regard the position in South Africa as a favourable ground to breed Marxist revolutionary ideas, whose spread they are determined to stem.

Herein lies the contradiction between foreign investors and the national bourgeoisie. The adoption and determined implementation of apartheid ensured suitable conditions for the growth of the Afrikaner bourgeoisie, and in spite of changing conditions they still support it and at best are only prepared to consider the relaxation of petty apartheid. The white working class, which is overwhelmingly Afrikaner, also still supports apartheid because of unearned benefits which they enjoy under an apartheid policy. For instance, the Nationalist government has so expanded the public sector that 35 per cent of the economically active whites are employed in this sector. The non-Afrikaner national bourgeois, too, have benefited from apartheid especially in so far as it guaranteed them unlimited supplies of cheap regimented labour. An example of their appreciation of this is the 30 per cent English and Jewish vote in support of the Nationalist government in the last elections. Afrikaner bourgeoisie have become strong enough to link up with the non-Afrikaner bourgeoisie, and are, in fact, more closely linked by class interests than divided by white ethnic considerations. The national bourgeoisie today stands united in relation to foreign investments. The South African Foundation which was established to defend South Africa abroad and to act as apologists of apartheid consists of white national bourgeoisie.

Although the national bourgeoisie are willing to effect some marginal changes in black labour conditions, such as have been included in recent labour legislation based on the Wiehahn Commission report, they are not going far enough to allay the fears of foreign investors. A number of measures are being taken, e.g. the relaxation of exchange controls to encourage a greater flow of foreign investments, which are declining. At the political level there is hardly a meaningful move to bring about changes that blunt the contradication between foreign investors and the national bourgeoisie.

As far as the extent to which we can exploit the contradictions between foreign and national capital interests is concerned, this is a matter which is being handled effectively by the Organisation outside. What measures are taken, other than military ones, are matters which the comrades, who are in contact with the developing and fluid situation, are in the best position to examine and apply.

Fraternal greetings to all comrades.

*Amandla! Matla!*

# A Note on the Comment
# on the Paper on Apartheid

But for the fact that you specifically asked me to comment on your Note, I do not think I would have found it very necessary to do so. I might probably have sent word to say: Thank you. You preface your comment, on my Note to SOM, with a clearly set out statement of the premises on the basis of which you proceed to set out your views on my Note to SOM. A long time has elapsed since you did this, and in case you have by now forgotten, it is worthwhile reproducing it: 'We, the people of South Africa, black and white, in the liberation struggle are, through the joint strategy of our political organisations (the ANC, SACP, SAIC, CPC, COD) our trade union organisations (SACTU), our political party (SACP), our military organisation (MK) and many others of our institutions engaged in a revolutionary struggle to seize power from the present minority dominant class, the bourgeoisie and its henchmen, into the hands of the present immense majority of the dominated classes, the proletariat, the peasantry and the general masses of the oppressed of all races and colours.'

Comprehensive! I may probably in the course of my comments have a word or two on this.

I like your forward-looking approach. In a revolutionary struggle one cannot and should not expect to muster the support of the masses of the oppressed and exploited by pointing to beacons that have been passed along the road. Our finger must point forward to a horizon, to a goal to strive for with all the resources available to us, with all our might. We are in a very happy position that the National Liberation Movement is spearheaded by the ANC in alliance with the CP. It is almost a unique relationship and provides a suitable climate, which makes it relatively easier to conduct a politico-educational campaign. This climate provides an opportunity to enlighten those among the oppressed who, as you say, are still confused about the nature of the democracy we are striving to establish. For this task we require on the part of our comrades, the patience of a conscientious class teacher who does not judge the overall progress of the class by the attainment of the above-average pupils, but by the progress of those on the lower levels of attainment. That requires patience and hard work, and we are capable of both.

The Organisation has clearly stated the objective, viz that after overthrowing apartheid we aim at establishing a Democratic People's Republic. This has implications the appreciation of which must call forth greater resourcefulness on the part of our advance guard. The next question that springs to mind is: what will be the relative strength of the classes in such a situation? And what must we do to ensure that the Party of the working class is in a strong enough position to assume the responsibilities it will be called upon to fulfil, if the fruits of revolution will not be lost at that stage when the capitalist vested interests, using bourgeois aspirants from the masses of the oppressed, will use every trick to gain ascendancy?

It appears to me we should also bear in mind and be on guard for an eventuality whereby the government may seek to avoid a final reckoning by military means. What if the contending forces should be forced by the concrete facts of the situation to resort, at some stage, to seeking a settlement by negotiations? In the light of known facts about the existing organisational groupings and their interests, I think we are entitled to forecast what the situation would be. And this is no idle exercise. If the Nationalist government found itself compelled to yield to a combination of pressures, and thus rather than fight to the end, decides to convene a national convention to discuss the future of the country, it is not difficult to visualise what would happen. A number of organisations would come forward claiming representation. And presto!, like the Holy Ghost descending on Pentecost Day, what a babel of tongues would be there! (Such as I witnessed many years back in Rev. Chiliza's Full Gospel Church along Mngeni Road in Durban, when suddenly the whole congregation was up dancing, shouting in a medley of tongues.) Other than delegations drawn from the ruling class parties, there would be PAC, BPC, APDUSA, AZAPO, Labour Party, the Freedom Party, Gatsha and his ilk, 'moderates' of all description, NAFCOC and similar business organisations amongst coloureds and Indians, etc. The PFP which represents the powerful interests of monopoly capital is angling for such a situation. It hopes that the white bourgeois parties would forge a real 'unity' of all anti-working-class interests, irrespective of racial origin or colour of the skin. Such developments, which we must watch carefully, are taking shape. In November 1979 the Prime Minister, P.W. Botha, convened a conference at which he sought to bring about a closer working together between the public sector (government) and the private sector. He assured the latter of the government's determination to foster private free enterprise, and simultaneously announced a plan for a Constellation of States in Southern Africa. High-sounding words, behind which lurk the forces of monopoly capital determined as ever before to advance their interests under this smokescreen. In a piecemeal fashion, indications are being thrown out of the 'benefits' the petit bourgeois from the ranks of the oppressed should expect as the 'plan' is being implemented. A 'Multi-state Development Bank' is to be set up to provide credit facilities for small business. To facilitate the realisation of this objective, all bantustans are advised to seek 'independence'.

In welcoming the government move to bring about a partnership between the public and private sectors, Nicholas Oppenheimer, Harry Oppenheimer's son, dangles a bunch of carrots and says if the 'plan' is to be a success, 'A new economic regime, with significant social and economic and ultimately political implications, is called for,' but 'a precondition of success must be employment in, and indeed a vested interest for all in, the free enterprise system' – i.e. capitalism.

What must make it easier for the 'plan' to succeed is the fact that Afrikaner and English alike are wedded to capitalism, and both groups are sharing business opportunities on such a scale that Nicholas Oppenheimer made bold to say with no fear of contradiction that 'by no stretch of the imagination can business any longer be thought of as the exclusive domain of a particular tribe'.

The impact of this pronouncement in the context in which it appears is obvious. The Afrikaner and the English business interests should seek common solutions to the problems of the country based on class and not racial groups. If the Afrikaner and the English would go into such a consultation/conference with an agreed strategy, it does not require much foresight to forecast the effect of their concerted action on such political organisations from the ranks of the oppressed as would be represented there. The offer: 'A new economic regime with significant social . . . and political implications . . . and a vested interest for all in the free enterprise system.'

The price to pay for this: all, black and white, must join hands in the fight against 'Communism' and in fact against the interests of the masses of the oppressed and exploited people to ensure a new lease of life for monopoly capital. The difference being that monopoly capital will have drawn into its service sections of the oppressed who will go out to the oppressed to preach the dawn of a new era of fulfilment of hope and promise for them. But even after considering, as briefly as we have done, this second option to which the ruling class may resort, we are back to the question: what must we do to ensure that the Party of the working class is in a strong enough position to take over power at the crucial moment and set up socialism?

At the beginning of your Note you complain that my Note was full of 'provocative assertions, hints and undeveloped points' which have set your mind athinking. Blame my training as a teacher, which was entrenched in my mind by having to teach others to be teachers. One of the most important lessons in Psychology of Education and in School Method was the injunction to draw the answers from the pupils. They should work out answers from hints thrown out. When I write I so often forget that my position is no longer that of a teacher. But in our political work I have found the approach fruitful. It sparks off discussion and a search for a solution. In what follows in Section IV of your Note you and I are largely in agreement.

I need now only comment briefly on the question you pose as to whether there is any similarity between the statement by Dobb on industrial capital's 'internal colonial policy' in Europe and our characterisation of the policy of apartheid as it applies to Africans in particular as 'introverted colonialism' and 'colonialism of a special type'. Everywhere in the process of the development of capitalism or of the industrial sector, the agricultural sector has fulfilled the following key functions:

(1) For the rising industrial economy it has provided agricultural raw materials on terms of trade which are loaded in favour of the industrial (manufacturing) sector. At a stage when few foreign exchange assets have been built up or few colonial possessions have been acquired to provide such raw materials at low prices, industrial capital relies for its supplies of agricultural raw materials on domestic agriculture. Thus in the absence of colonies

it applied policies which otherwise would have been applicable to the colonies.

(2) Agriculture provides food for the masses of people who in the process of capital accumulation are displaced from the land and forced to rely for their living on wage labour as does the proletariat in the urban areas.

(3) The rising capitalist class and their governments did not hesitate to resort to controlling measures to prod agriculture to produce at least enough food to support the local market in order to avoid importation of food and finding foreign exchange to pay for it, at a stage of economic development when exports and markets had not been adequately developed.

Thus the relationship between agriculture and industrial capital was a phase – a passing phase – in the evolutionary development of capitalism.

On the contrary, the creation of bantustans – at a stage when the South African economy was already well developed with a well-established industrial capital sector, export sector and export markets, and an agricultural sector that was but one of the sectors of the overall economy – aimed at cutting the Africans off from the main economic stream. It was an exercise at creating areas within the broader national economy which would have a permanently established Lazarus–Dives relationship. In other words, for the Africans apartheid seeks to reverse the forward process of economic development. It does so not because it expects peasant farming in the bantustans to play the role which agriculture played in the course of capital accumulation, but to supply the one important factor which creates value, viz labour – unlimited supplies of labour. Apartheid creates 'introverted colonialism'; 'colonialism of a special type'.

A couple of years back I prepared a paper on the peasant question. If you have time and the paper is still available it may be pertinent to refer to the section that deals with the part African farm labourers played in the development of white agriculture.

All I may now add by way of emphasis is this: to attain the goals you have spelt out so well requires a strong working-class party – the CP – strong in members and single-minded of purpose. This, of course, does not suggest that in the process of building and strengthening itself and its position, it would allow its relationship with Inqindi and other allies in the Congress movement, as well as any others that may crop up, to suffer. On the contrary as the situation becomes more fluid and the Nationalist government seeks in a desperate hurry to shore up the disintegrating apartheid structure, the Party and its allies should step up the pressure and give the Nationalist government no breathing space until it collapses.

*'Dici'* (I have spoken), frequently would Cicero so end his orations in the Roman Senate, even when it was no more than a whirlwind of words.

# A Discussion Document (3/B)

## GENERAL APPROACH

1. In the situation that has arisen the most important thing and, therefore, priority number one is to ensure that two views do not become rallying points around which two groups may form. It should be stressed that this is nothing more than a political discussion in which there may be differences of views which should not be allowed to become a dividing line. If anything, there should emerge at the end a clearer understanding of certain issues now in question. In that way the discussion will have borne fruit.

2. It would appear the sharp reaction sparked off by the document (1/B) calls firstly for a self-critical examination on the part of the authors. The question must arise: what did they set out to do and why? In attempting to do that, did they not go beyond the scope of what they sought to do? In dealing with the policy as enshrined in the Freedom Charter (FC), was there any justification for giving their own interpretation of what the Freedom Charter aims to achieve?

3. It seems to me before we venture out to examine the main issues raised by commentators on the original document, we must answer the questions posed above. It is only after we have done this that we could be in a position squarely, and in a manner that may be convincing to others, to be able to answer questions that stem from statements made in the documents.

4. We must concede that in drawing the document, the authors acted on information from an individual; that while our youth concentrates on the study of Marxism they did not know much about the national liberation struggle and were in fact placed at a disadvantage in discussions with their counterparts in other organisations here. If we had, before writing the document, sought first information from the proper channels – D.C. – the

problem might have been posed in a less alarming manner or the
D.C. might have taken steps itself to correct any imbalance in the
political education programme in their syllabus. The document,
being based on a report, which on the face of things is not borne
out by facts, went further than just recommending to the D.C. to
make the desired adjustments in their education programme.
It bypassed the D.C. and directed its message to the general
membership, by way of not only drawing attention to the
imbalance in the political education programme, but launched
into an explanation and interpretation of policy. By so doing the
document went much further than what the authors had originally
set out to do.

By failing to observe the correct procedure and going beyond
the scope of what was intended to be done, the authors have erred.
It seems to me this error must be conceded, if not to right the
present situation, at least to warn us for the future.

5. On the question of whether the Liberation Movement
favours capitalism or socialism, the Freedom Charter is silent, and
for those of us who have been in jail for the greater part of two
decades – '60s and '70s – this matter has not arisen as an issue. It has
all been for the better that the position has remained like that
because in our circumstances we are not in one way or another in a
position to influence the direction of the Liberation Movement
outside. To the extent that the document expressed itself specifically on a matter in which the Freedom Charter is itself silent is
unfortunate. The document correctly points out: 'the central
point to bear in mind is that the Congresses provide a home for all
shades of political opinion . . . nationalists, conservatives and
progressives, capitalists and communists . . .'. It must be conceded
as a slip-up that, contrary to their advice, the authors of the
document should state categorically the Freedom Charter's bias
for capitalism; a fact which must be expected to raise alarm on the
part of those who are committed to a struggle against capitalism.
The 'central point to bear in mind' is to keep together the diverse
forces in the Liberation Movement to fight for the overthrow of
fascism. Issues that would arouse differences among the diverse
forces should, therefore, not be given prominence, nor even be
raised where the guiding policy is itself silent.

6. Having made these concessions, what the authors set out
primarily to do must yet be clarified. We must however, first give
attention to some of the issues raised in the various documents.

## BOURGEOIS DEMOCRACY OR PEOPLE'S DEMOCRACY

7.  On the question of bourgeois democracy (BD) the document cites the programme of the CP as a source which is alleged to say 'the CP expressly welcomes the Freedom Charter as a progressive step towards a bourgeois democratic republic'.

8.  The central issue around which the controversy has come to rage is whether the Liberation Movement (as consisting of the ANC with its open membership, the various Congresses and the CP in so far as it supports the Freedom Charter) aspires to set up a people's democracy or a bourgeois democracy. Two documents and the main body of opinion in the third claim the people of South Africa are engaged in a national struggle against the National Party fascist regime. A victorious struggle will usher in a people's democracy – a grey-dawn state between capitalism at its highest and final stage and the emergence of socialism. The other view expressed in two documents (F/24 and F/12) supports Document 1/B and states that a successful liberation struggle will usher in a bourgeois democracy. Both views claim their conclusions to be the correct projections of policy as based on the Freedom Charter.

9.  Now for a brief examination of 1/B, F/24 and F/12. In 1/B it is stated that it is the programme of the CP, which regards the Freedom Charter as a 'step towards bourgeois democracy'. Here, therefore, there is no claim made that the Congresses have come out specifically or by implication to state what they aim to set up, beyond what is expressed by and stated in the ten clauses of the Freedom Charter. But if read together with other interpretations of the charter, e.g. 'the Freedom Charter is based on the principle of private enterprise' (i.e. capitalism), and 'the clause that demands nationalisation is an exception in an economy that allows individual ownership', then one would be hard put not to come to the conclusion that apart from what the CP programme is stated to say, the aim of the Freedom Charter, which is based on the principle of private enterprise, is not to establish a bourgeois democracy. Taken to its logical conclusion this interpretation would imply that if the demands of the Freedom Charter were met by any white minority government the Congresses would require no more than that whether political power was in their hands or not.

10.  In F/24 as well as F/12 the position is put categorically that the 1963 programme of the CP states that the Freedom Charter would establish a bourgeois democratic society whose 'nature will be such that it will give the working class a good base from which

to continue the socialist revolution'. There is something of a paradox here: that in order to pave its way for a thrust into socialism, the CP must encourage the demobilisation of the forces that have overthrown national and class oppression so that those forces may themselves become capitalists in place of their former capitalist oppressors. And who is it intended to persuade to believe that such an arrangement 'will give the working class a good base from which to continue the socialist revolution'?

At this point the question arises whether, in fact, the CP is cooperating with the Liberation Movement in order to induce into capitalism (bourgeois democracy) new candidates from the ranks of the oppressed? In the South African situation, where are such candidates to find the materials to build themselves such capitalist castles? For all the floods that have flowed under the bridge, one cannot recall that the CP programme sees the Freedom Charter as 'a progressive step towards a bourgeois democracy'. Rather would one expect that the CP would regard the strengthening and reinforcing of capitalism at the end of the struggle for national liberation, as a retrograde step, rather than a progressive one.

In quoting Mao (pages 10–11) F/24 states that he 'describes the nature of the revolution in China as being to bring about bourgeois democratic changes but not to set up a socialist state'. Well and good! But Mao does not say the nature of the Chinese revolution is to establish a bourgeois democracy. What then must we understand by bourgeois changes? It means to bring about such reforms as will place all the sections of the population on the same footing with respect to the enjoyment of rights as they were denied before the liberatory revolution was victorious. But the bringing about of such reforms does not necessarily mean, more particularly where the liberatory revolution is led by the working-class party, that the liberatory revolution aims at setting up a bourgeois democracy, i.e. a capitalist state. In citing the revolution in China, and those mounted by anti-fascists fronts in Eastern Europe, F/24 states that people's democracies were set up both in Eastern Europe and in China. With the anti-fascist revolution here which is led by the working class, the CP and progressive intelligentsia, why should it not be expected that after liberation the struggle of the people will not have been hoisted to a position above capitalism in its naked brutality, though not to socialism as was the case in China and Eastern Europe? The Freedom Charter itself opens its preamble thus: 'We the people of South Africa . . .' and the opening article says: 'The People shall govern'. How much more is required to elucidate what the Freedom Charter aims at setting up? It restores to the people their rightful place – a people's democracy; and not to a section of the people – the bourgeoisie – a bourgeois democracy.

From reading the documents, everybody is agreed that for the plunge to socialism it is the CP that will lead the overwhelming majority of the population, the working class and the peasantry.

On page 13, F/24 trips and is thrown into confusion, in which a people's democracy and bourgeois democracy are synonymous. Referring to the popular fronts in China, Eastern Europe and presumably at home, he states: 'The objectives of all these fronts were (and are) freedom from fascism and the establishment of a National Democracy in which all the people irrespective of class or creed, would be involved. That is in fact the logical meaning of bourgeois democracy'. Needless to say, that is what bourgeois democracy is not, and what people's democracy is.

In conclusion, F/24 switches over from its support of the bourgeois democracy interpretation, which it has become clear it has never understood in the same light that 1/B and F/12 do. On page 13–14, F/24 cites Lenin on the question of imperialism and monopoly capital as saying: 'The working class (party) should strengthen its position at the head of the national liberation struggle against colonialism and at the same time against imperialist exploitation.' Following Leninist teaching and in support of it, F/24 concludes: 'This has been the essence of our national liberation struggle ever since it emerged at the end of the last century. It has also been the basis of the unity of purpose between Inqindi and CP.' With that F/24 drives the last nail to seal the coffin of a bourgeois democracy being the aim of the Freedom Charter.

11.   Let us now examine briefly how realistic it is, in the South African situation, to expect the forces lined up against the fascist regime to work for the establishment of a bourgeois democracy. We do not have to examine closely the composition of the membership of Inqindi and that of its allies to observe that it consists in overwhelming numbers of the working class. This trend has been increasingly so more particularly since the fifties when the Nationalist government embarked on a sustained programme of repression. Add to this the fact that the population group from which such membership is drawn has no significant rentier class which has large accumulations of idle funds that are

looking for opportunities of investment. The wages of Africans, for instance, as has been established by survey after survey, are barely above the poverty datum line, i.e. the lowest level at which the worker can barely manage to pay for the barest necessities of life for himself and his family. This refers to those employed in the secondary and tertiary sectors of the economy. If we bear in mind that 'in 1970 only 58 per cent of the economically active African men held jobs in sectors other than agriculture and domestic service' we shall realise that with the best will in the world this section of the working class cannot be in a position to invest, not to mention the 42 per cent employed in agriculture and domestic service. In the September 1977 issue of the *South African Journal of Economics*, H.J. Reynders, dealing with 'Black (African) Industrial Entrepreneurship', points out that Africans are particularly lacking in capital and entrepreneurship. He goes on to say: 'In both the Homeland and the urban townships the practice of home crafts, handicrafts and home industries still prevails.' Against this background, to encourage or support the establishment of the bourgeois democracy would in reality amount to the perpetuation of the control of the economy by capitalists drawn from a white minority which is running the bourgeois democracy that presently prevails in the country. It is inconceivable that the Freedom Charter could be aiming at the establishment of a bourgeois democracy other than the one that exists when the people whose policy document it is have not got the means to turn such a bourgeois democracy to their advantage. In short, they have not got the capital to make capitalists of themselves. Without basing himself on the policy of the Liberation Movement, Reynders, executive director of the FCI, shows himself as having his finger on the pulse of the oppressed when he says, 'We [would] do well to take cognisance of the feeling among some Blacks that the Free Enterprise system is to blame for the plight in which they find themselves. This is a tragedy, and a further deterioration in Black attitudes towards the Free Enterprise system might well result in its disintegration in the only part of southern Africa in which the system is soundly based' (p. 242).

If the Freedom Charter does not stipulate expressly that it aims at fighting capitalism, there is no implication in it either that it aims at saving capitalism from disintegration, an end which Reynders, an avowed supporter of apartheid, sees as inevitable given the prevailing conditions.

12. If the statement in 1/B that 'The clause that demands nationalisation of mines, financial institutions and other monopoly industries is an exception to the rule in an economy that allows individual ownership' were a correct policy interpretation of what will happen after the triumph of the people's struggle for liberation, that would mean that the victorious liberation forces would reverse, much to the advantage of the captains of private enterprise in the present capitalist set-up, a trend which presently points to increased nationalisation. In a review of A.D. Wassenaar's book *Assault on Private Enterprise: The Freeway to Communism*, Wassenaar is quoted as saying that the public sector has become so big that 'in 1960 it was estimated that 30 per cent of all economically active white persons were employed in the public sector; 6 years later this had increased to 35 per cent'. It goes on to say that in fact the public sector has become so big that 'it has become well-nigh impossible to trace the ramifications of State enterprise which have already permeated the economy along a broad front' (Sept 1977, *SAJE*, p. 285).

For what good reason would a people's government – a government that is pledged to rule in the interests of more than 4/5ths of the people who have through blood and bitter struggle shed oppression – wish to reverse the process of nationalisation?

13. It is important to emphasise that outside the areas presently occupied by state enterprise (nationalised areas) and monopoly industry and finance, there is only room for small businesses sharing a limited market. A recent commission report on an enquiry into the Monopolistic Conditions Act and study on the concentration of economic power in the South African manufacturing industry by P.G. du Plessis states that a high measure of concentration (i.e. degree of monopoly à la Kalecki) is shown in a summary of statistics 'which reveal that in the manufacturing, wholesale and retail, construction and transportation sections, 10 per cent of the firms control, at least, 74,6 per cent of their respective markets'. The commission concludes that 'Economic power is largely concentrated in a relatively few hands, and that by international comparison an exceptionally high degree of concentration of economic power prevails'.

If nationalisation of such enterprises were to be 'an exception to the rule', that would mean taking off the hook a large number of monopolists who use a variety of sophisticated techniques to effect monopoly: take-overs, mergers, pyramiding. If a victorious

185

people's revolution relaxes, instead of stepping up, nationalisation as envisaged in the nationalisation clause, it will have thrown away the main instrument in its hand to control the economy, for the benefit of the erstwhile oppressed as provided for in another clause of the Freedom Charter. To relax this clause to provide for individual ownership would be tantamount to sacrificing the interests of the overwhelming majority for an insignificant minority – bourgeois democracy – what a price!

One must go further and express the hope that when the opportune time comes Inqindi will carry out a decision it publicly announced in 1959. Then Inqindi called upon foreign investors not to support and strengthen the apartheid regime by continuing to invest in the country. The announcement warned that when Inqindi took over it would nationalise all foreign investments made after that public warning. Nationalisation on a big scale is the only meaningful way in which the victorious liberation forces through their own people's government in a people's democracy could control the existing resources to the immediate benefit of the millions of the oppressed and exploited masses in our country.

## THE LIMITS OF THE FREEDOM CHARTER

14. That the Freedom Charter is a policy document as well as a programme which sets out clearly the main objectives of the National Liberation Movement seems to be clearly understood and accepted by all the contributors to the current discussion. To the extent that it is thus understood and accepted, so is the distinction between Inqindi and Marxism understood.

If we understand policies in general to 'represent the totality of standards or norms that govern the conduct of people in an organisation' there should be no difficulty in realising the fact that over time advances take place in thinking and application of policy. Such advances in thinking and application as a result of changing circumstances may result in policy variations. Keeping an eye on changing conditions, our leadership outside (external and internal) will from time to time make statements which have the effect of varying policy in certain respects; e.g. about twenty years ago the demand for the calling of a national convention was such a powerful weapon in the hand of the Liberation Movement that the government was placed on the defensive. Today the conditions are such that the Liberation Movement rejects this call when made by the agents of imperialism because it is intended to dilute the demands of the Liberation Movement, which alone are a true reflection of the aspirations of the oppressed masses in this country. The statement by O.R. [Tambo] that they are troubled by reformists and that the Organisation aims at the seizure of power becomes plain. With the victory of the present struggle, political control must pass from a government that rules in order to further only the interests of the capitalists to one that is representative of the people: 'The People shall govern.'

It must be borne in mind that race oppression as well as all other forms of oppression are born of class conflict, in which the dominant class – the capitalist class – seeks to keep the masses of the people, mainly the working class, in a position where they will serve the interests of the capitalists. With the victory of the liberation struggle against the various forms of oppression, the liberation forces will have weakened the capitalists and tipped the scales vis-à-vis the capitalists in favour of the oppressed. We see, therefore, that the last word on the Freedom Charter is not yet said. The struggle is hoisted to a higher level when the people's government (i.e. a government representative of the forces that have won the liberation struggle) must remain in power to enforce the Freedom Charter in a milieu in which a people's democracy is the order of the day. At this stage the bourgeois economic order has not been changed but the people's government controls it to the benefit of the people.

## THE PLACE OF OTHER POLITICAL GROUPS

15.  The correct assessment of the role played by other political organisations outside the Inqindi alliance is a matter that can be arrived at after careful observation and study over time. Sometimes new organisations spring up when its founders believe that the old organisation has become a fetter restraining the people's ability to strike the enemy. This was the case in Zambia when UNIP sheered off from the ANC and successfully led the struggle for independence. When Impama [PAC] came into being its founders believed that Inqindi's ability to fight the Nationalist government regime was hampered by factors outside itself. But the growing strength of Inqindi has belied the hopes of the founders of Impama, which has now become bedevilled by fragmentation into splinter groups. The Abamnyama [Black Consciousness organisations], with BPC as their central political pillar, claim also that their line is the surest road along which to

lead the oppressed to freedom. All these streams in varying degrees receive support from the masses of the oppressed.

As the struggle takes a sharp upward turn and pressures from many fronts increase, as is the case here today, a motley crop of organisations springs up like mushrooms after a thunderstorm. All seek to cash in — some hope to forge links with the more 'enlightened elements' to establish a government that will bring about reforms that suit their interests most, e.g. the merchant classes. Others link up with political organisations that have strong links with the far-flung imperialist forces, e.g. the Blackists. Yet others will see in the long-standing oppressive regime an invincible force with which they must seek accommodation, e.g. the bantustan rabble. Before categorising these political groups, we should take careful observation and study. Among them there may be people who genuinely believe they are acting in the best interests of the oppressed. It may pay better dividends painstakingly to show how the road they are following can only end up to the disadvantage of the oppressed on the basis of pointing out the correct line.

## CONCLUSION

16. The programme of the CP correctly sees the Freedom Charter as a progressive step towards the establishment of a National Democratic Republic, and not a bourgeois democracy. The premise of a bourgeois democracy cannot be sought, therefore, in either the CP programme or the Freedom Charter. The stand taken in 1/F as well as in A and E is the only rational basis on which the close relationship between Inqindi and the CP can be explained. In conducting political education it is important that a study of both Marxism and the liberation struggle should receive due consideration. And it is important that attention should again be directed at arming the young comrades with as much theoretical knowledge as will prepare them for the task ahead.

# Supplement to 3/B

*INTRODUCTION*

1. First one must point out an irregularity that is dismaying. The units were instructed to discuss the various documents and submit their views, from which the HO [High Organ]* would compile a representative comment on polemic. As units, at least some of them, got down to this task, a three-man group set about drafting a reply without canvassing views of membership. At least three units submitted their considered views. But Section now orders units to discuss the draft of the three-man committee and submit their comments.

If HO wants to issue a representative comment on polemic, it must build on views of membership. The manner in which this matter is handled is, to say the least, unsatisfactory. The membership cannot feel involved in this exercise.

2. In dealing with issues of such importance as have been raised in the various documents it is important that all matters which tend to cloud the main issues, and whose exclusion from replying documents would not detract from their argument, should not be brought in. The first 8 to 10 pages of the draft paraphrase the various documents, and in doing so an opportunity is given for replying arguments to say they have been misrepresented. If statements which appear in documents are to be used, they should be correctly quoted in the course of the argument. A paraphrased version allows too much room for subtle insinuations to bring more to the surface the paraphraser's viewpoint. If this is detected by the scanning reader against whom the slant is intended, it can only result in a boomerang effect, viz undermining confidence on the part of the reader in the draftsmen.

---

*The High Organ provides the leadership echelon for the membership of the ANC in all the sections.

**Wherein lies the difference?**

3. The point in 1/B which gave rise to the polemic was what would happen after a victorious struggle for national liberation. The document 1/B visualised the continued existence of a bourgeois democracy in which the objectives of the Freedom Charter would be put into practice. Whether this view was taken from what was believed to have been stated in the CP programme or was accepted to be what the Freedom Charter expressly stated, does not make any difference.

The other point of view led by 1/F saw the triumph of the struggle for national liberation as terminating the control of a bourgeois democracy and its replacement by a people's democracy – a transitory phase from which the CP would lead the working class into socialism.

One question is: where does this draft stand in relation to the one point of view or the other, i.e. 1/B or 1/F?

4. The draft concedes two points which were raised in 1/B, viz the reference to bourgeois democracy as coming from the CP programme is incorrect and that a bourgeois democracy which will be set up when the Freedom Charter is being implemented will pave the way for the CP to launch into socialism.

In conceding the point so far as the programme of the CP is concerned, the draftsmen do so with their tongues in cheek. They state that for purposes of the present discussion we shall assume that the programme of the CP does not say so and that in place of bourgeois democracy, it says a national democracy. In other words, except for our assumption for purposes of the present discussion the CP programme in fact says 'the Freedom Charter is a progressive step towards setting up a bourgeois democracy'. With this reasoning one must expect that with all other facts and assumptions remaining unchanged, a bourgeois democracy and national democracy must be interchangeable concepts. And in reality that is what takes place in this draft – a situation in which F/24 found himself.

Various economic arguments raised in various and varying contexts in the body of the draft, show that the draft has not departed from the contention in 1/B that the Freedom Charter aims at setting up a bourgeois democracy or, presumably, at supporting the present one if it should accommodate the liberatory forces by granting the demands set out in the Freedom Charter. In the circumstances the bourgeois democracy/national democracy as seen by the draftsmen seems to be poles apart from the people's democracy/national democracy as seen by the people's democracy school and supporters.

5.   It is difficult to imagine that in fact the draftsmen visualise a situation in which after the struggle for liberation has been won, the liberatory forces could find some accommodation with the bourgeoisie to implement the Freedom Charter. Can anybody realistically expect the bourgeoisie to man the scaffold to hang themselves by nationalising banks, monopoly industry and finance houses? On page 20 the draftsmen say: 'The Freedom Charter will take away from private enterprise the power of exploitation, and a public sector will emerge which will strive to promote .the welfare of all people. The controls exercised by the State over the other industries and trade will check the rise of new monopolies and strengthen the roots of the new democracy.'

If the South African economy or 'bourgeois democracy is of a special type' because it has deviated from the path of 'a classical bourgeois democracy', where in the capitalist world do they find an economy that answers to the four characteristics of 'pure competition' – the only situation in which 'capitalism among Africans would flourish'?

7.   Many enlightening arguments have been advanced to show that in fact if the National Liberation Movement was to set up a bourgeois democracy after freedom it would be to entrench capitalism to the detriment of the oppressed. This is contrary to the claim that when the 'Freedom Charter is implemented' (page 16), which means after a victorious struggle for liberation, 'capitalism among Africans would flourish as never before. For the first time since conquest they would have the right to own freehold land, factories, commercial establishments and to form all kinds of companies . . . the realisation of the Freedom Charter would open up all the fresh fields for a prosperous African population of all classes, including the middle class'.

The Africans before have had the right to own these things. In a number of cases they have exercised that right. They have owned freehold land, they have set up commercial establishments, e.g. freehold farms in the Eastern Cape, commercial establishments there, freehold properties in the towns of the Eastern Cape. The question to be asked is how these slipped out of the hands of African ownership decades before the Group Areas Act and before there was any law to force Africans to part with such properties. The answer is the poverty of the Africans. The African-owned farms in the East London, King, Peddie, Komgha, Stutterheim, Queenstown and Glen Grey areas were bought over by whites over time because the owners had no means to invest in the farms for profitable production; they sold underdeveloped properties in the towns because they could not build on them; commercial establishments failed for lack of funds to run them and others switched over to running boarding homes (coffee shops). What prospects are there now to support the statement that with the implementation of the Freedom Charter 'capitalism among Africans would flourish'?

8. On the basis of empirical evidence and the direction of the trend with regard to the African share of non-wage income, the prospects for the growth of a big capitalist class among Africans are bleak in the foreseeable future. (We are concentrating on analysing the African position to meet the argument of the draftsmen — not that the position class-wise is very different for coloureds and Indians, although it is slightly better.)

What name do the draftsmen give to this 'new democracy' whose public sector (i.e. the government sector) 'will promote the welfare of all the people'? A bourgeois democracy/national democracy, as they see it, aims to advance the interest of 'private enterprise', in other words, the interests of a class — the capitalist class — and not that of 'all the people'. Herein lies their dilemma: the class in a bourgeois democracy framework, or the people in a people's democracy/national democracy framework (where 'national' means with all barriers of race or any other group interests pulled down).

## ECONOMIC REALITIES IN SOUTH AFRICA

6. In putting forward the point for a bourgeois democracy, this school does not seem to take into account economic structural developments that have been taking place over the years throughout the capitalist economy and in South Africa, especially, in the post-World War Two period. As a result the draft persists in visualising a situation in which after a victorious struggle for national liberation, the decks will have been cleared for 'capitalism among Africans to flourish as never before' (page 16). The draft sees the bourgeois democracy in South Africa (page 12) in which 'nationalisation of commanding heights' occurs, as a deviation from a 'classical bourgeois democracy'. It therefore sees the

' South African 'bourgeois democracy as of a special type', simply because there is nationalisation on an increasing scale.

This means that the draftsmen still entertain in their own minds the idea(s) of a 'golden era' in which there will be restored 'perfect competition' after attainment of freedom through a struggle in which political power will have been wrenched by the liberatory forces out of the hands of the capitalists. And so they would like to see the restoration of the economic ideas of what Marx, more than a century ago, referred to as the 'classical school' because then it was so out of step with reality. Thinking among bourgeois economists themselves had by the 1920s undergone such transformation that by 1933 Joan Robinson and Chamberlin had, independently of each other, published books to debunk the idea of 'classical bourgeois' economics, viz pure or perfect competition, whose characteristics were (a) homogeneity of product among the sellers; (b) many sellers of the product, i.e. enough sellers so that no one is large enough relative to the entire market to influence product price; (c) an absence of artificial restraints on demand, supply and product price; and (d) mobility of goods and resources.

On page 25 of the draft appear the following statements: 'A small class of rich African farmers (in the bantustans) is emerging whose outlook is capitalistic', and in the urban areas 'a top layer of well-to-do black workers is emerging who are investing in 99-year leases, motor cars, refrigerators, television,' etc. The draft is overrating the recent upward movement of African wages. Although they have used these developments in a different context, they remain the only basis on which buoyant hopes for building capitalism among Africans may be justified.

Making allowances for the increases in African wages as from 1974, let us examine the position. Of the economically active population, Africans constituted 70 per cent. Of the labour force in the modern sector they constitute 72 per cent and it is estimated they will form 75 per cent by the year 2000. This shows that more and more Africans are joining the ranks of the working class, which, as experience shows throughout the capitalist world, does not invest in production simply because working-class incomes cover the family consumption expenditures with difficulty. As it is, '43 per cent of total African expenditure' is accounted for by foodstuffs (Jill Nattrass, *SAJE*, Dec 1977, page 425). By generally accepted standards such a high expenditure of income on foodstuffs is a pointer to low incomes.

In any case, how much difference have those increases made to improve the African workers' standard of living, to say nothing of entertaining any sanguine hopes of building investible funds from that source to make 'capitalism flourish among Africans'? The following statistical excerpt should suffice to illustrate the point (*Marketing Research and Media*, Autumn 1978):

**Table 1. Gross earnings by sector of employment 1974–1976.**

|  | Average annual earnings per earner (Rands) | | | | Percentage increase 1974–76 | | Annual % increase 1974–76 | |
|  | 1974 | | 1976 | | | | | |
|  | Whites | Africans | Whites | Africans | Whites | Africans | Whites | Africans |
|---|---|---|---|---|---|---|---|---|
| Mining | 6 747 | 545 | 8 554 | 1 058 | 26,78 | 94,12 | 12,59 | 39,32 |
| Manufac-turing | 5 385 | 1 052 | 6 851 | 1 496 | 27,22 | 42,20 | 12,78 | 19,23 |
| Retail trade | 2 562 | 737 | 3 064 | 984 | 19,59 | 33,51 | 9,35 | 15,54 |

The three sectors of employment selected above are among the biggest employers of African labour from which 'a top layer of well-to-do Black workers are drawn'. The figures show to what extent the statement is overrating the impact of wage increases made after the widespread 1973 strikes and also show to what extent the wage gap between Africans and whites has been narrowed. The press reports on which the draftsmen base their statement quote percentage increases without stating the baseline figure. It was to warn the unwary reader who is carried away by reading these big, big percentage increases for African workers while white workers have received much smaller increases percentage-wise that the 1974 *Survey* of the South African Institute of Race Relations brusquely states: 'Africans cannot buy food with percentages. They need hard cash' (quoted by Selby Ngcobo in *Public Policy and the South African Economy*, page 84). And again, what prospects are there that from this class may flow investible funds to make Africans participate as capitalists in a capitalist economy in South Africa? In today's investment scene in South Africa, the main sources of investible funds are companies' retained profits, institutions (e.g. pension funds, insurance companies, etc.) which command large funds, rentiers and foreign capital.

The figures in the table above show that, in spite of the increases, wages still fall short of the accepted Minimum Effective Level (MEL) of living, which in Johannesburg was estimated at R122,87 per month for an African worker with a family of 5 or 6 (Truu: *op. cit.*, page 85).

9.  On the question of the emergence of 'a rich class of African farmers whose outlook is capitalistic', it is hardly necessary to comment. Commenting on the poverty of the bantustans, Dr Selby Ngcobo states: 'the performance of agriculture appears to have remained disappointing', and in this connection referring to the reports of the Bureau of Economic Research re Bantu Developments, he adds: 'The general impression gained from these reports is that the long-term trend of rural stagnation and retrogression . . . may at last have come to a halt' (Truu: *op. cit.*, page 88).

10.  The reference to [Maurice] Dobb in the draft, about the coexistence of giant monopoly concerns and small business, seems to be making a case for the need to preserve the capitalist system in order to give the African petit bourgeois a chance to participate in capitalism as a capitalist. It was, of course, not Dobb's intention to put·up a case for small business. He was explaining why small business is still there, which we do not go into here.

What one would like to emphasise here is that it is unrealistic to seek to preserve capitalism in order to give the African an opportunity to be a capitalist even if his participation is limited to small business. Even the opportunities to operate as a small businessman are shrinking at a fast rate. For instance, in the case of retail trade the growth in numbers of hypermarkets in the main industrial centres is sounding a death-knell for small retail trade business. Commenting on the performance of the hypermarket in Johannesburg's Norwood suburb, the general manager gave some outstanding information. On the opening day, which was a Wednesday, the takings amounted to R300 000 and at the close of business — midday Saturday — $3\frac{1}{2}$ days later, 'sales of more than R1 million had been recorded'. The general manager comments: 'It is claimed that these giant emporiums have forced the small trader out of business.' 'Lacking the hypermarkets' bargaining power, traders in the Black townships buy their goods at higher prices and therefore charge Black consumers more.' In fact 'the rich of Houghton can buy mealie meal, the Blacks' staple food, cheaper than in Soweto' (*Panorama*, September 1978, pages 20–21).

195

In the face of these realities, if the African businessman would be kept in business after freedom is won, it would only be in segregated areas like the present townships and at great sacrifice on the part of the African consumer – the working class. Needless to say, this cannot be what the bourgeois democracy school wants to see. But how would it be prevented in a situation where 'nationalisation would be an exception' to the rule?

11. The direction which the thinking in Inqindi is taking is indicated in its elaboration on the land clause which, according to Brownlee, appeared in a special issue of *Sechaba* in 1969: 'The land must be taken away from exclusive European control, from those groupings (i.e. corporations and state capital enterprises) and divided among small farmers, peasants and the landless of all races who do not exploit the labour of others. Farmers will be prevented from holding land in excess of a given area, fixed in accordance to concrete situation in each locality.' This elaboration makes it abundantly clear that the Organisaiton does not intend land to be a dancing ground for capitalists. If anything, the statement is closely in line with the practice on state farms in socialist countries where the farm worker is allowed sufficient land to till on his own on condition that he does not employ anyone to work on such land, and is even allowed to sell his produce on a free market.

## RESTATEMENT OF POSITION

12. The position must be clearly stated. From the various documents no claim has been made to change the Freedom Charter. The point of difference is what is projected will happen after the struggle for liberation will have been brought to a successful end. The bourgeois democracy school says it will be desirable to entrench capitalism in order to give the Africans in particular, and the oppressed in general, an opportunity to play the capitalist game from which they have been excluded.

The people's democracy school, on the other hand, says that the way the bourgeois democracy school sees things is incorrect. In the first place the Freedom Charter itself does not envisage the establishment of a bourgeois democracy, i.e. an entrenching of capitalism. The Freedom Charter says: 'The People shall govern' . . . not a class, as is envisaged under bourgeois democracy. The Freedom Charter says: 'We, the People of South Africa, declare that . . . only a democratic state based on the will of all the People can secure to all their birthright without distinction of colour, race, sex or belief.' 'The People of South Africa' – not the bourgeoisie, as must be the case in a bourgeois democracy. The Freedom Charter therefore envisages the establishment of a 'democracy based on the will of the people', in other words, a people's democracy.

The people's democracy goes further to say, in the light of the disadvantageous economic position in which the oppressed are placed in relation to that of the white capitalist class, the salvation of the oppressed, the overwhelming majority of whom are working class, lies in using the transitory phase of a people's democracy as a launching pad for the CP to go into socialism.

The case put forward by the people's democracy school is certainly in the best interests of the people of this country.

13.  Much else of what is dealt with in the draft is just irrelevant: the intentions of those who mooted the idea of the COP [Congress of the People] or what the Congresses understood by the Freedom Charter when they adopted it; who drafted it and what they had in mind other than what is set out in the Freedom Charter; this introduction of personalities into the discussion serves only to remove the attention of the reader from the real issue.

14.  Further views on the Freedom Charter and the place of other political organisations of the oppressed need not be repeated here, as they are set out in 3/B.

15.  What seems to be clear is that since this is an open discussion there should be no attempt to compile a representative document. One may well say with Mao: 'Let a hundred flowers bloom.' We should however agree to send out a representative statement which endorses the statement issued in the sections, calling upon us all to regard this discussion as one of the political discussions that will continue to crop up in the course of our work. As stated in 3/B, if such discussions are conducted properly our understanding of the problems that face us will be enhanced.

Mok. supports the above point of view.

Keto supports the draft.

# The ANC and Student Organisation

Let's clear a few matters first. Yes, in your previous note you have made some reference to the Afrikaanse Studentebond and its relationship with Nusas [National Union of South African Students]. I was aware of the error but I had my eye on other matters and therefore did not bother to point out the error. But the more important point you were raising really was the need for our students to participate in Nusas activities. I agree with you although I am not going to elaborate on this here. Probably even more important is the need for the Organisation, i.e. both the ANC and the Party, to take an active interest in students on both sides of the colour line. The role which comrades S.O. Man and Comrade Soldier and others played about the middle 1970s was good and it bore quick results. One must only hope that the Organisation has intensified its activities in this direction. S.O.M. gave me a very good and enlightening account after Comrade Soldier had referred me to him. I do not know Fatima personally and only began to hear about her on the island. But in this connection, what I am particularly interested in is the little bit of light you throw on the attitude of the Organisation to the Black Women's Federation. I recall vividly that last conference under legal conditions in 1960, at a time when Natal was afire from end to end. I still have a vivid picture of Mandlovu in all her sangoma [diviner's] regalia and gesturing with the ox-tail. I was damned angry with Tennyson or Joe for not being at the hall at the time to capture Mandlovu with a camera. In the spirit of the time you were right to have sought a discussion of the uprisings, and the spirit was very high throughout the country. Hence the organisations were not caught unaware by the April bannings of Inqindi [ANC] and Mpama [PAC]. Enough of the past.

A small correction: the leaders' conference in 1960 took place in Donaldson Hall in one of the large community rooms. The Rev.

Tantsi was chairman, and I led the ANC delegation. That's how I could deal with those Liberal Party disruptions.

The resolution put before the All-In African Conference was for the government to convene a national convention. The resolution then went on to say that if the government failed to do so before the end of May when a Republic was due to be declared, the ANC would call for a three-day stay-at-home (29–31), after which the ANC would embark on a path of non-cooperation. That is the gist of the resolutions adopted at that conference, and the resolution was drawn up after a lengthy discussion at a CP meeting and adopted by the ANC working committee. (To be correct, that resolution was adopted by the seven man committee, most of whom incidentally were members of the CP. When the history of the period is written, much will be unravelled concerning the quality of functions of executive members of the ANC at all levels, i.e. the Party and ANC top-level positions. It might not be opportune to do so before the struggle is over. I am happy you attach the significance you do to the All-In African Conference (1961) at Maritzburg. It marks a new watershed in the development of our struggle. That is material for the historian.) Yes, MK was formed after.

It was in June when the ANC put the proposition before a joint sitting of the Congresses. You will appreciate that I am here giving you the bare bones. Correct, at top of the structure of MK was the High Command (HC), on which both the ANC and the Party had each a representative, as MK was seen as a joint venture by the two. Lower down were the Regional Commands (RCs). In practice a member of the HC was commander at the regional command. In addition, a political representative was attached to an RC although in practice this might not have been observed in every region. All this was in the first instance machinery that was located inside the country and was at its early stages of development. Since the Morogoro Conference [1969] we are informed that a Revolutionary Council was set up with such arrangements for recruiting and training in all the necessary aspects indicated in your note, and in so far as I am aware nobody questions this.

On those aspects in your note which refer to the current polemic I quite understand and appreciate the impatience which I sense in your note. At present I would like you to bear with me. During all the time that these discussions have been going on, we have been as involved in them as elsewhere. It is understandable that since the joint declaration a few months back, you should not be regarded as indifferent. Until such time, which I hope won't be long now, I feel rather constrained to say nothing as much as I would like to meet your wish on the issues you raise.

Time marches on, comrade, and the hours of motion which the physicists laid bare in respect of matter have an equal applicability in respect of social phenomena. In my last note I should have added by way of a postscript what some comrades have come to regard as an obsession on their part. I would make no apologies for that. If it is an obsession I would say with Stanley Jones, it's a 'magnificent obsession'. I am referring to what I regard as an urgent need on our part, viz to cut direct to the coloureds to set up units both of the MK and the Party in the coloured townships, and there to recruit them for MK. The coloured population is running close to three million. The Nationalist government is being pressurised both from within the ranks of the National Party and from opposition ranks to absorb more and more coloureds into the army as it does with Africans and Indians also. But the impression I have is that the CPC [Coloured People's Congress] machinery which was only beginning to take shape in the Western Cape and hardly at all in the Eastern Cape, to say nothing of the Transvaal and Natal, has been largely crippled. Now that the ANC is open to all, it should no longer rely on the CPC or the SAIC to reach out to these groups. Membership of the ANC entails a special duty, viz recruiting for MK, and the carrying out of this task must not be left to chance.

The fighting ability of the coloureds is second to none; if the larger part of their active population should fall on the enemy side, our task will be made ever so much more difficult.

Enough for today, regards to all Comrades.

*Amandla! Matla!*

# Index